# From Anger to Action

# From Anger to Action

*Inside the Global Movements for Social Justice, Peace, and a Sustainable Planet*

Ben Jackson and Harriet Lamb

ROWMAN & LITTLEFIELD
Lanham • Boulder • New York • London

Published by Rowman & Littlefield
An imprint of The Rowman & Littlefield Publishing Group, Inc.
4501 Forbes Boulevard, Suite 200, Lanham, Maryland 20706
www.rowman.com

6 Tinworth Street, London SE11 5AL, United Kingdom

Copyright © 2021 by The Rowman & Littlefield Publishing Group, Inc.

*All rights reserved.* No part of this book may be reproduced in any form or by any electronic or mechanical means, including information storage and retrieval systems, without written permission from the publisher, except by a reviewer who may quote passages in a review.

British Library Cataloguing in Publication Information Available

**Library of Congress Cataloging-in-Publication Data**

Names: Lamb, Harriet, author. | Jackson, Ben, author.
Title: From anger to action : inside the global movements for social justice, peace, and a sustainable planet / Harriet Lamb and Ben Jackson.
Description: Lanham, Maryland : Rowman & Littlefield, 2021. | Includes bibliographical references. | Summary: "From Anger to Action tells the stories of the citizens' movements charting new paths to tackle the big global challenges that lie behind the political upheavals of our times. Drawing on candid insights from citizens, activists, and innovators, and their own experiences as leaders of advocacy organizations, the authors give an insider account of the battle for change"—Provided by publisher.
Identifiers: LCCN 2020048577 (print) | LCCN 2020048578 (ebook) | ISBN 9781538141328 (paperback) | ISBN 9781538141335 (ebook)
Subjects: LCSH: Social justice—Citizen participation. | Peace—Citizen participation. | Sustainable development—Citizen participation.
Classification: LCC HM671 .L358 2021 (print) | LCC HM671 (ebook) | DDC 303.3/72—dc23
LC record available at https://lccn.loc.gov/2020048577
LC ebook record available at https://lccn.loc.gov/2020048578

# Contents

| | | |
|---|---|---|
| Acknowledgments | | vii |
| Prologue: Hope Is Happening | | ix |
| 1 | The Journey to Change | 1 |
| 2 | Citizenquake | 11 |
| 3 | The Timed Test We Cannot Fail | 33 |
| 4 | The Doves Take on the Drones | 65 |
| 5 | Seeds of Hope among Displaced Lives | 87 |
| 6 | The 99 Percent Fights Back | 109 |
| 7 | A Tale of Two Pandemics | 137 |
| 8 | The Past as Prologue to Our Future | 151 |
| 9 | The Three Wheels of Change | 169 |
| Notes | | 183 |
| Index | | 199 |
| About the Authors | | 211 |

# Acknowledgments

All social change is the product of collaboration. This book reflects what we have learned from the many activists, colleagues, and campaigners we have had the privilege of working alongside, involved in all kinds of struggles for change across the world. They are far too many to mention individually, but we remain grateful to them all just the same.

Our fantastic editor and collaborator, Kay Parris, transformed the final outcome of our book with her ideas, sense of narrative, razor-sharp copy-honing skills, and persistent advocacy for you, dear reader, when NGO jargon and activist waffle reared their ugly heads.

We are enormously thankful to Jon Sisk, Benjamin Knepp, and all the team at Rowman & Littlefield for believing in this book and backing it through the pressures of the Covid-19 crisis. Harriet would like to thank Clare College Cambridge for the Eric Lane Fellowship and its role in kicking this book off—as well as Ashden's chair, Sarah Butler-Sloss, together with Anita Henderson, Jo Walton, and all the rest of the Ashden team for their generous support in helping it take flight. Ben would like to thank the Institute of Development Studies, Sussex University, for his time as a visiting fellow, which so helped in developing ideas—especially professors John Gaventa and Melissa Leach for all their support and insights. We would like to thank all those who contributed support, interviews, ideas, and feedback, including Richard Adams, Ayham Alsuleman at GLA, Joe Barrell at Eden Stanley, Mark Campanale at Carbon Tracker, Marike De Pena at Banelino, Jonathan Ellis, Rachel Griffiths, and Dalya at Herne Hill Welcomes Refugees, Mark Heywood at Maverick Citizen, Abir Haj Ibrahim at Moberadoon, Zamzam Ibrahim at SOS, everyone at International Alert, Nick Jeyarajah, Peter Martin, Nick Martlew at Digital Action, Ed Mayo at Co-operatives UK (and now Pilotlight), Gemma Mortensen at More in Common, Agamemnon

Otero at Repowering, Nicola Reindorp at Crisis Action, Madeleine Rose at Pacific Environment, Will Shanks, Nirvana Shawky, Michael Silberman, and Jacqui Howard at MobLab, Danny Sriskandarajah at Oxfam GB, Sue Tibballs at the Sheila McKechnie Foundation, Louisa Waugh, and Sam Worthington at InterAction. While we appreciate their contributions enormously, all opinions and any errors are entirely our responsibility. We are also hugely grateful to Emily Johns for her beautiful illustrations. Finally, we would both like to thank our families for their unstinting support and all their input of ideas and words to the writing of this book, as well as their forbearance. So thanks to Steve, Oscar, and Neena Percy (Harriet) and Gill, Rhona, and Angus (Ben).

# Prologue

*Hope Is Happening*

People mill excitedly around the towering bronze statue of transatlantic slave trader Edward Colston in the British city of Bristol. It is 7 June 2020. Everyone's phone is out, Black Lives Matter placards waving, and Covid facemasks on as demonstrators heave back, their body weight pulling on the white rope around Colston's neck. Heave! Suddenly, cheers fill the air as he topples, crashing to the ground, his smart, pleated coattails breaking off. A young man jumps on the fallen statue before demonstrators drag it to the water's edge and roll it into the harbour. Just like the 20,000 slaves 300 years before—who perished on Colston's ships en route from West Africa to the Americas and Caribbean, their bodies thrown into the sea—it sinks and disappears.

This reckoning with history in Bristol Harbor was one flame in a wildfire sweeping the world. Everywhere, the momentum was unstoppable. Years of suppressed frustration that people's lives and neighbourhoods are still shaped by racism and global exploitation had exploded.

The use of lethal force by US police against men of colour is not an unusual event—indeed, research suggests that about one black man in a thousand "can expect to be killed" this way.[1] Yet the choking of George Floyd under the weight of the Minneapolis police system, filmed in heartbreaking phone video, was the spark that ignited global protests off the back of decades of mobilising by activists. This forty-six-year-old African American father epitomised the inequalities of race and class: he had Covid-19, he had lost his job because of the lockdown, he was accused of using a counterfeit twenty-dollar bill, and he was restrained by a police officer who knelt on his neck for eight minutes and forty-six seconds as he begged for his life and his dead mother.

In anguished, furious response, protests in support of the Black Lives Matter movement—which had been organising for years—mushroomed throughout the United States and far beyond, on every continent, reaching even war-ravaged countries. Protesters came out for weeks on end, often in defiance of Covid-19 lockdowns, sometimes confronted by far-right counter-demonstrations. They marched in solidarity, demanding justice for every African American killed or abused by police brutality, as well as an end to structural racism and oppression in their own countries.

Like so many others, we were stopped in our tracks by these extraordinary events. Amid lockdowns, in the dystopian world of silent and sterile streets, boarded-up cafés, and closed offices, struggling people were rising up in anger—and hope.

Leading American historian of race and Africana Ibram X. Kendi has long decried his country's inability to face up to its deep-rooted racism but believes that we are now "living in the midst of an anti-racist revolution." The extremes of the Trump era, he says, "held a mirror up to American society, and it has reflected back a grotesque image that many people had until now refused to see." Now citizens both black and white "weren't merely advocating for a few policy shifts. They were calling for the eradication of racism in America once and for all."[2]

The energy generated by the historic summer protests of 2020 has not dissipated. It has rippled out, joining the eddy of a million social movements battling for change.

Bristol mayor Marvin Rees, seeking to heal the polarisation in his city, called on people to "listen to those who found the statue to represent an affront to humanity."[3] As the drama unfolded, he talked of the need for change to respect all voices, citing the African proverb "If you want to go fast, go alone. If you want to go far, go together." We want to go far in Bristol, he says. During a climate conference they were both attending, Harriet enjoyed a bus journey chatting with Rees, a social activist in both the United States and the UK before becoming the first directly elected black mayor of a British city. Bouncing along on the back seats, Rees argued passionately that measures to combat climate change must also meet the needs of his most disadvantaged city inhabitants. He is now pushing ahead with plans for Bristol to grow back better from Covid-19, connecting with citizen groups and tackling social injustices such as child hunger and fuel poverty while squaring up to the climate emergency. Impatient climate activists have been calling for just such action, with Extinction Rebellion bringing parts of Bristol to a standstill for five days and Swedish teenager Greta Thunberg leading, just before Covid-19 hit, possibly the biggest march in Bristol's history. Momentum builds.

During the early months of restrictions to control the Covid-19 pandemic, Harriet helped out a couple of hours a week in her local volunteer-run community shop, which was also organising deliveries for those self-isolating. A myriad of such voluntary, community, and mutual-aid groups had sprung up, throwing a lifeline to vulnerable people in lockdown, bringing a sense of cohesion and kindness into barren months. On the shop counter, as she rang up the milk and eggs on the cash register, her phone kept buzzing with messages from the wider world: colleagues texting about indigenous people in Brazil hit by Covid-19 and Ben venting his fury over poisonous far-right social media campaigns scapegoating refugees. Behind the scenes, he was leading work to build a coalition of refugee organisations united in their long-term strategy as, day after day, the British government lashed out against people fleeing their conflict-torn countries, desperate enough to board small, flimsy dinghies to cross the dangerous Channel waters from France.

Here we all stood in a moment of history as four global crises converged: the climate emergency, soaring inequality, conflict at a twenty-five-year high, and thus more refugees fleeing their homes than ever before—and, enveloping them all, the pall of Covid-19. Yet we also felt, in our souls and almost in our bones, the urgency and the clarity of people's calls to change—to refashion and renew our societies—rising up from city streets and dusty village tracks to international arenas.

These challenges have brought forth an extraordinary renaissance in citizen action as movements of people, in their tens, hundreds, and thousands, group and regroup to put compassion first, take grassroots initiatives, or press governments to use their power to put people and nature at the very centre of their planning. Long-nurtured visions of a new economics have been slapped down on the desks of government ministers looking for fresh answers to the entrenched, painful, ugly problems brought into sharp relief by Covid-19.

We can choose to go back to the old ways, or, from this crisis, people movements can lead us into a different world that addresses the intertwined roots of the injustices that ultimately hit us all. Indian author and environmental activist Arundhati Roy sees the pandemic as a portal we must pass through while making a choice. As she says, "We can choose to walk through it, dragging the carcasses of our prejudice and hatred, our avarice, our data banks and dead ideas, our dead rivers and smoky skies behind us. Or we can walk through lightly, with little luggage, ready to imagine another world. And ready to fight for it."[4]

*Chapter One*

# The Journey to Change

*How we started, what keeps us going,
and our view of the road ahead.*

"Stop biting your nails!" Ben hissed as we hopped nervously from foot to foot in the daunting grey stone lobby of the High Court in central London, then promptly returned to biting his own. Lawyers swept past in their gloomy black gowns and old-fashioned wigs, reinforcing our impending sense of doom. Absurdly, Harriet started wishing she had worn a suit, smarter shoes—anything to feel less vulnerable, less like a young activist kidding herself we could take on the pillars of the establishment: government ministers, arms dealers, big business, and the law.

It was November 1994, and our landmark case was up for judicial review: the first ever court challenge over the misuse of Britain's aid budget. Billed by the media as David against Goliath, our tiny campaigning organisation, the World Development Movement (WDM), was taking the fight directly to the government.[1] The stakes could not have been higher: if we lost, the organisation could be bankrupted, and the use of development aid for commercial gain, even to sweeten arms deals, would continue unhindered. If we won, we would put a stop to the government misusing aid to clinch a billion-pound weapons deal with Malaysia—and help ensure that aid in the future would be focused on ending poverty.

How had we, a couple of scruffy, inexperienced young campaigners, found ourselves in this position of grave responsibility? All we had were a sense of outrage at the injustices meted out by rich countries against poorer ones and a small citizen group determined to do something about it. Yet here we were.

As eager advocates for more and better international aid, we had spent months holed up in our office in a cold, dank back alley of Brixton, South London, scrutinising the £234 million aid package for the controversial Pergau Dam project in Malaysia. Despite admitting that the dam was "uneconomic"—there were cheaper ways to generate electricity—the government was doggedly defending the project, even as Friends of the Earth (FoE) slammed its destructive environmental impact and a group of members of Parliament (MPs), journalists, and nongovernmental organisations (NGOs), including ours, dug away at this perplexing use of Britain's then small and highly constrained aid budget.

Through our investigations, we became convinced that the aid must have been linked to a £1 billion weapons sale that the Thatcher government had signed with the Malaysian prime minister Mahathir Mohamad back in 1988. We did not have the smoking gun, but an official audit and our own research uncovered suspicious coincidences everywhere. We scrapped our previous plans for the year and swung into hunting down clues. For weeks we pulled all-nighters in the grimy office—a particular challenge for Harriet, who was breastfeeding her first baby at the time. Our team poured over details and dates of arms sales and piles of newspaper clippings (no Google to help us then), cross-referencing them with aid packages, checking the law on aid. Endless exhaustion and cravings for decent food were punctuated by rare moments of exhilaration as we scrabbled to pull together our evidence.

Two parliamentary inquiries were next to haul the government over the coals but still nothing happened to stop the dam from going ahead. Ben was called to give evidence to the Foreign Affairs Select Committee as part of a panel of NGOs. The government MPs on the committee had decided that the scandal was starting to hit the credibility of the government itself and embarked on a tough barrage of questions to take our position apart. In the debriefing afterward, Ben was hoping for a sympathetic chat through his bruising ordeal. "I *told* you we should have prepared more thoroughly!" Harriet thundered. She was right; another lesson learned. The whole case threatened some big interests, and they were not going to take it lying down. Arriving for work one morning soon afterward, Harriet was alarmed to find a journalist from the *Sunday Times* on the office doorstep, but he just said, "So what's your next angle on the story? My editor wants the scoop." We had counted ourselves lucky to get a journalist to pick up the phone in normal times. Now they were beating a path to our door.

Later, as we sat scratching our heads over how to move the campaign forward, Ben hit on an idea: "It must be illegal to spend aid money on an uneconomic project, and even more so to link aid to an arms deal. Why don't we take the government to court?"

Leading human rights law firm Bindmans agreed to take the case but put our chances at no more than fifty-fifty. We did not have the money to pay legal fees, but we did have thirteen thousand members to whom we appealed by stuffing envelope after envelope in our musty basement. In response, to our relief and growing excitement, hundreds of checques and scribbled messages of support began landing on our doormat each morning: our members and wider supporters were backing us in droves. It strengthened our resolve. They swung behind the wider campaign, writing letters to their MPs, upping pressure on the government.

Having convinced the distinctly conservative judges that WDM had the "standing" to take the case, we waited anxious months for our High Court hearing date finally to arrive. Then, in his ruling, to our initial disbelief, Lord Judge Rose pronounced the aid "fatally flawed" because the project was "economically unsound" and so could not promote the development of the country's economy as required by aid law.[2] Slowly, slowly the news sank in. We had won the case. We would have hugged the barristers or done cartwheels around the High Court, but it is not that kind of place.

The chief aid civil servant, Sir Tim Lankester, who had internally opposed funding the dam, said afterward that the court decision had come as a "big shock" to the government and its lawyers. They could not have been more shocked than we were. The phones never stopped ringing while the press ran stories about "the whole dam scandal," as the *Independent* newspaper put it. All aid to the dam was stopped. The contract had to be funded instead from central Treasury funds, winning a tidy £234 million back for the aid budget to be spent on more deserving programs. Three other aid projects we had been investigating over their use of aid to subsidise British companies to win contracts were likewise deemed at risk of legal challenge and had their funding returned to the aid budget, too.

"Pergau marked a watershed," said Sir Tim in his tell-all exposé of the sorry saga.[3] Revealing the lobbying faced by the government from British companies bidding for the arms deals and contracts for the dam, he wrote in 2012:

> It led to a rethink of aid policy in both main political parties. In retrospect, Pergau came to be seen as a turning point when British aid moved away from being so closely geared to British commercial interests and moved toward becoming today possibly the most highly respected amongst all the donors with a much-strengthened focus on poverty alleviation.[4]

According to Sir Tim, our campaign and landmark court case had not only secured this fundamental shift in aid but hastened setting up the separate Department for International Development, precisely to prevent development objectives from being overruled by UK commercial or foreign policy interests.[5]

Pergau also revealed how the arms industry had penetrated to the heart of government, with its own taxpayer-funded promotional body, the Defence Export Services Organisation (DESO)—headed at the time of the deal by Sir Colin Chandler, who had been seconded into government from British Aerospace, the main company to benefit from the arms deal. It was only in 2007 that DESO was finally closed down.

Pergau was a milestone in both of our lives. We learned how an audacious move by a tiny pressure group, with determination and conviction, could get to the heart of government power and forge change. It propelled us both forward through a lifetime of campaigning because we learned that we could take on what have sometimes seemed—and sometimes proved, of course—insurmountable obstacles.

Oddly, and more by luck than our judgement, we had followed a classic model of securing systemic change: we had struck fast when an opportunity arose but had been guided by WDM's long-term strategy to end business hijacking of aid; we took risks and adapted our short-term tactics; we worked in a pincer movement with MPs, the press and other NGOs, later discovering that our best allies were in fact civil servants on "the inside"; and we turned to our base, organised over years, for funds and support, and they responded because they knew and trusted us. Our court victory had repercussions beyond the specific project, cementing the shift in the aid program, with the old commercial links ruled out of order. We learned that you can win, and unlock bigger change, against all the odds. We learned quite a lot about the science and art of changing the world, although we didn't fully appreciate it at the time—we were too keen to catch up on some sleep.

We also learned, over subsequent years, that campaigns for change are rarely done and dusted. In 2018, critics condemned the renewed transfer of aid funds to the International Trade Department as "a slush fund to pay for developing the UK's diplomatic, trade or national security interests."[6] When in June 2020 the UK government announced a decision to merge the Department for International Development with the Foreign and Commonwealth Office, without consultation, this same logic was driven further—provoking three former British prime ministers from both main political parties to join a chorus of condemnation. Danny Sriskandarajah, chief executive of Oxfam GB, said the merger was "scarcely believable," adding, "This decision puts politics above the needs of the poorest people and will mean more people around the world will die unnecessarily from hunger and disease."[7] Many critics referred back to the Pergau Dam scandal as an object lesson to governments on the need to keep development interests separate from commercial or diplomatic ones. As former secretary of state for international development Hilary Benn, MP, put it while condemning the merger: "The then Conservative Government decided to give money to a project to build a dam.

Why? Because it thought it would help it to get an arms deal . . . the legal focus of our development assistance has to be the reduction of poverty."[8]

The merger was part of a deliberate effort to reverse the gains on aid policy won by progressive civil society campaigning since Pergau. For example, the right-wing foreign affairs think tank the Henry Jackson Society, which sees itself as the home of US-style neo-con foreign affairs thinking in the UK, had advocated just such a merger as part of a wholesale repurposing of post-Brexit international aid toward "British culture, values and history."[9] Shortly before becoming prime minister, in an approving foreword to the Henry Jackson Society's report making this case, Boris Johnson said: "The authors are to be applauded for some radical thinking about reform . . . to ensure that these vast sums do more to serve the political and commercial interests of the country." In response, NGOs have been working to rebuild grassroots organising on the issue as well as more united campaigning through coalition initiatives such as the Campaign to Defend Aid and Development. They stepped up further after Chancellor Rushi Sunak announced in November 2020 he was slashing the UK's foreign aid by £4 billion a year, reversing a promise to keep meeting the UN target of 0.7 percent of national wealth for aid and instead switching the funds into increasing military spending. Part of the campaign strategy is about reframing the media narrative to show how efforts to address poverty and environmental destruction head-on also tackle root causes of the climate change, conflict, engrained racism, forced migration, and grotesque inequalities that plague ordinary people across rich and poor nations alike.

## BRINGING THE GLOBAL BACK HOME

We both cut our teeth working with dynamic activists overseas—Ben in Uganda and Harriet in India. These activists campaigned alongside indigenous communities, pushing for policies to end poverty and saw no separation between "environment" and "development," which dominated the West's siloed thinking of the 1980s. We each took from this experience that, above all else, for those of us working for change, wherever we may live, it all starts back home: we have to find the solutions to our ever-more integrated world on our own doorsteps. In our case, as Europeans committed to ending global injustices, our role is to change the policies and practices of Western governments and companies that fix global structures and trends. And these can be transformed when civil society operates at its brightest and best.

So, what is civil society? There is no single accepted definition, but we take it to mean those parts of society outside of government and business where people come together to work for the common good—each in their own areas of particular interest. For us, that stretches from the droves of concerned consumers shopping for fair trade goods in the supermarket, the car-free families showing how we can cut carbon emissions, volunteers helping settle refugees, and people protesting against local fracking, to entire grassroots movements or huge NGOs whose operations span the globe. It is where people are creating a better society, whether in a neighbourhood support group caring for people self-isolating to avoid Covid-19 or a campaign team lobbying for new global trade rules. In this book, we focus especially on those parts of civil society aiming to address the big global challenges we face. This is the civic space where we both, in different ways, have spent our lives and which, we believe, has the power to change the world—but it is a space threatened by powerful moves away from international rights and responsibilities. This is the decade when we have to build together from the grass roots up, and from the top down, to find compelling new solutions to our global challenges. Our very future hangs in the balance.

## BURNING ISSUES OF OUR TIME

In the years since we stood shaking in our shoes in the High Court, we have driven a Challenger army tank through the City of London to campaign against arms sales; danced around high streets, dressed in banana outfits to promote fair trade; met Nelson Mandela when we stood in solidarity with post-apartheid South Africans; supported peacebuilding and refugees in our communities; fostered civil society coalitions; and nurtured solutions to climate change.

Today, like so many concerned citizens, we feel ever more viscerally the heat of the global fires burning fiercely across our world: rising inequality and persistent poverty; a dire climate emergency; escalating or entrenched conflicts within and between nations; unprecedented numbers of people forcibly displaced from their homes, and often their countries, to live year after year as refugees. These fires are all connected, the flames of each fanning the other.

And then the catastrophe of Covid-19 blew up, adding existential urgency. Pundits had long predicted a global pandemic and now here it was, a threat at each of our doorsteps, demanding both global and very local solutions. The havoc it has wreaked on our lives and economies demands urgent government action. But no one government can tackle the virus or its long-term fallout alone; global cooperation is needed. At the same time, so many people have gotten through this crisis with the help of groups springing up spontaneously in streets or rural neighbourhoods, or building off existing networks, offering a million acts of kindness in their communities every day.

We know that many who believe in international solidarity feel lost today, unsure of our vision, battered by these catastrophic challenges. Populism has made things worse—muscling into our societies, upturning all of our cosy assumptions about progress, enticing people to turn their backs on these burning global and pushing an inward-looking nationalist agenda against hard-won multilateral rules-based agreements.

The outlook can seem bleak. But today, more than at any other moment in human history, even if we want to shut out global issues, they are going to come walking, swimming, or—as the coronavirus did—exploding into our lives. Over the last few decades, through technology and breaking down barriers to trade, we have created a globally connected society: social media gives us followers in countries we have never visited; factories in one country affect the weather in another; companies move their money at will and switch sourcing for their products across continents in an instant. Inequalities, conflicts, and ideological battles seen as "overseas" end with terrorists killing people on London Bridge and with refugees clinging to the underbelly of trucks to reach safety, while pandemic disease and climate change swirl into every corner of the world.

Millions of people are looking in the mirror and facing up to the utterly interconnected—and yet strangely disconnected—world we have created. Western nations, having been prime architects in the creation of globalisation, are at the centre of those webs. So, we cannot now just "Globexit," even if we wanted to.

Instead, civil society is flexing its muscles and responding at a pace and scale never seen before. Of course, citizen-led movements cannot replace, or afford to ignore, the decisive battlegrounds of electoral politics or mainstream democracy. But change is not up to politicians alone. Citizens can reshape the terms of the debates and win support for approaches that deal with the root causes of our problems and achieve a just, sustainable world. Indeed, our decisive role in transforming change and creating defining moments has been grossly underestimated and needs more recognition. So much social change has come about only because citizens have imagined, acted, and organised, pushing politicians to take "new" issues seriously and creating the inspiring visions that help people see how a better world would look. In a "good society," people feel able to shape their lives for the better and to live, work, and connect with their neighbours in the local, national, and global villages. Especially in dark times, it is up to us as citizens to take the initiative. No one else will do it for us.

## A NEW WORLD ON ITS WAY

Anyone who has yet to see a murmuration of starlings, soaring and swooping by the thousands into ever-changing formations in the open sky above, has a wondrous experience still in store. Their breath-taking synchronicity happens because each tiny, vulnerable bird is hyper-connected through instantaneous communication and response with the birds closest to it, their flying creating a rapidly changing domino effect, so that the local change becomes "global," and ever more starlings are attracted to join and benefit from the protection and spirit of the group. We draw inspiration and hope from this phenomenon for civil society, made up as it is of millions of individuals who, in coming together, create something spectacular.

Through the myriad initiatives of vibrant individuals and loose groups, through large, organized NGOs or citizens' spontaneous protests, the rough outlines of a new international vision are being sketched out. In the words of Arundhati Roy: "Another world is not only possible, she is on her way. . . . On a quiet day, if I listen very carefully, I can hear her breathing."[10]

In the decisive decade ahead, we believe civil society will find its momentum in surprising new ways that catapult big, transformative changes. Citizens will push the boundaries forward, sometimes against all odds, unearthing those sweet spots of radical, deep-rooted and systemic solutions that carry wide appeal, rooted locally but with their eyes on the global prize. For the two of us, while we have learned much over our years of civic participation, we have no sense of the "good old days." On the contrary, despite so much that is daunting, we believe the 2020s could be the most exhilarating time ever to be engaged in civil society as it spins forward, reinventing itself for the new age to which it is urgently called.

We are not academics surveying the sector, analysing how governments, companies, and a plethora of stakeholders are acting; nor are we serving up a full menu of policy solutions. Instead, we are exploring trends, highlighting the compelling ideas for citizens' movements and, most importantly, sharing humbling stories of how individuals and civil society are finding means to address the burning issues of our time. Obviously, we could not begin to showcase a fraction of these inspirational initiatives, and we have drawn mainly from our own context and experience. We make no claim to cover here all that citizens are doing to create change within their own societies in Somalia or Vietnam, for example.

Yet we do feel confident that civil society can take the strain and reinvigorate from below, creating a fighting-fit movement, on the front foot, outward looking and ready to go to scale. That is easy to write about and very hard to do. But people have always chipped doggedly away at issues until solutions emerge like sculptures from stone. We grew up with Northern Ireland mired in "The Troubles" and South Africa ruled by apartheid—both seemed intractable, yet both found ways forward. We predict that civil society will, by trying and succeeding, trying and failing, again and again, finally crack the Rubik's cube of a new global settlement. We are convinced that our best bet for finding that will be led, not by companies or the market or party politics—critical though those will be to its formation—but by citizens who are already trialling and nurturing the big ideas, as individuals and organised into movements and groups.

This hope is not cheap and cheerful, or eyes shut tight with our fingers crossed. Ours is a hard-edged hope, wrestled out of our own campaigning struggles, and out of walking alongside people who have sacrificed, had multiple setbacks, and are yet pointing the way to a new international vision—a kinder way of living that puts people and the planet first.

*Chapter Two*

# Citizenquake

*How the last decade of public revolt turned our world upside down—and how citizen movements can reshape it in the next.*

It didn't seem like the calm before the storm. Ben's Egyptian colleagues led his small group weaving through a phalanx of cars eight lanes wide through the roundabout in central Cairo. Hooting yellow cabs, buses full of students, pickups piled with sacks of vegetables, mopeds, cars of every vintage. They were in the middle now, and every driver was looking for the next gap to dart into. "Keep going, keep going," said Ben's colleague Nirvana Shawky, a local. She was right. The only way was to dare them to run you down. The van driver who had seemed menacing a moment before smiled and spread a hand over his steering wheel, a gracious concession in the battle of wills.

They reached the other side and hurried on to their meeting in the towering white headquarters of the Arab League, where Ben's colleagues from Crisis Action had been lobbying for months to secure support for peace efforts on the civil war in South Sudan. None of them knew that just four days later, on 25 January 2011, that roundabout—Tahrir Square—would be transformed into the epicentre of a citizen uprising that, within three more weeks, would force the country's thirty-year dictator, Hosni Mubarak, from power and send waves of inspiration across the world.

An idealistic young former journalist at the time, Nirvana is still deeply affected by what unfolded:

> Anyone who tells you they knew the revolution was just about to happen is lying. Police brutality was the initial spark. But the long-term causes—growing economic division and an elite that didn't even pretend to have a social contract with the majority—had been clear for a long time. Yes, we were

standing up against an autocrat. But dictatorship was the elite's tool to protect their money-making interests.

Really—we were so shocked at the numbers who turned out to protest on the twenty-fifth. Social media was going crazy. It was a public holiday; of all things, for Police Day. But then it escalated. More people. More cities. And when the government blacked out the internet, we started saying to each other, "Something really must be going on."

The movement declared that Friday a "Day of Rage." More and more people poured out—many heading to Tahrir Square, which was soon permanently occupied by thousands of citizens. For days, they protested in the square, planned, blogged, and debated. They organised clinics, kindergartens, art displays, and better rubbish collection than in most of the city. A tent city sprang up where Ben and his colleagues had struggled to cross the road. Even the army tanks that had taken up position at the uprising's start were immobilised by protesters lying inside their tracks, day and night.

Across the Middle East, the momentum that had begun in Tunisia a month before, sweeping dictator Zine al-Abidine Ben Ali from power after twenty-three years, seemed unstoppable. Full-scale uprisings took off in Bahrain, Libya, Yemen, and Syria, with popular protests in more countries, including Lebanon, Palestine, Jordan, Kuwait, Oman, and Sudan. In the end, much of this citizen momentum was stopped in its tracks—either by military coups snuffing out the move to democracy, as in Egypt, or a combination of brutal repression and militant armed Islamist groups seeking to exploit the flux. In Libya, Syria, and Yemen, uprisings descended into repression and civil wars fuelled by outside powers with terrible human suffering and millions forced to flee.

When asked how she looks back on the Tahrir Square protests, Nirvana's voice falters: "It's still very hard to talk about it all even now, to be honest. The problem for our generation was that we touched our dream. For a short glimpse of time, we tasted it, smelled it, saw it. We could really feel the sense of change, of freedom. Then it was taken away from us. The experience has marked us as a generation. I think forever." But does she regret being part of the citizen revolution?

Not for one moment. That is what they want you to feel. That there are only two choices. Either their brutal "security" or religious fanaticism. They want you to believe that you don't have the right to aspire to freedom, democracy, equality, international solidarity—that somehow you are a second-class human being. That that is not for people in the Middle East.

Of course, I wish we had thought more about strategy back then; about how we could have negotiated and organized better. I wish we'd not allowed the glow of seeming to win so quickly and being at the center of global attention to distract from the forces we were up against. But I'm not torn, I don't regret it. The regimes have put change on pause for now—but when it comes again, it will take off from where we'd moved it to.

She draws hope from the success of revolutions in Sudan and Tunisia, which removed dictatorships and secured gains toward democracy, and from a resurgence of protests in countries such as Iraq, Lebanon, and Algeria:

> Even after everything the regimes have done—the terrible suffering of Syrians, including six million of them being forced into exile, the appalling suffering of the people of Yemen—yet the human spirit rises again to defy them. What is clear is that we need to combine our street protests with deeper organizing. We need to reach out and build alliances with a wider range of people, not just those we arrogantly see as "pure" progressives like us. We need to organize better to win. We need to use social media more strategically. I believe we can, and we will.

## AN AGE OF RAGE

The Arab Spring marked the start of an unprecedented, decade-long surge of citizen uprisings and populist rebellions, which still grip our world. Of course, every generation has its movements and protests. The 1980s, for example, had the antinuclear peace movement, anti-apartheid struggle, British miners' strikes, the Nicaraguan solidarity movement, and the risings against the Communist regimes of Eastern Europe of 1989 that shaped our political comings of age. The 1960s saw independence struggles as in Mozambique, the movements for civil rights and against the Vietnam War, and the 1968 revolutionary events. But analysts argue that ours is an exceptional age for system-challenging nonviolent rebellion—whether judged by the numbers of people taking part or their spread across all regions, in rich as well as developing nations.

"People in more countries are using people power than at any time in recorded history. Nonviolent mass movements are the primary challenges to governments today," according to Harvard political scientist Erica Chenoweth.[1] She led a pioneering global study of the patterns of resistance, which concluded that between 2010 and 2016 alone, there were more new nonviolent "maximalist" campaigns (those aimed at overthrowing a country's existing order) than during all of the 1990s.[2] She also says there is a marked shift toward nonviolent strategies as the lead route for citizen movements: "There is a falling away from the consensus that you need armed struggle. . . . People are not picking up guns as they did in earlier eras. They're instead looking to civil resistance to assert their claims and seek transformation."[3]

## Chapter 2

## OCCUPY: RADICAL DEMOCRACY

As spring 2011 moved into a hot summer of protest and citizens continued to occupy Tahrir Square, on the other side of the world, the radical anti-consumerist magazine *Adbusters* emailed its subscribers, declaring, "America needs its own Tahrir." In a July 2011 blogpost, it noted that "a worldwide shift in revolutionary tactics is underway right now" and called for people to adopt the "spirit of this fresh tactic." It made the link back to earlier anti-globalisation movements such as the running street protests against the 1999 World Trade Organization meeting in Seattle, but noted that the strategy now needed to be different—to mobilise a swarm of people to take action right inside the heart of the problem. "We go out and seize a square of singular symbolic significance and put our asses on the line to make it happen. . . . The time has come to deploy this emerging stratagem against the greatest corrupter of our democracy: Wall Street, the financial Gomorrah of America," the message proclaimed.[4] It advocated that the call to action should be to end the corporate control of politics—though, over time, the movement's proposition was diffused.

The Occupy movement came together after months of discussion by diverse activist, labour union, radical artistic, and internet-based groups thinking along similar lines. These streams coalesced around a growing citizen outrage that those responsible for the financial crash of 2008 faced few consequences—and that the opportunity for system change was slipping away. Instead, ordinary people were facing the brunt of cuts, austerity and plunging incomes while the richest held on to their position. The movement's rallying cry—"We are the 99 percent"—drew inspiration from a *Vanity Fair* article by Nobel-prize-winning economist Joseph Stiglitz a few months earlier. Titled "Of the 1%, by the 1%, for the 1%," this distilled the escalation in US inequality over previous decades to a point where "1% of the people take nearly a quarter of the nation's income."[5]

Protests took place around Wall Street, the heart of American—and indeed global—capitalism. Street artists stripped outside the New York Stock Exchange before the police arrived: Eric Clinton Anderson as a naked janitor with dustpan and brush remarking to bemused passers-by, "Somebody needs to clean up Wall Street"; a shirtless Zuni Tikka declaring, "Wall Street has stolen the shirts from our backs."[6] A mass rally on 17 September 2011 ended in the occupation of nearby Zuccotti Park where protesters set up tents for a round-the-clock presence. Occupy Wall Street had begun.

Occupy was an experiment in radical democracy, embracing all manner of critiques of the system and routes for change. By October, the movement had spread to 951 cities across 82 countries.[7] One sprang up on the edge of the City of London in the shadow of the domed St. Paul's Cathedral. But on

Wall Street, two months after the occupation started, the New York police moved in to clear the site. Other crackdowns followed.

For a crucial moment, Occupy shone a direct light on the grotesque ballooning of inequality and the steady growth in the power of the banks and financial corporations across economic and political life, as well as their role in corrupting democracy. While castigated by some for lacking a set of clear demands, to others that was Occupy's strength, allowing a diversity of radical critiques of the system. Its lack of alignment to established political parties or organisations showed the potential of a movement not in hock to them—even if its disintegration highlighted the resulting absence of its organising depth. Instead, it embraced creativity, deflating humour, constructive confrontation, and spontaneity, with the voices of all people in the movement shaping its stance.

In its untidy, broad-brush way, Occupy put an argument that had languished on the fringes of public and political debate—the need to challenge global neoliberal capitalism—into the mainstream. It showed how a street movement could become global to match the globalised system and helped inspire later protest movements. Ultimately, the harsh truth is that Occupy secured little direct change to global business or ever-growing wealth disparities. But such movements for change have long fuses, and Occupy was the initiation for many activists still mobilising today, sharing their learning with Extinction Rebellion or the Sunrise movement on climate change, for example.

## "PEOPLES OF EUROPE RISE UP!"

In Europe, Occupy ran alongside a series of mobilisations against government cutbacks and soaring unemployment. Just months after the 2008 market crash, banks and governments in Europe started to declare they could not pay their debts—and were forced by the IMF and the EU to make severe spending cuts in order to bail out banks and the financial system. Businesses closed, unemployment soared, and construction projects shuddered to a halt, leaving the skeletons of half-formed buildings abandoned as a rebuke to the property bubble.

From 2010 onward, one after the other, EU member states including Cyprus, Greece, Spain, Italy, Portugal, Ireland, Hungary, Latvia, and Romania declared they could no longer pay their debts or stop banks from going under. Outside the EU itself, but within its orbit, Iceland's overheated financial system suffered the biggest banking collapse, in relation to the size of its economy, ever recorded. The government collapsed; its citizens took to the streets and ushered in a new political era when they refused to bail it out.

At one point, the euro itself looked as though it might collapse—a crisis staved off by an emergency bailout package agreed to by EU leaders just hours before the markets opened on the next Monday. The head of the European Central Bank, Mario Draghi, declared famously that he would "do whatever it takes" to shore up the euro—a boldness replicated by governments investing billions in job retention schemes under pressure from trade unions and citizens after Covid-19 forced huge swathes of the global economy to shut down. During the financial crisis, as now, however, joblessness soared, and citizens' spending power was decimated. People took to the streets in 2010 and 2011 to protest across Spain, Ireland, Portugal, Italy, France, and—perhaps most dramatically—Greece, where youth unemployment grew to 62 percent, and citizens' buying power fell by 40 percent.[8]

As in Egypt, a digitally fuelled protest movement exploded. On 5 May 2010, after the Greek government put forward another devastating round of EU and IMF austerity cuts, the country saw its biggest protests since the 1973 student uprising against the Greek military junta, and trade unions called nationwide strikes. On May Day 2010, activists broke into the Acropolis, the symbol of Ancient Greece as the birthplace of democracy, to hang a huge banner declaring: "Peoples of Europe Rise Up!"[9] Outside the Greek Parliament, protesters chanted: "Let the rich pay for the crisis!" They condemned the centre-left government of George Papandreou, a grandson in a political dynasty representing the essence of a complacent political establishment.

The march ushered in months of popular resistance organised by citizens beyond the political parties and trade unions, while people's assemblies in Athens's Syntagma Square debated alternative solutions. The government approved the austerity packages in the midst of continued protest. But on the back of the social movement, the radical left-wing Syriza party was propelled to power under Alexis Tsipras in 2015, only to fracture after it, too, accepted an EU loan and cuts package, finally losing power to the centre-right in 2019.

Spain also faced huge anti-austerity protests that swept a social movement into power. The Take the Squares movement occupied central squares across Spanish towns and cities, including on a mass scale in Madrid's Puerta del Sol in 2011. The linked Indignados movement ("the outraged ones") established Occupy-type encampments with action sustained over many months. This progressive social movement also gave birth to a new political party, Podemos, in 2014, led by political scientist and activist Pablo Iglesias and signing up a hundred thousand members within three weeks of being launched. Podemos rejected coalition with the social democratic PSOE after the inconclusive April 2019 election. However, it agreed to do so seven months later when a rerun election saw gains for the far-right populist party Vox, which openly lauded the fascist former dictator General Franco. Having made the transition from citizen movement to left-wing populist politics and power, Podemos struggled to sustain the mass support of its social movement base.

For anyone who thought the tidal wave of citizen demonstrations would ebb as the financial crisis appeared to recede, a further resurgence in 2019 and 2020 proved them wrong. In Lebanon, amid economic turmoil and fury over political corruption and neglect, mass protests brought the resignations of two prime ministers: in October 2019, that of Saad Hariri, who had introduced a tax on WhatsApp, and less than a year later, that of Hassan Diab after the devastating explosion at the Beirut port killed 170 people, injured thousands and destroyed a large swathe of the city. In Hong Kong, a new law enabling citizens to be extradited to mainland China for trial was the first in a series of oppressive national security laws that triggered months of mass public rallies. In France, an increase in gasoline prices set off the *gilets jaunes* protest movement voicing the frustrations of peripheral France at roundabouts, highway bridges, and finally in angry demonstrations week after week in the heart of Paris on the Champs-Elysées. In Algeria, the president's announcement that he would seek a fifth term in office sparked over a year of weekly anti-corruption mass marches in the capital, only brought to an end by Covid-19. In Chile, the spark that set a tinderbox of resentments alight was a thirty-peso (four US cents) increase in Santiago's metro transit ticket prices.

## CHILE: "IT'S NOT ABOUT 30 PESOS. IT'S ABOUT 30 YEARS"

Sometimes, it is a constant wall of sound. In the next moment, it picks up a beat from someone and morphs into a pulsing, defiant collective rhythm. The *cacerolazo* (literally, stew-pot-striking protest) rises from an orchestra of a million people who have brought every kind of pot, pan, or metal dish from their kitchens across the Chilean capital, Santiago, onto the streets around the Plaza Italia in October 2019. "Oh, Chile despertó" ("Oh, Chile woke up") is the crowd's chant. It rings as a rebuke to the complacency of the political and business elite and their international allies, who vaunted Chile as the poster child for radical free market economics; this, they advocated, was the route to peace and prosperity for a developing nation.

In common with the new wave of rebellions, it was mobile phones and social media that enabled the flame to spread like wildfire. Fast-moving digital swarm tactics had replaced the slower and easier to repress command-and-control organising of the past. Students moved fast to call on fellow citizens to support mass fare-dodging and the occupation of stations and trains. Before long, *#EvasionMasiva* had taken on a life of its own. Caught off-guard by the movement, the government declared a state of emergency for the first time since the ending of dictatorship in 1990. Chile's billionaire president Sebastian Piñera deployed the police and army in force, declaring, "We are at war." Tear gas, water cannons and even live ammunition were unleashed on the protesters. Dozens were killed, thousands arrested.[10] But street protests, sit-ins, strikes, and violence between protesters and security forces escalated. Trade unions, the urban poor, and older generations angry at pitiful pensions in the country's privatised system joined the protests, which spread to other cities.

The cacerolozo continued from people's windows and balconies even as a curfew was declared—one reason the tactic has a long history in Latin America. "This sound is so strong, with the military on the street, it is the only way we can protest peacefully and show discontent with the government," Tatiana Moyano, a hostel owner says. Another protester, seventy-three-year-old Gustavo González says, as he claps his hands in time to the street chants, "Chile thinks it is a stable country, but it has a lot left over from the dictatorship, a lot of discontent of the population. . . . The country is unequal, the rich are rich, the poor are poor. The metro was the fire that lit this movement."[11]

When President Piñera's hard-line tactics failed to quell the riots, he abruptly changed tack, appearing on television to apologise to citizens and express understanding for their plight. He reversed the fare increase. He promised to increase pensions, health coverage, and the minimum wage and cut politicians' pay. He asked his cabinet to resign. But the young protesters were no longer satisfied with such concessions. They wanted system change. And many in their parents' generation now joined them. They had all known someone among the thousands killed and tortured under General Pinochet's military regime. Now the citizen movement was demanding a new national constitution to replace the one inherited from the bloody Pinochet era.

The young people were no longer constrained by the implicit deal made during the 1990 transition to democracy that overthrowing the dictatorship meant it was not possible to demand bigger change. They were shaped by this history. "We are the generation for whom the joy never came," says twenty-six-year-old Nicole Martínez—a bitter twist on "joy is coming," the rallying cry of the citizen movement to end military rule.[12] Three decades later, the protesters in Plaza Italia gave voice to their demand for full system change by repeating another popular slogan among the beating of the pans: "It's not about 30 pesos. It's about 30 years."

In November 2019, the movement secured a major concession when the government agreed to a referendum on a process to replace the constitution into which Pinochet had hardwired his regime's extreme free market ideology. Its approach had been shaped by the so-called Chicago Boys group of Chilean economists cultivated by the high priest of the radical free market revolution, American economist Milton Friedman, who saw Chile as the lab test for the liberalisation unleashed on the wider world during the 1980s. Thus, the social movement's victory is significant not just for Chile but for the wider citizen battle for deep change, away from the model that has underpinned the escalation of inequality worldwide. While the constitutional referendum had to be delayed due to the Covid-19 pandemic, Chilean activists started organising to ensure that this would not become an excuse to block the long-term change they had fought so hard to win.

## RISE OF THE POPULISTS: "TAKE BACK CONTROL"

While many citizen movements stem from a liberal, progressive base, the right wing has been on the march, too. Fascist and neo-Nazi movements have been resurgent in Europe and the United States, with a surge in attacks on migrants and ethnic minorities. More broadly, nationalist populist movements have upturned the accepted political order with a dramatic series of victories, from such parties taking power in Poland, Hungary, and Italy to the lurch to the right in Brazil with the election of President Bolsonaro and in the Philippines with President Duterte and with the hold on power of Hindu nationalist Narendra Modi in India and conservative Islamist Recep Tayyip Erdoğan in Turkey.

Previously concentrated in emerging democracies, the populists have spread into established liberal democracies. Sometimes, they come as insurgent new movements and parties, like Matteo Salvini's anti-immigrant League Party in Italy, which grew out of a regional separatist movement. In other cases, a populist faction has taken control within an established party, as President Trump did in the Republican Party and the hard-line pro-Brexit right in the British Conservative Party.

*Populism* can be a slippery term. It can be seen as a way of appealing to and engaging people. Or it can mean an ideology that puts "the people" (who are good and share a true, common-sense will) versus "the elite" (who are bad, self-serving, and corrupt).[13] Often added to this is a strong, authoritarian leader who can cut through to save the people from the elite who ignore or belittle their values and favour outsiders. In the populist narrative, the leader will restore direct democracy to this silent, ignored majority and "get things done" by bypassing the usual institutions of liberal democracy, such as the mainstream media, courts, parliament, and—quite often—civil society organisations, which are portrayed as part of the problem.[14]

Unlike earlier populists, those in the new wave have generally followed a democratic route—positioning themselves as insurgent anti-establishment players who need the people's support to overturn a globalised elite. However, where they have won power, populists have often used it to subvert democratic checks and balances, and to entrench elite advantage. For example, for all his talk of it being a "big, beautiful Christmas present" for ordinary Americans, President Trump's 2017 tax-cut package benefited the wealthiest people and big corporations far more than ordinary workers.[15]

For a movement that often focuses its fire on globalisation, right-wing populism has been remarkably successful as a worldwide phenomenon. The populists have harnessed digital technology effectively, spreading fears of the "other," going for the mainstream media and its "fake news," and using big data to micro-target voters with a version of their message designed to press specific personality buttons. Populists have exploited people's fears about migration and globalisation's impact on areas suffering industrial decline and feelings that the established political order does not listen to them. They have exploited divisions between those with more socially conservative values of locality, family, and nation (and sometimes religion) and those more outward-looking "progressive" values of global connection, universal human rights, and equality. And they have played upon people's sense of powerlessness to influence their lives and the breakdown of community solidarity. It is no wonder that the Brexit slogan of "take back control" had such resonance with many who have indeed felt left behind.

Strangely, some issues we have both worked away on in NGOs for years to promote the political agenda—such as the impact of international trade rules on workers and farmers—but that remained on the B list of public debate, have been thrust centre stage by the populists. During the Brexit turmoil, suddenly public debate and street placards started featuring obscure trade terminology for years restricted to the briefings of NGO trade policy nerds like us. Pro-Brexit placards outside Parliament read: "Let's go WTO!" or "WTO Rules: Set Britain free!" But any common ground ends there. The populist analysis promotes a retreat from exactly the collaborative international solutions we need more of, not fewer.

## A NEW GENERATION GRASPS A NEW POWER

Today's surging movements reflect their differing contexts, but they share three common characteristics that will affect the strategies for winning progressive change in the coming era.

First, the movements reflect people's yearning for deep change and their belief that the traditional political order will not deliver this. Many more people now believe that they, as citizens, must remake a broken politics. In a number of liberal democracies, people have rejected parties seen as just different flavours of the same establishment. In Britain, for example, over seventeen million citizens voted to take the country out of the European Union after forty years, rejecting what they saw as a cosy establishment consensus, while representatives of the centre ground of politics, of left and right alike, the media, and other national institutions looked on aghast. In regions such as the Middle East, people rally behind the cry "We are no longer afraid" and come out against sclerotic, oppressive systems of patronage and corruption that have kept elites in power for decades. As Dany Yacoub, a young protester on Beirut's streets in October 2019 put it: "They are stealing and pretending that they aren't. Who's responsible, if not them?" A trained teacher, she could not get a job because she does not have the right political connections. She added, "We don't believe them anymore."[16] Hardy Merriman, president of the Washington-based International Center on Nonviolent Conflict (ICNC) argues:

> When governments become more authoritarian, they become less accountable and are likely to become more corrupt and abusive. The wave of current uprisings shows that many people have concluded that the traditional institutional means of making change—elections, the legal system, and dialogue with elites—by themselves are insufficient to address their concerns and make the changes they want to see.[17]

Second, citizen movements have mobilised a new generation that feels robbed of a better economic future and thwarted by older generations. Across the world, more young people are going to universities, but many cannot get the skilled, secure jobs they had imagined because of the long shadow of the financial crisis and the shift to casual, deregulated work, creating what Paul Mason describes as a "mass transnational culture of disillusionment."[18] In the Middle East, two-thirds of the population is now under thirty, and even before Covid-19 hit, up to a third of young people, including graduates, had no job. The pandemic has triggered a job crisis on a scale not seen since the Great Depression, with young people even in wealthier Organisation for Economic Co-operation and Development (OECD) member countries facing unemployment rates of over 18 percent—more than twice those of older adults—and with little recovery expected until after 2021.[19]

Third, digital technology and the shift to a network mindset has enabled fast-igniting, fluid, and loose-knit movements able to change shape to outwit and surprise the authorities. It has provided a transforming ability for people to connect, organise and act cheaply and effectively without the command-and-control central leadership of the past. It provides a way for information and inspiration to proliferate—including across borders, as when the Arab Spring spread across the Middle East.

The hallmark of so many of the new citizen movements is that, through social media, they have mobilised people rapidly, both physically into street protests and virtually through a myriad of actions and debates in cyberspace. At the same time, this strength has sometimes also been a weakness for movements that may struggle to sustain large, fast surges and move from protest into negotiation on specific demands for change. Moving forward, groups are finding effective ways to address this vulnerability, as we will see in later chapters. The digital revolution is doing more than providing new tools for citizen revolutions. It is changing the entire way people think and act in movements. It is the shift that Jeremy Heimans and Henry Timms have called the move from "old power" to "new power." They present the following argument:

> Throughout history, movements have surged, people have organized collectively. . . . But until recently, our everyday opportunities to participate and agitate were much more constrained. Thanks to today's ubiquitous connectivity, we can come together and organize ourselves in ways that are geographically boundless and highly distributed and with unprecedented velocity and reach. This hyperconnectedness has given birth to new models and mindsets that are shaping our age.[20]

People's constant exposure through social media to collective comment, interaction, and action among their peers can give a stronger sense of the individual's power to act—and to do so immediately. In mobilising movements, it is often the so-called network effect that is crucial: having many people in a network in itself stimulates action because, as some start building for a particular action, the promise of mass take-up will encourage others to join the surge.

## CIVIL SOCIETY IN THE NEW WORLD ORDER

New activist movements are bursting with radical responses, showing creative ways forward and channelling people's fear, anger and hope into tackling specific issues. Many harness social media and bottom-up decentralised networks to call for change: from the school climate strikers to the struggle of Black Lives Matter against police killings of African Americans and from the #MeToo stand against sexual assault of women by powerful men to the call of #BringBackOurGirls for the return of the over two hundred schoolgirls abducted by Boko Haram from Chibok, Nigeria, in 2014. Alongside these has been the advent of digital-first campaigning organisations such as Avaaz, Change.org, and 38 Degrees, which, unlike the established, agenda-specific NGOs, work a spectrum of issues to build and mobilise large numbers of supporters in quick-response online campaign actions, providing surge pressure at key moments when an issue is live in the public's attention.

Over the last decade, the upsurge and dynamism of citizen street protests, the hashtag campaigns, and the digital-first campaign groups have often overshadowed the more established civil society organisations—despite closely shared agendas on human rights, corruption, peace, global poverty, environmental threats, racism, and xenophobia. With other NGO leaders in these sectors, we have both wrestled with how to respond to this sharp change in the campaigning terrain.

We know the critical role that the more formal civil society organisations have played over the years in putting issues onto the agenda and steadily pushing them up in it. They provide evidence and analysis to underpin tangible solutions and positive alternatives. They help develop long-term strategies on how to outwit powerful opponents and build alliances. They can fight long-term battles to win round after round of changes in policy and practice from governments and companies, doggedly building toward bigger change and shifting the social consensus. They can nurture organised constituencies of citizens and build living alternative models of a better future. This capacity for sustained organising, influencing, and pioneering new social change models remains as vital as ever. It also complements the street protests, hashtag movements, and digital groups, which, while strong on mobilising big-scale pressure for change and upwelling at critical moments, sometimes struggle to sustain momentum over the long haul or to translate this pressure into negotiations with power brokers to secure tangible concessions, even when mass protest has brought them to the table.

The new context is challenging for mainstream NGOs. Many find themselves with a set of well-honed tools based on lobbying for step-by-step change, using rational case-making, raising the profile of issues in the mainstream media, or lobbying decision-makers in the political centre ground. Yet these NGOs find little traction in a world of nationalist populism, angry street politics and fast-response social media movements.

The NGOs are under attack from the right for being "too political"—told, by one British government minister to "stick to the knitting" of traditional charitable good works and to keep out of campaigning.[21] But they also stand accused by social movements of not being political enough—for example, ready to point fingers at inequality overseas but cautious on the same issues at home. They are criticised for making too many accommodations to the powerful by accepting funding and a cosy relationship from corporates and governments, happy to rub shoulders with global celebrities and mega-rich philanthropists. Dazzled by the invitations coming in thick and fast to mingle with the global elite at Davos, critics argue, the NGOs became compromised as the darling cause of the very people responsible for the inequality and climate change they claim to stand against.

It has not been the best decade for these more established organisations, which have also been drawn into a bureaucratic treadmill, reliant on funding from large donors, acting as major service contractors to governments with work on the ground becoming cautious, technocratic, and unimaginative. Former-NGO-worker-turned-academic Michael Edwards says they have been left offering "thin answers to thick questions."[22] This has contributed to a loss of connection with the grass roots, which is often treated as a passive base, providing funding for the professionalised campaigns at headquarters or urged to click on quick-and-easy email petitions rather than being part of an active movement for change that they own and shape. The charge is that traditional NGOs care more about protecting their brands and their funding base than delivering transformative change.

During a year-long review with frontline campaigners working for social change in Britain, the support and training organisation the Sheila McKechnie Foundation was told that

> many civil society organisations have allowed themselves to become too focused on the model and the money, rather than their mission. . . . [Campaigners] regularly articulated the need for bolder leaders willing to realise the sector's potential by challenging the status quo within their own organisations and beyond. There was a strong desire for a greater sense of solidarity and common purpose across the whole of civil society.[23]

The report concluded with a call for a "new conception of civil society potential called 'Social Power' . . . which comes from both the way civil society works at best, and the resources it holds," arguing that we should accord this social power "equal status with political and economic power."[24]

Some of these difficulties may be inevitable, as Harriet knows from personal experience at Fairtrade International. As the organisation professionalised its system and introduced good management and efficient processes, it moved further away from its campaigning roots in more radical movements. Civil society thinker Mark Heywood, who cofounded the Treatment Action Campaign in South Africa, similarly watched his organisation grow from grassroots activism to internationally acclaimed NGO. Reflecting on this, he articulated his wider worries:

> There's a real danger of the NGOs becoming too close to the elite, of imbibing their bad habits and outlooks. Of course, people need a way to earn a living. But we all need to be careful this doesn't make us risk-averse and cautious. I sometimes reflect on the way people in South Africa were prepared to risk their lives for the struggle against apartheid. We don't take enough risks today in civil society, we're not bold enough. People are dying because of the poverty or repression we campaign on and we should be much more outspoken. These are gross crimes that are preventable—and we should continue to be outraged and driven to urgent action. We've accepted there is a normality to all this too much, become too complacent. Of course, we should celebrate the amazing victories we have won, but this too should drive us on.[25]

With the glass shaken and "globalist" assumptions under attack and in retreat from nationalism, many of these NGOs have been left associated with a discredited form of elite globalisation and unable to break the ice in the populist political discourse that shouts: "Charity begins at home!" International NGOs have been blindsided and bewildered by the earthquakes around us—often left handwringing and impotently fulminating about the "madness" overtaking our world or doggedly pressing on with well-worn narratives from a time when globalisation reigned unchallenged.

Meanwhile, the cutting-edge movements driven by young people have picked up that more radical baton and are pressing on out in front. The big organisations now need to remake and widen their approach for a new age with guts and creativity. They need humbly to contribute their greater resources and capacity for sustaining pressure at the service of wider movements for change—as indeed many are doing, such as Greenpeace supporting the climate school strikes behind the scenes.

Danny Sriskandarajah, chief executive of Oxfam GB—and on the board of peacebuilding organisation International Alert when Harriet was CEO there—told us:

> How we balance and reconnect the institutional parts of civil society with the voluntary, grassroots base is one of the biggest challenges. Take Oxfam and International Alert. They are both good stories of good people coming together to solve a pressing problem—meeting humanitarian need, how to build lasting peace after war. They then build organisations to be more effective in doing this, but in so doing the organisations become institutionalised bits of civic life. These institutions can play a positive role—using their clout to open doors for lesser-known groups, throwing their strength behind issues championed by social movements, using global networks to drive change across borders—but they also need to collaborate better with social movements and avoid crowding out other bits of civil society. A key question is how we build better links between the institutional and informal bits of civil society.[26]

In the next decade, the better-resourced NGOs in the rich nations of the global North need finally to grasp the nettle and seed power and resources to civil society in the global South. They also need to reinvent themselves for the new age, finding the winning combinations of serving local movements, harnessing the reach and power of the internet, and connecting people globally. This will mean finding innovative ways genuinely to empower local groups, and more generously contributing their resources in long-lead research, convening and alliance building.

## MOVEMENTS UNDER ATTACK

The rise of civil society action for progressive change has triggered a counter-reaction by the powerful interests it threatens. Governments are cracking down on people-power movements, part of a wider retreat from the global democratic gains of the twentieth century. In its *Freedom in the World 2020* report, monitoring group Freedom House documented 2019 as the fourteenth consecutive year of decline in global freedom in every part of the world.[27] Some of this is violent repression, with regimes using a "stability first" argument to justify the need to stave off chaos, as in the Middle East. But governments are also using a wider range of tactics—including becoming more adept at thwarting online organising by social movements that had outmanoeuvred them at first. Maria Stephan, who heads up the Program on Nonviolent Action at the US Institute of Peace, says:

> Authoritarian regimes have a learning curve and they are clearly adapting their strategies and tactics. . . . There are many similarities in regimes' responses to nonviolent movements: they blame opposition activities on outsiders; they characterize the opposition as traitors and terrorists; they co-opt the opposition through legislative reforms; they pay off their inner entourage; they counter-mobilize their own supporters; they employ agents provocateurs to foment violence in the ranks of the opposition; they outsource repression to thugs; they master the art of censorship and surveillance; they keep journalists out; they use pseudo-legitimate laws to keep their grip on power; and they assemble a coalition of allies to share techniques and tactics.[28]

More widely, civil society organisations have been in the firing line from right-wing populists, painted as another elite institution getting in the way of ordinary people's common-sense views. This becomes especially true where organisations defend the rights of minority groups and other "outsiders." In Hungary, for example, right-wing leader Viktor Orbán has railed against NGOs as agents of foreign forces undermining the nation and has instituted a series of crackdowns on independent NGOs and human rights groups to restrict their activity, funding, and voice. Organisations are required to have national security clearance and permits and pay a 25 percent tax on foreign funding for activities "supporting migration"—with huge fines for failure to do so. The government dubbed these the "Stop Soros" laws as Orbán, during his successful 2018 re-election campaign, deployed vitriolic, anti-Semitic attacks on the Hungarian-born businessman and philanthropist George Soros. Soros's Open Society Foundation and the liberal university he founded in Budapest have had to withdraw from Hungary, unable to operate, though the foundation continues to support Hungarian civic groups that are under intense pressure.

Similar attacks have escalated in countries such as Poland, Turkey, and India, with its vibrant civil society made up of three million organisations and movements. In 2017, international civil society network CIVICUS, which monitors the space for civil society to operate internationally, downgraded India's classification to "obstructed." In a special report on India, the group noted:

> The government uses such tactics as restrictive legislation to deny civil society organisations (CSOs) their right to register, and in some cases suspends or withdraws CSO permits to operate. Resourcing of CSOs is also being targeted: some CSOs have been prevented from receiving funding from external sources, and some have had their bank accounts suspended.... It has become common for human rights defenders and those who expose government malpractice to be threatened and attacked, with the aim of silencing them and intimidating others.... Some have been assassinated. Indian authorities have also used the media to demonise human rights defenders.... Activists have been subjected to smear campaigns and accused of promoting anti-nationalist agendas or of being the agents of western power.[29]

In 2019, matters worsened when the Indian authorities shut down the internet and banned protests to try to block the largest nationwide demonstrations in four decades against the Modi government's anti-Muslim discrimination in its new citizenship law.[30] In September 2020, Amnesty International made the shocking announcement it had been forced to halt all of its work in India after a sustained program of government harassment culminating in its bank accounts being frozen.

CIVICUS has rung the alarm on this wider trend of "closing civil society space," saying the sector is under serious attack in 111 countries—well over half.[31] This marks a major retreat from progress after the fall of communism in Europe and the shift from dictatorship to democracy in many parts of Latin America, Africa, and Asia. Most in the firing line are indigenous people, trade unions, and groups defending the rights of minorities or fighting for social and environmental justice.

Leading NGO Human Rights Watch reports that in the last decade, for example, more than three hundred activists have been killed in the Brazilian Amazon over land and forest disputes, many by illegal loggers.[32] These have escalated as President Bolsonaro cuts back on enforcing environmental laws, weakens environmental agencies, and lashes out at those defending the rainforest. In December 2018, after Gilson Temponi, president of a farmers' association in Placas, Pará state, reported illegal logging and death threats from loggers, two men knocked on his door and shot him dead. Dilma Ferreira Silva, an environmental activist in the same state, and five other people were killed in 2019 under orders of a landowner involved in illegal logging.

Media and social media campaigns are also vilifying and undermining civil society. In Britain, for example, a narrative has been propagated that big charities have become "politicised" by head office staff and trustees taking up left-wing campaigns, away from their true mission of helping people. Particular vitriol has been reserved for attacks on international NGOs in an almost daily drumbeat of exposes, from levels of CEO pay to corruption or over-aggressive fundraising techniques. Of course, international NGOs should be subject to scrutiny and their malpractice exposed and addressed, as they have been, for example, following a series of serious safeguarding breaches, including sexual exploitation of vulnerable groups. But other attacks have proved groundless and have been part of wider right-wing agendas to push back against campaigning by NGOs who championed Britain's commitment to meet the UN target to spend 0.7 percent of GDP on international aid.

When Ben headed up Bond, the membership network for international development NGOs, these simmering hostilities between charities, the media, and the government intensified following the appointment of liberal-turned-neo-conservative former journalist William Shawcross as chair of the Charity Commission, the regulator for England and Wales, along with a group of likeminded new board members. Overlooking other pressing issues, Shawcross identified Islamist extremism in charities as the "most deadly" problem the charity sector faced,[33] even though the commission's own lead investigator, David Walker, had previously said that "terrorist abuse is actually very rare in charities."[34] The new board members set about pursuing their agenda, with statutory investigations against Muslim-based charities soaring to over a third of the total investigations (despite Muslim charities being less than 1 percent of the total number of charities) and created a new category of inquiry labelled "extremism and radicalisation"[35] They used the commission—with allies in newspapers they briefed off the record providing covering fire through hostile stories about Muslim charities—to prosecute a relentless campaign to find evidence for this theory, with little success. Ben worked closely with large Muslim development charities as they became tied down in a barrage of inquiries, which led nowhere but diverted huge management resources away from their frontline responses to pressing humanitarian crises.

In one instance, board members of the commission pressured staff to tell two respected human rights foundations, the Joseph Rowntree Charitable Trust (JRCT) and Roddick Foundation, to cut off their funding to Cage—an organisation working with communities affected by the war on terror—and say they would never fund it again, threatening them with intrusive investigations if they refused. This was shown in emails disclosed later when Cage challenged the action in the High Court. In the end, the court forced the Charity Commission to climb down and admit it had exceeded its remit.[36] After Ben spoke out in the media on the issue, he was given a friendly off-the-record warning by an official to be careful, as the board members involved were furious about the whole episode.

## BALLOT BOX OR CITIZEN ACTION?

In the coming decade, can civil society find its way through the threats it faces from external opponents and the dangers it faces from within? Can it find a path from mass street protest to securing concrete advances for people and planet? Can it compete in an era of noisy populism and toxic public debate via social media? We emphatically believe it can and, indeed, that we will see citizen movements come into their own to reset our world's direction.

Conventional thinking grossly underestimates the role of citizens in achieving change compared to electoral politics. And yet many social transformations have come about only because citizens have imagined, acted, created, and organised. Workers have come together in trade unions, friendly societies, and cooperatives to fight the exploitation of the industrial age. In more recent times, feminist, civil rights, and green campaigners have pushed new agendas from the margins to the mainstream. In some cases, these movements gave birth to political parties, as when the environment movement spawned green parties across Europe; in others, what started as fringe social movements have gone on to transform the priorities of mainstream politics.

But the reshaping influence of citizen movements is often drowned out by the obsessive daily chatter of the minutiae of electoral politics.[37] Mark and Paul Engler observe in their outstanding study of nonviolent resistance:

> Decade after decade unarmed mobilizations have created defining moments. . . . That most pundits have little to say about social movement eruptions, no matter how often they seize the spotlight, reflects a bias in their thinking about how social change happens. The same analysts who invariably describe waves of unarmed revolt as spontaneous and uncontrolled spend endless hours speculating on which candidates might enter into elections that are still years away.[38]

Often, commentary focuses on the relatively short period at the end of the process when elected politicians enact laws or policies on which civil society has campaigned for decades. Take, for example, the advance in the past decade in country after country to legalise same-sex marriage. Decades of tough campaigns to shift laws and social expectations made the final legislative step possible—helped along at times by new narratives celebrating shared positive values of love and equality, as in the successful campaign for equal marriage in Ireland.[39] Sometimes we all talk as if making change is up to politicians, with the role of citizens being only to cast a vote every few years or knock on doors to get the right party elected; yet we have power in our own hands to set agendas and forge concrete change.

There are particular times when citizens are called to reset the basic assumptions and frameworks of mainstream politics and wider society. We are living in just such a time. Our traditional nation-based politics and the free market dogmas of the last four decades have left local communities battered and hollowed out and have failed to resolve the deep contradictions thrown up by global challenges. In this dark landscape, the siren call and simple answers of populist politics will continue to resonate until citizen movements reshape the terms of the debate and win support for approaches that deal with the root causes of the global and local challenges we face, not just their symptoms.

Our call for citizen-led change does not involve a plague-on-all-your-houses dismissal of mainstream democracy. Electoral politics is obviously a vital battleground for what the future holds. But for those interested in big change, there are good reasons to focus on civil society. For a start, it can ensure governments are kept accountable—not just every few years at elections, but constantly. A patchwork of pressure groups and charities do this vital job day-in-day-out, formulating proposals for better policy (often drawing on their frontline practical experience), lobbying officials and politicians, spotlighting hidden citizen concerns to journalists, calling policy makers to account on unmet promises. Movements also play a key role in expanding the sense of belief in the possibility of bigger change among the wider public that is needed for progressive electoral politics to win.

Indeed, citizen action through civil society can also remake the very essence of how we think about political power. Veteran activist and writer Hilary Wainwright argues for a new type of thinking about how we "win power" to make big change happen. Radicals have often focused on how to gain control of the levers of the state to meet the needs of the people through, say, redistributing resources or putting in place social justice measures. Whether won through the ballot box or revolution, this is what she terms "power over." This type of power is important, of course, but Wainwright urges us to look more toward "power to" or "power-as-transformative-capacity" noting that:

> The distinctive feature of the 1960s and 70s was that people took power into their own hands, discovering through collective action that they had capacities of their own to bring about change. These were not simply exerting pressure on the governing party to do something on their behalf. Their approach was more directly transformative . . . a pervasive and self-confident assertion of people's own practical knowledge, as well as their collaborative capacity. It was pitched against the claims of those in authority to know "what people need" and accompanied by an inventiveness about the forms of organisation that would build that capacity.[40]

Digital technology has supercharged this strategy. Citizens and movements have harnessed it to connect decentralised networks, channelling their ideals, knowledge, and creative energy into "power to" manifest change for themselves. We see many examples of this in action, from new forms of leaderless protest to the emergence of socially and ecologically driven economies beyond profit or reliance on the state. Such examples model what a different future could look like and reveal new sources of citizen power bending the status quo toward an arc of transformation. Better linking these myriad initiatives into a grid more powerful than the sum of its parts is the key connector that will transform citizen movements in the coming era.

Building citizen power in this way should not be a separate route up the mountain of transformation from that of government and politics. Rather, the two paths need to crisscross each other all the way up. A vital part of the strategy ahead will be seeking ways to maximise the symbiosis between the two. Just as citizens push local authorities, governments, and companies to change their policies, government at local, national, and international level can enable positive civil society action through better laws and policies, and by adopting or helping to scale up viable citizen alternatives for a "good society." As Compass think tank head Neal Lawson argues, the role of government should now be all about helping to "join up, scale up, accelerate, replicate and project these emerging forms of collaborative action to ensure they become the predominant form of 'deciding and doing' in the 21st century."[41]

At its best, this can become a virtuous circle with government-led and civil society–led changes supporting each other to move forward. In campaigning, civil society often needs to force a reluctant government or company to take action. Sometimes the campaign then reaches a tipping point where insiders see they will have to move—but need the public pressure to take wider society with them. President Obama was fond of retelling the famous story of the legendary civil rights and labour organiser A. Philip Randolph's meeting with President Franklin D. Roosevelt at the White House to push for an expansion of civil rights. "I agree with you in every respect," said the president. "Now you have to go out and make me do it."[42]

The urgent need to address major global challenges has never been more pressing: fewer than ten years remain to avert climate catastrophe; wars have escalated after decades where peace was at last gaining the upper hand; soaring numbers are forced by war and persecution to flee their homes and seek sanctuary in other countries; and persistent poverty is compounded by grotesque inequities based on race, class, and geography. Just when we most needed international solutions, we faced the dangerous growth of xenophobic blind-alley politics. And then Covid-19 ambushed our world, adding fuel to the fires.

## A DIFFERENT PATH

These are dark times. Yet, like many who long for a saner, safer world, we both believe this is a moment for real hope—that the last ten years have brought us to a point where the stark choices facing our global community can inspire unprecedented action. Mass uprisings of citizens have shown the level of yearning for change across the world. Now, people are forging the advance guard of the different paths we need to take, showing a determination only strengthened by the sudden, global horror of the pandemic—first, armies of volunteers rushing to support the most vulnerable, then a healthy proliferation of new visions and strategies for recoveries that could create radically fairer, greener, and more enlightened societies than what came before.

We imagine citizens travelling the path to change on a sturdy adult tricycle of the future—perhaps one of those three-wheelers developed to provide car-free transport for kids, or an electric cargo bike delivering our shopping. The wheels represent the three vital elements of progress: believe, battle, and build. Our beliefs ride out in front. They guide the direction, provide the framework for all our decisions, and enable humanity to nurture once more values such as empowerment, collaboration, hope, and compassion that enable deep change to occur. At the back, one wheel powers our campaigns, which must be bold and ambitious to meet the scale of the problems we face—focused on securing changes that kick off a chain reaction toward transformation. Meanwhile, the third wheel is turning as citizens build new models for living today. The future, they say, is dappled in the present. And a quiet revolution is underway through the abundance of initiatives in the social economy and experiments in sustainable and democratic living, from energy cooperatives to Fairtrade. These schemes provide a beacon on the hill lighting the way to a better place where people would rather live.

We see in their undaunted courage and creativity the beginnings of a more coherent citizen strategy for change, which we can all join, and which show a better way forward for communities, nations, and the world. People are fighting the fires—and none burns more fiercely than the climate catastrophe.

*Chapter Three*

# The Timed Test We Cannot Fail

*How civil society is driving change with
ten years to prevent climate catastrophe.*

It is a grainy photo of an unknown, fragile girl with tight pigtails pulled back from her face. Behind her loom the sombre stone blocks of the Swedish Parliament, granite to her hand-painted, flimsy cardboard sign. This is the teenager who sparked school strikes across the world, becoming the living symbol of today's citizen activists.

The school strikers surprised everyone. The rise of this movement was not planned. No one would have dared to dream so big. It was the simple courageous action of one schoolgirl who stood upon decades of research, science, and campaigning and gave them a new, unstoppable heart and soul and momentum.

For years, scientists and NGOs had kept on arguing the science. Again and again, they would throw up the graphs and thermometers to prove that the globe was warming. Dangerously so. Every time their results were questioned, they doubled down and found yet more evidence.

In 2006, US vice president Al Gore was wowing audiences around the world with *An Inconvenient Truth*, a strangely compelling film of line graphs and scientific calculations. Harriet arranged a babysitter so she could pedal over to London's Shepherd's Bush and watch a special screening organised by Save the Children to galvanise international NGOs. In the silence of the cinema, you could hear the pennies dropping.

Harriet's anecdotal experiences fit into this large analytical frame. She had been a childhood climate denier. Growing up, her mother regaled the family with tales of how it used to be colder in her childhood when, evacuated to Badger Farm in Somerset, in the West of England, during World War

II, she used to skate on the frozen watery Levels. In Harriet's own shaming proof of how people can dismiss facts, she told herself that her mother always exaggerated—that she was, as always, spinning a good old yarn about the good old days. But Harriet was absorbed with pain about animal species being made extinct by human action. Still at primary school, she was moved to tears by the words of the naturalist and author Gerald Durrell and copied out in big rounded letters: "Man is sawing off the very branch on which he sits."

Fast forward several decades, and Harriet was working for Fairtrade. As a global movement, they were finally gaining significant enough market shares to shift agendas by being ruthlessly single-minded. They had one objective only: to win fairer prices for smallholder farmers and workers in developing countries. Full stop. While people were bringing up other issues, they kept on marching down that one clear track.

But climate change kept coming up—as when Harriet visited the Kagera Co-operative Union in the foothills of Mount Kilimanjaro, Tanzania. These old coffee farmers, mostly missing a few teeth, were among the founding fathers of Fairtrade and of the cooperative model in the new nation of Tanzania back in 1961. Standing, sweating, on their small, dusty plots, Harriet listened as they talked about the changing weather. This was a serious matter: their whole income at stake. The climate, they told her, had gone mad. When it used to rain, it was now sunny; when it used to be sunny, it was now raining. They could no longer rely on the farming rhythms learned from their parents and grandparents.

Back in London, their words haunted Harriet. Then came news from Uganda, where one coffee cooperative saw members killed and whole villages swept away by torrential rains. Just weeks later, the Fairtrade office heard from Nicaraguan coffee farmers caught in catastrophic weather, then farmers in the Caribbean as their banana trees were devastated. The roll call grew and grew. It seemed so strange; how could this be happening? In the cinematic dark, listening to Al Gore, Harriet finally understood how science explained the stories: the coffee farmers were living today's reality of this global catastrophe. From that moment, she realised that the global issues of our time are poverty, conflict, refugees, and climate change—and that they are all interconnected. For example, climate change is an exacerbating factor of conflict and of poverty, and the most vulnerable are the hardest hit by changing weather. So our responses as civil society must be better interconnected, too.

At the time, the big environmental NGOs were pushing climate change up the agenda, chipping away at major political players to build support for action, securing government and multilateral commitments. In Britain, Friends of the Earth ran a classic three-year campaign with 130,000 people lobbying their members of Parliament, supported by the band Radiohead, involving all political parties in the demands, spreading the campaign to Europe—until 2008, when the UK Climate Change Act came into force, committing the government to its first fully binding legal targets to cut greenhouse gases by 80 percent by 2050. Decades of campaigning by such NGOs worldwide fostered a long, slow burn of raising public awareness, building a bedrock of knowledge among opinion leaders, and winning changes from governments and companies.

Then the 2008 financial crash pushed attention and resources away, as governments focused on saving the banks and cut budgets that could have funded tackling climate change. One casualty was the utter failure of the 2009 international UN Climate Change Conference (COP) talks in Copenhagen (dubbed "Brokenhagen")—a salutary warning for the delayed COP26 talks being hosted by Britain in 2021. As a result, government actions on climate fell far short of what was needed, good work was abruptly stopped, and the public was preoccupied by coping with austerity.

The climate activists had underestimated the scale of the opposition from some countries that derailed the global talks—and from the fossil fuel industry. Directly copying tactics from the tobacco industry, oil and gas companies created confusion and doubt, tying the climate movement up in proving facts while the climate deniers and delayers spoke directly to people about lost jobs, deserted towns and coal miners' futures. In the United States, Australia, and Brazil, right-wing populists who disputed climate change were voted into government.

Meanwhile, year by year, reports by the UN's Intergovernmental Panel on Climate Change (IPCC) became starker, consistently proving beyond a doubt that the world was warming up to dangerous levels, getting close to reaching 1.5 percent above pre-industrial levels, the point at which a series of feedback loops will be set off, further entrenching warming and sea-level rise as ice melts. We have, the scientists say, ten years to stop the most dangerous temperature increases. We are "likely" to reach 1.5 percent between 2030 and 2050 if the world continues warming at the current rate. So, to keep the temperature increases below 1.5 percent, we must halve $CO_2$ emissions by 2030 and, by 2050 at the latest, reach "net zero"—the point at which our carbon footprint is effectively zero because we offset remaining emissions. Even these estimates are now thought to be too conservative. This is the make-or-break decade to avert calamity. And the temperatures keep rising relentlessly, and biodiversity is collapsing.[1]

In response, a new wave of protest movements—from school strikers, the Sunrise movement and 350.org—have exploded onto our streets, transforming the political urgency and ambition. These grassroots activists are tearing up the campaign rulebook and transforming what is politically possible in the 2020s.

As international civil society network CIVICUS suggests, such new movements should set "the path for a radical re-haul of civil society in order to get back to our roots and organise to build people's power and define a future based on local initiatives and organising."[2] International NGOs that do not see this risk, CIVICUS warns, will become more irrelevant in the lives of people who should be their natural constituency, those on the frontline of poverty, austerity, and climate change, whether in the global North of rich nations or the global South.

The breadth and depth of today's climate movements are up to the challenge—if they can deepen and sustain their momentum. They stretch from Amazonian indigenous people to Indian farmers, from community initiatives on marginalised public-housing sites to school strikers in Malawi, and from progressive companies to city mayors. Some are organising nonviolent direct action or seeking to cut off the finances flowing into fossil fuels, while others build the alternatives that foreshadow the future and develop technical, political, and business solutions. Sometimes, each plays to its strengths; other times, they need to come together if we are to converge on a carbon-free future. It is an extraordinary global whirlwind trying to win the political agreements and implement the practical solutions in time. The clock is ticking: we have just ten years.

There can be no doubt that it is thanks to civil society that, finally, people are taking climate change more seriously. Of course, the shifts to a low-carbon world will depend upon the whole of society, from businesses to consumers, governments, and civil servants, with an untried level of collaboration. But civil society has shifted global agendas and is pushing for the levels of radical government actions needed, at pace. The opposition is hefty. But this is not the proverbial David against Goliath, with Greta Thunberg going it alone against Trump and Mighty Oil and Gas. This is much more like Goliath slugging it out against Goliath. The forces arranged on each side are formidable. The climate movement boasts some of the world's brightest minds, strongest campaigners, and biggest strategic thinkers and a mass of ordinary people with deep determination, as well as those with deep pockets—and they are ready for the struggle of our lives.

## SCHOOL'S OUT FOR CLIMATE

It took a teenager to say: "Listen up!" Greta Thunberg speaks directly, shaking people out of their lethargy. She tells it like it is. She is angry, blisteringly angry, her eyebrows knit in fury, and she has inspired a movement that has flown around the world.

On 20 September 2019, according to organisers 350.org, a reported four million people from nearly all US states and 165 countries took to the streets in the biggest climate mobilisation in history, starting in the Pacific islands and Australia and moving gradually around the world, like a New Year's celebration. For this "general strike," adults were encouraged to support the young people—under strict instructions not to bring branded banners. Over 70 trade unions, 3,000 businesses and 800 civil society organisations got behind the young people, from Bangladesh and Kenya to New York, where Greta received a rock-star welcome. After sailing across the Atlantic, she led a march through the streets to the United Nations Headquarters, surrounded by chants of "Fossil fuel lobbyists have to go!"

At the United Nations Climate Action Summit days later, Greta did not mince her words: "This is all wrong. . . . You have stolen my dreams and my childhood with your empty words. People are suffering. People are dying. Entire ecosystems are collapsing. We are in the beginning of a mass extinction, and all you can talk about is money and fairy-tales of eternal economic growth. How dare you!"[3]

Her bleak words, delivered with raw emotion, resonated with the visceral anger felt by so many young people in the face of government inaction. In a rallying call for civil society everywhere, Greta Thunberg said: "We proved that it does matter what you do and that no one is too small to make a difference."[4] Now #FridaysforFuture is far from small. A quick visit to its basic website is always motivating, with school strikes recorded in Burkina Faso, Zambia, Azerbaijan, Afghanistan, and Iraqi Kurdistan—the list rolls on.

Of course, young people have always been in the forefront of environmental struggles.[5] The difference is that, this time, the young people have united, across continents, behind one startlingly new technique—the school strike—often acting on the same day. That has given them a break-through.

The school strikers are now well organised, using their phones and the internet to plan—often supported with logistics behind the scenes from the traditional environmental NGOs such as Greenpeace. This is unlike any generation before, any global campaign before. The young people have a compelling case and have found their voice to speak from the heart about their futures being stolen from them. As people have lost trust in institutions, young activists have won respect in new ways. The messenger is key: people know they are campaigning in their own time, with no other agenda.

Initially, the school strikers mostly kept a laser-like focus on highlighting the problem, urging others to work out the solutions. But in the UK, one group has gone a step further. In February 2020, they crowded into a room in Parliament, as MPs supported the first bill ever drafted by students, calling for a new climate change act to transform education and ensure that all educational buildings reach zero carbon. "We have done our homework," enthused the bubbly twenty-five-year-old Zamzam Ibrahim, then president of the National Union of Students and cofounder of the initiative #TeachtheFuture, presenting the young people's proposed legislation. "To avoid us repeating the failures of the past, our education system must do better to equip young people with the knowledge, the skills and the agency to tackle these crises."[6]

Born in Sweden to parents who were refugees from the war in Somalia, she came to live in a working-class community in Bolton at age nine, going on to study finance and accounting at Salford University, with climate change never featuring once in her whole education—a situation she is determined to remedy. Describing herself as "opinionated," Zamzam is constantly seeking to tie together the big issues of climate change, inequality, racism, and sexism, and to ensure that people who are disproportionately affected by climate change—such as climate refugees overseas—are given more of a voice. Sometimes, she tells Harriet with frustration, people stay in their silos and look only through the lens of climate change, but she believes that how we talk about climate justice must take into account wider injustices and how all the issues connect. She took hope, she says, when climate strikers came out against restrictive immigration moves by the government. "As activists, we have to be ready to constantly challenge ourselves, to question our own status quo, to make sure our work is always relevant and impactful and go to the root causes."[7]

Part of that constant questioning in the environmental movement has more recently included the challenge of being too white and too middle class, and many movements are actively seeking to better engage with black and minority ethnic communities and to address their priorities. As Black Lives Matter exploded, an Ashden colleague of Harriet's from Haiti, Jennifer Lauture, remembers being one of very few black students studying environmental sciences in the United States; she said: "For the first time in years I've felt that there is momentum to change. . . . In a lot of the places in the US affected by environmental issues like dirty water and coal pollution, you see indigenous people fighting for their land rights, against environmental racism. In the US, a lot of climate activists are minority groups. I'm hoping that now their stories will come up more in the media."

## INCONVENIENT ACTION FROM EXTINCTION REBELLION

It is not just the young ratcheting up the urgency. On 31 October 2018, Extinction Rebellion (XR) burst onto London's streets in all their Technicolor glory. A fast-spreading movement, XR include many retired people from genteel English country towns, ready to be arrested to get action on climate change. They argue that democracy is broken, that polite petitions, behaving well, and meetings with elected representatives are not getting results. With their hourglass symbol representing time running out, a typical leaflet reads:

"We are in trouble. Sea levels are rising. Heatwaves are killing crops. The Arctic is melting, and Africa and the Amazon are on fire." Like the school strikers, XR believes in telling it like it is, churning out terrifying facts and figures, pointing to research that shows that over 40 percent of insect species are declining, and a third are endangered.

Once you read the science, it is hard not to be messianic about climate change—and XR most certainly is. Some environmental charities have shied away from bombarding the public with negative, horrifying imagery. The thinking was that this put people off and made NGOs sound hectoring. But XR is not pulling any punches. It believes in creating moments of civil disobedience to demand attention and compel government action to avoid climate and biodiversity tipping points. XR is getting noticed as a result and has mushroomed across 58 countries from the United States to Austria, from Australia to India.

Will Shanks, a charming, redheaded scientist fresh from the university who worked for a French company refitting homes to reduce their carbon footprint, was among the first to join XR. He did not think it was brave to court arrest; he found it a release. He told Harriet, "I would sit at my parents' dinner table, and everyone would be chatting as normal, and inside my head, I would be saying: 'Can't you see? We are doomed. We have to do something about this.' I couldn't believe how much people are behaving as normal when the world isn't normal."

XR cofounder Dr. Gail Bradbrook argues that the truth is painful; that you have to hold it in your heart and not just in your head, so local XR groups dedicate whole meetings to their feelings of grief. Surprisingly, there is more talk about grief and pain in the XR movement than in most of today's peace groups seeking to end violent conflicts.

XR's threefold commitments are: tell the truth, halt biodiversity loss and reduce greenhouse gas emissions to net zero by 2025, and hold a citizens' assembly to draw up policies to create climate and ecological justice. When the movement spread to the United States, XR added a fourth commitment to a just transition: prioritising vulnerable and indigenous peoples. At first, members purposely did not have policy positions on the exact route to reach their goals, arguing that a legally binding citizens' assembly should determine them. XR believe that not getting drawn into specific policy debates enables them to keep the focus on the big-picture crisis. That is frustrating for some policy makers, keen to engage in solutions, and for some members who feel invigorated by the actions—only to return feeling disempowered by not moving on to the solutions. But local groups, for whom building community is key, are supporting solutions in their areas.

Now, across the UK, the first citizens' assemblies, conventions, or resident commissions, have met to discuss solutions to climate change. The most significant was established by six House of Commons Select Committees, with 108 people selected randomly but adjusted to ensure a spread of age, class, ethnicity, and views—including sceptics—since everyone will be affected by government measures to meet the legal commitment to reduce carbon emissions.[8] In autumn 2020 they reported, with their clear list of priority recommendations, that steps taken to recover from Covid-19 should also cut greenhouse gases and green all our lifestyles, from encouraging cycling to discouraging flying.

Such inclusion is a key point for advocates pressing for radical changes to meet the goal of net zero, arguing that we must involve people in decisions and show the side benefits of climate action, such as improved health if air pollution levels decrease. The citizens' assemblies follow the "deliberative democracy" model pioneered in Canada, and picked up in France, enabling people to discuss difficult options in more detail. Experts guide discussions, while questions for the assemblies are submitted by environmental groups, businesses, and trade unions—but, for XR, such assemblies must be given power to ensure their recommendations are followed. Meanwhile, the XR rebels want to be seen and heard, and to do that they are ready to break the law and fill the prisons.

They take their inspiration from a long history of nonviolent civil disobedience, from the Indian independence struggles to the American civil rights movements, pointing out that everyone makes heroes of past rebels such as Nelson Mandela, but, often, they do not like today's rebels disrupting their lives. Nonviolent direct action is a fully developed methodology for citizens to effect large-scale change peacefully. It includes mass noncooperation with the state or active civil disobedience by large groups to disrupt or defy the law, without using violence, as part of planned strategy to force an opponent to change. As its famous proponent Martin Luther King Jr. said, "Nonviolence is a powerful and just weapon. Indeed, it is a weapon unique in history, which cuts without wounding and ennobles the man who wields it. It seeks to secure moral ends through moral means. I believe in this method because I think it is the only way to re-establish a broken community."[9]

So, believing that public disorder and mass arrests focus government minds, XR's strategy is one of escalating civil disobedience, to the point of paralysing the government and its agencies. "Get like the French, stop being so polite, get your tractors onto the streets and have debates," Dr. Gail Bradbrook exhorted a group of farmers in 2019.[10] Dagan Jones is a buffalo farmer from Hampshire who followed that call, driving a pink biodiesel tractor to "take Westminster Bridge."[11] And XR has "taken" other bridges, blocked the roads outside Parliament, and glued themselves to walkways and buildings, including Shell's HQ.

In October 2019, Harriet cycled to Trafalgar Square, London, head down in the pouring rain. The vast stone lions gazed over an eerie quiet as people scurried past to enjoy the National Gallery's art or get to work. Then, suddenly, a message ran through phones and, from nowhere, hundreds of people appeared; hourglass banners fluttered, tents popped up, including the trademark "wellbeing tent," music played and the protesters settled in. Soon the police appeared in their yellow jackets, faced with their constant dilemma of how to handle the protests.

Interestingly, and perhaps surprisingly, at first XR seemed to take the public with them. People chatting on buses and trains murmured respect for what XR was ready to do, and for their views—even if they disagreed with particular actions.[12] Even establishment figures, such as Sir David King, the UK government's chief scientific adviser on climate change from 2000 to 2007, say that "XR have a point" or, "It's hard to disagree with them."[13] By November 2019, over 11,000 scientists from 153 countries had come out in favour of action on the global crises from protecting ecosystems to tackling fossil fuels, saying that, in this gloomy situation, citizen movements give them hope.[14]

XR pulled off its most dramatic stunt at London City Airport where a smart man in a suit grounded a plane before take-off by refusing to sit down while he read his demands; a fellow protester glued himself to another plane fuselage. Eighty-two-year-old Phil Kingston was among those arrested. XR spokesman Rupert Read said, "By nonviolently shutting down this airport, in homage to the style of the Hong Kong democracy protesters, we are demonstrating the utter frailty of the transport systems that countries such as ours, unwisely, have come to depend upon." The group said hundreds of people had signed up to "nonviolently use their bodies" to close the airport.[15] More controversial was the decision by the Canning Town group in October 2019 to stop a rush hour Underground train. That tested the public's patience, especially working people on their commute, sparking deep reflection in the movement with many uneasy about the action while respecting the devolved decision making that, within basic principles, empowers groups to decide on their stunts. A year later and, to some, more controversially still, XR activists blockaded printing presses to obstruct distribution of the *Times* and *Sun* newspapers as a protest against the power of climate change–sceptic billionaire newspaper owners like Rupert Murdoch, whom they accused of blocking the truth.

Both XR and the school strikers have become global movements while keeping decentralised local roots: an unpredictable model that has yielded phenomenal results. They are adding raw energy to the momentum already building through every channel, from Sir David Attenborough's devastatingly sad films of wildlife under threat, to scientists' mounting evidence and calls for actions, to mainstream NGOs solidly pushing the case. Indeed, whenever people talk about a campaign's "overnight, run-away success" you can be sure that it has been built on bedrock of long, slow awareness raising. At Apple, they say that each new product is but the springboard for the next.

The same applies to social movements. Just as the #MeToo match lit a flame that spread like wildfire because, for decades, women had been organising and demanding rights, so too the school strikes and XR have propelled change forward.

Following a fortnight of nonstop protests in April 2019, and after XR members met with leading politicians, the Welsh and UK Parliaments declared a climate emergency, which has no legislative effect but paved the way for government action. Then the UK government announced the 2050 target to reach net zero, while two-thirds of English local authorities have declared a climate emergency and are drawing up action plans.[16] These are huge victories, undoubtedly made possible by the protests that shifted public awareness and put climate into people's everyday discussions, thus creating a space in which government action became not only permissible but desirable.

Importantly, public concern held up despite Covid-19 and job losses rocketing up the worry list. Globally, IPSOS Mori reports that four in five people agree that we are headed for disaster if we don't act fast[17] and that 71 percent see climate change as significant a threat as Covid in the long run.[18] In a GlobeScan poll across 27 countries, 90 percent of people see climate change as a serious issue (in the United States, 81 percent, up from 60 percent in six years) with people in Kenya, Mexico, Argentina, Nigeria, and Turkey wanting the most urgent action from their governments. According to Eric Whan from pollsters GlobeScan, the Covid-19 crisis has increased people's sense of the threat from rising temperatures: "This is a year of vulnerability and exacerbation of inequality and those most susceptible to disruption feel the greatest level of seriousness."

Such heightened awareness may be starting to influence political behaviour, as a wave of Green Party candidates was unexpectedly swept into power in European Parliament elections in May 2019. Finland has committed to be carbon neutral by 2035, and Norway has a 2030 target[19] while the adoption of the European Green Deal on 11 December 2019, as the flagship policy of President Ursula von der Leyen's new European Commission, was almost certainly made possible by the pressure of social movements.[20]

## ONLY 3.5 PERCENT OF PEOPLE TO WIN CHANGE

XR's founders are influenced by Harvard University political scientist Erica Chenoweth, who argues that you need 3.5 percent of the population to actively participate in protests over a sustained time to secure political change and open the window of acceptable policy shifts. In the United States, that would mean 11 million citizens actively engaged in a movement, or 2.3 million in the UK.[21] Her research finds that sustained nonviolent civil disobedience, as well as being the moral choice, is the most effective way of achieving goals—in fact, twice as effective as violent campaigns. Chenoweth underscores the rich US history of resistance, from economic cooperatives and empowering the labour movement to putting climate reform on the agenda and winning "voting rights for women and for African Americans living in the Jim Crow south. . . . In fact, it is hard to identify a progressive cause in the United States that has advanced without a civil resistance movement behind it."[22]

These movements work, she says, when "they constantly increase their base of supporters, build coalitions, leverage social networks, and generate connections with those in the opponent's network who may be ambivalent about co-operating with oppressive policies." She continues: "Crucially, nonviolent resistance works not by melting the heart of the opponent but by constraining their options."

She says of XR, "They are up against a lot of inertia. . . . But I think that they have an incredibly thoughtful and strategic core. And they seem to have all the right instincts about how to develop and teach through a nonviolent resistance campaign."

Critics argue that successful movements specifically target the systems of oppression they aim to overthrow, whereas XR, while seeking to tie up the workings of the state, including the police and courts, has impacted the general travelling public not directly responsible for climate policy. XR's answer is that only through maximum disruption can they reach policy makers; this, they say, is another form of democracy. But these are live debates as they review their strategies and their internal levels of accountability and consider how to engage a wider and, in particular, a more diverse membership. By September 2020, new strategies were emerging as XR evolved to maintain momentum. Some activists swung behind a new environment bill in Parliament while others shifted tack with different groups targeting the corporates, financiers, think tanks, or lobbyists.

For the campaigners, this is the fight of their lives, to save thousands of species—and humankind—from extinction. The stakes could not be higher. Nor could the opposition be tougher, more formidable or eye-wateringly well funded, with a powerful interplay between the interests of companies and national governments that either own or are comprehensively lobbied by oil and gas companies. That is why some sections of civil society are focused on exposing the companies' tactics.

## EXPOSING FOSSIL FUEL MERCHANTS

In 2017, fossil fuel companies benefited from subsidies of US$5.2 trillion a year.[23] It is hard to grasp such numbers: US$5,200,000,000,000. That is

US$14.2 billion a day, or US$9.8 million per minute. Every day. For a year. Which is equivalent to 6.5 percent of global GDP.

Who revealed this? The International Monetary Fund (IMF), the global body charged with keeping the world economy stable and a byword of conservative thinking, which called its own revelation "shocking," citing that the annual subsidy is greater than the total health spending of all the world's governments.[24]

The sum includes direct government subsidies at some US$500 billion a year, for example, to reduce the retail price of fuel. But the IMF takes a wider, less conventional definition of subsidies, including polluters not paying the costs offloaded onto governments and taxpayers—for example, the bills for dealing with flooding caused by climate change, or the harm caused to residents with respiratory problems in cities like Beijing or Delhi. The IMF calculated that, if fuel prices had included all these hidden costs and so changed behaviours, estimated global $CO_2$ emissions in 2015 would have been 28 percent lower, fossil fuel air pollution deaths 46 percent lower, and tax revenues higher.[25]

Nicholas Stern, the eminent climate economist at the London School of Economics (LSE), said, "This very important analysis shatters the myth that fossil fuels are cheap by showing just how huge their real costs are. There is no justification for these enormous subsidies for fossil fuels, which distort markets and damage economies, particularly in poorer countries."[26]

Clearly, argue activists, renewables would be even more competitive once these offloaded costs—or "externalities," as they are known—are taken into account. Yet subsidies are still going toward finding new reserves of oil, gas, and coal, which must be left in the ground if we are to avoid the climate crisis. So why, ask protestors, do governments not take action?

Indeed, campaigners find themselves constantly looking both ways like the fabled Push-Me-Pull-You in *Dr Doolittle*. Sometimes they are buoyed with hope by the shifts in public and political opinion or the spread of renewables and electric vehicles. Over the past decade, 2010–2020, Britain has gone from getting 41 percent of its electricity from coal to less than 2 percent while wind has whistled into second place, supplying 21 percent of electricity—up from 3 percent in 2010. Few predicted that in just ten years, Britain would shift to a cleaner electricity supply at this pace.[27] Campaigners have also notched up good wins such as when Shell Canada was forced by blockages led by the Tahltan First Nation to give up its coal-bed methane permissions in the Sacred Headwaters, which violated indigenous people's lands and rights; the regional government then imposed a permanent oil and gas development moratorium there.[28]

At other moments, activists have despaired as companies boost investments in a huge global expansion of oil and gas extraction, supported by governments. In 2019, their spending was set to increase to US$115 billion, with just 3 percent of that directed at low-carbon projects, while governments continue to issue licenses. In response, specialists are tracking fossil fuel companies' lobbying, nerds pouring over data patterns behind computer screens, who have as much impact as street protestors. Think tank Influence-Map has revealed that the world's five largest listed oil and gas companies spent more than US$1 billion touting their climate credentials since the 2015 Paris Agreement on climate change, while lobbying to expand their fossil fuel operations.[29] InfluenceMap revealed that the five major oil companies—ExxonMobil, Shell, Chevron, BP, and Total—have spent on average US$195 million each year on branding campaigns around renewables, while putting another US$200 million into delaying or opposing binding climate policies.[30]

Catherine Howarth, chief executive of UK-based ShareAction says, "These companies have mastered the art of corporate doublespeak—by boasting about their climate credentials while quietly using their lobbying firepower to sabotage the implementation of sensible climate policy and pouring millions into groups that engage in dirty lobbying on their behalf."[31]

Chevron, BP, and ExxonMobil lead the field in direct lobbying to push against or weaken legislation to tackle global warming, increasingly using social media to push their agenda. BP donated US$13 million to a campaign, also supported by Chevron, that successfully blocked a carbon tax in Washington state in the United States, with US$1million spent on social media ads. All five companies are members of the American Petroleum Institute, which successfully campaigned to deregulate oil and gas development in the United States and roll back methane emissions regulations.[32]

In a move called "astroturfing," companies also fund what look like genuine community groups but are in fact fake. For example, a state bill in Colorado, Proposition 112, aimed to increase the distance fracking wells are set back from houses, schools, and hospitals in order to protect communities and the environment. But the campaign by a "grassroots" group, Protect Colorado, helped to defeat the bill. Protect Colorado's Facebook page and website list it as a community organisation. But the organisation was given US$41 million by the oil and gas industry and its trade groups in 2018, according to campaign declarations to the Colorado Secretary of State. The *Guardian*'s analysis of Facebook's ad disclosure platform reveals that Protect Colorado had an influence reach of up to 3.3 million in the weeks before the vote, in a state with five million people.[33]

Anne Lee Foster, communications director at grassroots coalition Colorado Rising said, "It felt like an attack on our democracy, where you have these corporations spending millions and millions of dollars, often out-of-state interests, fighting citizens who are simply trying to protect their families." She continued, "We lost by 200,000 votes, so yes, 100% we believe the vote was swayed by the social media push they financed. They created doubt. They exploited people's fears that the setback would mean big job losses."[34]

Other organisations, taking their cue from successful campaigns against the tobacco companies, have been running #ExxonKnew and #ShellKnew exposés of how company executives knew about global warming; that they hid that knowledge from shareholders as well as the public and policy makers; and that they lobbied actively to undermine scientists, throwing seeds of doubt on the clear facts of global warming. They studied well at the school of the tobacco lobbyists.

Pulitzer Prize–winning non-profit *InsideClimate News* undertook an eight-month investigation to find out what Exxon knew:

> At a meeting in Exxon Corporation's headquarters, a senior company scientist named James F. Black addressed an audience of powerful oilmen. Speaking without a text as he flipped through detailed slides, Black delivered a sobering message: carbon dioxide from the world's use of fossil fuels would warm the planet and could eventually endanger humanity. . . . It was July 1977 when Exxon's leaders received this blunt assessment, well before most of the world had heard of the looming climate crisis.[35]

The group uncovered just how much Exxon learned—until in the late 1980s, when Exxon stopped the research, which posed an existential threat to its highly profitable oil business. The non-profit reported:

> Exxon worked instead at the forefront of climate denial. It put its muscle behind efforts to manufacture doubt about the reality of global warming its own scientists had once confirmed. It lobbied to block federal and international action to control greenhouse gas emissions. It helped to erect a vast edifice of misinformation that stands to this day.[36]

Likewise, in Europe, the investigative NGO Corporate Europe Observatory revealed that gas firms are spending millions in order to win European Commission backing for infrastructure projects that could lock in gas use for forty to fifty years. Between November 2014 and August 2017, the two European commissioners in charge of climate and energy policy and their cabinets met with the gas industry an astounding 460 times—compared to 51 meetings with public interest groups.[37] Overall, says the Observatory, gas companies spent €104 million (US$112 million) lobbying in 2016. Civil society groups pressing for a fossil fuel–free future spent 3 percent of that: €3.4 million.[38] The gas sector had 1,030 lobbyists, not to mention the 79 contracts with PR consultancies—over ten times more than the public interest groups' 101 people. This is what civil society is up against.

Pascoe Sabido at the Observatory said, "Turkeys aren't going to vote for Christmas. But the EU should know better than to listen to the fossil fuel industry. If we are serious about tackling climate change then the companies causing it should be kept as far away from policymakers as possible."[39] In

2019, they revealed that since 2010, just five oil and gas companies and their lobbyists have spent a quarter of a billion euros securing influence at the heart of European decision making. The Observatory mobilised almost two hundred groups, from Sweden to Spain, to campaign for an end to fossil fuel companies sabotaging climate action and demanding #FossilFreePolitics.[40]

## FOLLOWING THE MONEY

Some of the world's smartest brains lie behind civil society's varied responses to the climate crisis, none more so that those "following the money," a well-worn track for those seeking to shift corporate behaviour. The wry Mark Campanale, usually in a suit talking at high speed, has pinpointed shifting investors away from fossil fuels such as oil and gas as the single most effective strategy. He has three decades in sustainable finance for major institutional asset management companies under his belt; he cofounded some of the world's first responsible investment funds and is most at home talking financial risk to financial bodies. He is also a man who is shifting market behaviour.

Mark came up with the concept of "carbon bubble" and attached the term "stranded assets" to the risks that investors take by investing in fossil fuel–based companies. Morally, you might not care, but if your funds are tied to facilities that are going to be closed down because of the climate targets governments have set, the risk is surely too high, Mark says, taking the argument to investors' priorities. Therefore, investing in fossil fuels risks your assets being "stranded" and of no value.

Mark founded Carbon Tracker, a non-profit staffed with senior finance professionals and technical experts. Taken seriously as objective data providers, they aim to help financial markets understand and quantify climate risks, thus aligning capital market actions with climate reality. They are credited with having "changed the financial language of climate change" and with how investors assess oil and gas companies. Mark thinks at scale, strategically—you can almost hear his brain constantly whirring.[41] He figures that to turn the financial system against fossil fuels, Carbon Tracker needs now to change the minds of just one hundred key people in global finance.

When Harriet met with Mark, he was still seething from a recent meeting with Darren Woods, Exxon CEO, who has not yet accepted that renewable energy is cheaper in parts of the world than oil and gas, or that electric vehicles are cheaper: "He kept saying that we needed hundreds of billions spent on research to bring these alternatives to the market. He actually doesn't seem to hear what is being said."

Typically, Mark then rushes off to the United States to meet major investors, plotting his next move against the biggest companies on earth. He is generously advising a small NGO, plans to squeeze in a film with his family, and has just come from a breakfast with senior management of Blackrock, one of the world's largest asset managers. "I communicated my views robustly," Mark chortles. "I try never to lose the opportunity to make my point." The shift in Blackrock's position, to withdraw from coal and companies considered a sustainability risk, is being hailed as a victory for insider and outsider pressure coming together, given the huge activist and divestment campaign waged against Blackrock for financing fossil fuel companies.[42]

Carbon Tracker proves that you do not have to be a large organisation to have a large impact. Mark says, "We are like a judo move—we use the weight of the opponent to throw them; but you have to know exactly where the slight flick would make that work, where you—who are much smaller—can throw someone so much bigger than you."

Mark is clear that, to influence financial markets, you have to know how they work. "After 30 years I have a good sense. Well," he laughs, "apart from credit derivatives—I don't understand them." His razor-sharp analysis means he focuses on investors whom businesses cannot ignore. "We have to create the conditions so that no bank or pension fund wants shares in oil, gas and coal anymore. We can render the powerful powerless with relatively little funds."

He continues, "We have the insider game and the outsider game. Activism and being an activist are a mindset. You diagnose an issue and a problem from how you would do something about an issue; some people's minds are wired like that. I spent years in finance, so I know their Achilles heels." Now riding the crest of a wave, getting there has been far from easy. For years, Mark worked inside major companies, such as Henderson Global Investors, while also organising shareholder actions to hold companies accountable, frequently exposing malpractices. After giving a series of speeches to The Other Economic Summit (TOES), organised by the New Economics Foundation in the early 1990s, Mark became convinced his phone was tapped by Special Branch, due to interference on his home line. Then, he says, he got involved in the radical activist protest Stop the City, a precursor of the Occupy movement. Mark was arrested on conspiracy charges by the City of London police at the anti-globalisation protests of 1999 and was asked to give evidence against one of the main organisers. He refused. Then the police accused him of stealing his work computer, a breach of the Data Protection Act. One officer even visited his employer's human resources department to explain that Mark was in fact a communist.

While others from Stop the City were fined for breaches of the peace, Mark was one of only a few facing charges, warned he could spend three years in prison. Mark says: "I lost a load of weight and sleep. . . . It was a real struggle with the kids, unsure about money. . . . I felt vulnerable and I lost my mojo." London newspaper the *Evening Standard* ran headlines such as: "High-Flyer Arrested on City Riots" with their billboards screaming against the high-earning "son of an Italian waiter." It was a rocky time for Mark personally, and none of the environmental NGOs seemed to understand the financial theories he was exploring.

That all changed when Mark and Nick Robins, formerly at HSBC bank and now at LSE, wrote their first paper in 2011: *Unburnable Carbon: Are the Financial Markets Carrying a Carbon Bubble?* Originally it had taken them three years to raise the funds to test their hypothesis; they did not expect much attention; only a hundred copies of the report were ordered, and Mark missed the launch as his wife had bought tickets to a music festival. He says, "We were not planning to launch a campaign; we were testing a hypothesis."

Yet the study did get attention. One copy reached Canadian author Naomi Klein, who passed it along to environmentalist Bill McKibben, author of *The End of Nature* and founder of 350.org, who wrote the article "Do the Math" and launched a tour calling for divestment: "Naomi Klein and I each read the original Carbon Tracker report on the carbon bubble, and each of us ended up thinking the same thing: this changes the way people will henceforth think about the oil industry," McKibben says. "That led pretty directly to 350.org setting up a large-scale divestment movement."[43]

Mark's phone has never stopped ringing since that first report. Soon Mark Carney, then governor of the Bank of England, had lent his support to the "carbon bubble" theory and issued warnings about "stranded assets," for example to London insurers in 2015, as well as launching a taskforce on climate-related financial disclosures under the auspices of the Financial Stability Board.[44] Investment banks, fund managers, and regulators poured over the now seminal analysis, and soon the concept of the carbon bubble had become mainstream. Specialist energy news group EENews.net wrote:

> For about a decade, Carbon Tracker has been climbing out of obscurity to become one of the most influential climate change research organizations in the world, influencing government policies, banking rules and business decisions. The group's fingerprints can be found at the Bank of England, among European financial regulators, in the oil and gas sector, in the roots of the fossil fuel divestment movement, and even at the Vatican.[45]

Mark is frustrated that "most campaigners don't understand finance and even have a pride in not understanding finance. People say: 'Oh I hate bankers.' But they can be our allies. . . . Some colleagues don't believe Wall Street will attack the very industry they finance, but I think they will."

He is already plotting his next audacious judo moves to shift financial markets further. He wants citizens and workers to mobilise their latent power through divestments of pension schemes; he is planning how capital markets can better support social enterprises, including in less developed countries;

he wants to build out the "Social Stock Exchange" he founded and is thinking about fundamental reform of the financial architecture of capital markets with climate obligations taking precedence over World Trade Organization rules and investors considering the ecological limits in every sector. And, he says, "We need a fossil fuel non-proliferation treaty so that governments stop issuing exploration or mining licenses." After all his previous experiences, Harriet asks Mark if he feels nervous. "Am I nervous taking on these big companies? No. But I am nervous about us going to two degrees and sea levels rising by five feet and the Amazon and Siberia being on fire at the same time."

## DO THE MATH: 350.ORG

Click onto 350.org and up pops an invitation to join the US-led movement against climate change. A world map highlights its reach with campaigns dotted here, there, and everywhere. In the join box, Harriet types her postal code and, on hitting *return*, is immediately connected to the nearest group, with contact information and how to become active. Founded in 2008 by Bill McKibben and a clutch of university students, 350.org was an early adopter of internet tools to create a global movement focused on two core demands: "Stop fossil fuels" and "Create 100% renewables." Enter the world of climate activism, and you soon learn about 350.org's track record and how it has supported others in an inspiring example of civil society building a distributed network.

"Go-big" was the game plan from the start. In mid-2006, student Jamie Henn and some of his Middlebury College friends helped their guru McKibben organise a five-day walk across Vermont. Some one thousand people marched into Burlington, hailed by local newspaper the *Free Press* as probably the largest US demonstration yet on climate change. Henn wrote in a 2010 blog, "The march helped us realize the only thing missing from the climate movement was 'the movement.'"[46]

What followed, in 2007, was Step It Up, with the goal of organising climate rallies in all fifty states. Says Henn, "There were lots of factors that made Step It Up take off, but I think it was that big vision that acted as a center of gravity." Ambition is always inspiring. Their then-radical demand was to cut carbon emissions by 80 percent by 2050. Soon, future president Barack Obama and Senator Hillary Clinton endorsed the demand. Immediately, Henn and others upped their game. They dared to ask, "What if we could take the same Step It Up model of distributed actions around a common message and make it global?"

Thus 350.org was born, its name a reference to 350 parts per million—the safe concentration of carbon dioxide in the atmosphere. The target figure was seized upon as critical data that, if popularised, could radically alter the climate debate, writes Henn, now strategy and communications director:

> We decided to go global. I clearly recall an early conference call where our core team of seven friends (the same from back in the Middlebury days) divided up the continents. It was like a game of Risk. . . . We realised the ridiculousness in all this from the start, the hubris, but when you've got seven people and a global day of action to plan, there aren't too many other ways to go about it. For two years, I spent almost my entire life behind a lap-top, emailing and Skype calling anyone I could find that might work for us, become an ally, and take ownership of the campaign in their country or region. But the vision paid off, the ambition caught on.

Thanks to the digitally savvy 350.org, on the International Day of Climate Action, preceding the Copenhagen UN Climate talks in December 2009, over five thousand events were organised across 181 countries, proving 350.org's strength in combining on- and off-line campaigning. Website Criticalmass.com described it as one of the strongest examples of social media optimisation the world has ever seen. But Copenhagen was a disaster, with no binding agreement on emissions. With the clock ticking, campaigners came to believe that shifting public attitudes and government behaviour were never going to create enough change fast enough. They needed to target fossil fuel companies, and their investors. So, in 2010, students on US campuses began calling on university administrations to take endowment investments out of the fossil fuel industry—and instead to invest in clean energy and communities most impacted by climate change. Then, following the 2012 Carbon Tracker report, 350.org launched its Go Fossil Free campaign. This divestment movement escalated tactics in spring 2015, with nineteen students arrested at Yale, a weeklong blockade of Harvard's administrative buildings, and a student sit-in at Tulane University.

The movement won support from veteran campaigner Archbishop Desmond Tutu, who drew the historical parallels: "We must stop climate change. And we can, if we use the tactics that worked in South Africa . . . using boycotts, divestment and sanctions, and supported by our friends overseas, we were not only able to apply economic pressure on the unjust state, but also serious moral pressure."[47]

The momentum continues to build. By early 2020, US$14.14 trillion had been divested, with 58,000 individuals and 1,192 institutions shifting their money out of fossil fuels, from the University of California to Glasgow University (Europe's first to divest in 2014), the city of Copenhagen, the New Zealand Pension Fund, the Rockefeller Foundation, and Norway's sovereign wealth funds.[48]

McKibben says of the pressure that divestment is putting on industry: "This all could, in fact, become one of the final great campaigns of the climate movement. . . . Shell called divestment a 'material adverse effect' on its performance."[49]

Harvard University student Alli Welton argues, "It really feels as though divestment is a very clear way that we can effect change. . . . These local-level initiatives make climate change more accessible for people and make it more possible for them to get involved. We can see very clearly that we're part of something gigantic, and that definitely creates identity for a national and even international movement."[50] That is the holy grail of all movements: to help people see how their small actions fit into a larger goal, the total becoming more than the sum of the parts.

Increasingly, the "divest" call is matched by the "invest" part of the equation, a move lead by private philanthropists in the United States and UK such as DivestInvest, calling for a rapid increase in investments in the climate-positive solutions that are crying out for capital in order to get to scale. Mainstream investors have shown that they can deliver just as good rates of financial return while minimising the reputational and real risks of investing in fossil fuels. Whether investors will dial up the solutions—such as renewable energy, retrofitting social housing or building liveable cities around walking and cycling—is the question.

## CRITICAL CRY

From the outset, McKibben's mass-mobilisation strategy provoked heated exchanges. "Holding rallies about solutions will never replace the need for actually doing the messy business of electing politicians who support tough climate laws," Joe Romm wrote in a Think Progress blog after McKibben accused him and the Washington, DC, green movement of being too Washington-centric and obsessed with lobbying.[51] McKibben charged that Romm "paid less attention to the emerging popular movement on climate change than to the machinations of the Senate, but if we're going to get change on the scale we need, it's quite possible it won't happen without an aggressive, large and noisy movement demanding that change."

For Romm, 350.org needed to step up to the political mark. He believed pressure was required on foreign states that were not doing enough to tackle climate change, while on the home front, progress would come only when politicians feared the political costs of voting against climate change. Getting engaged in politics is a common challenge to civil society, perhaps especially in the United States. Others argue that it is only by staying out of the political dogfights that campaigns can bring in the focus and energy from the public, while delivering a mandate to politicians to take action; they have applauded 350.org's ability to forge broader alliances, as with women's groups and trade unions.

McKibben is no naive lightweight, having brought his kudos and style of politics to Vermont senator Bernie Sanders's 2016 Democratic presidential primary campaign. He states that climate change is becoming Democrats' number-one or number-two issue and is the most important issue for young Americans of all political parties. "So, we're going to see political action. The question is, will it be enough?"[52]

## INTO THE POLITICAL RING

"Forests still standing, chemicals banned. The world is a better place because Greenpeace did that work," says Greenpeace USA executive director Annie Leonard, "and if we did the same things in the next 50 years, we're toast." She reflects, "The movement has evolved, because it wasn't working. The science is stronger than ever, and we're still losing."[53] While some NGOs have pursued causes with popular appeal, such as protecting endangered species or banning plastic bags, what has been missing, she says, is a mass movement to galvanise public sentiment on climate change and be overtly political. That is where the Sunrise movement comes in.

In 2019, a gaggle of children crowds into the offices of California representative Nancy Pelosi. Standing in a semicircle, clutching their handwritten letter, they start putting their case to the coiffured congresswoman in her blue trouser suit. She does not listen. She starts talking about her own resolution. What is most remarkable is just how clever the children are in arguing back: when she says that there is not enough money, one of them pipes up, "We have tons of money going to the military," while another argues that inaction will cost more in the long run. When she says they can do it their way once they are elected, quick as a flash, they reply that it will be too late then. "We're the ones who are going to be impacted," they reply, politely holding their ground. It is a scrappy moment captured in a shaky video. Such are the turning points for social movements.

The video went viral with three million views, shooting the Sunrise movement to fame. An extraordinary ability to play the game of hard politics is what differentiates Sunrise. Cofounder twenty-six-year-old Sara Blazevic says of the group's founding in 2017:

> Initially we thought, if we can build the public support and the public pressure, our political system will follow. We'd be a movement that was pretty solely focused on the outside game strategy: building public pressure, elevating the urgency of the crisis in the eyes of the American people and demonstrating it to political leaders and forcing them to reckon with it . . . then when Trump got elected, and we realized there was just no credible path to passing any type of federal legislation on climate in four years, we realized that we also had to contend with how to win political power pretty seriously.

Realising that they needed to connect with hard politics, Sunrise shifted to calling for the Green New Deal to address climate change and inequality, a rallying cry with a clear vision of the changes the movement seeks. It was initially mocked as they pushed for Democratic support.

A week after the 2018 midterm elections, Sunrise organised the protest in Nancy Pelosi's office, calling on her to support the Green New Deal. New congresswoman Alexandria Ocasio-Cortez launched a resolution to create a committee on the plan, her backing transforming the group's fortunes. As Ocasio-Cortez said, "The way things are done has not been getting results. We have to try new methods."[54]

Sunrise has propelled the Green New Deal right up the political agenda and into the national conversation. On 10 January 2019, 626 organisations signed a letter sent to all Congress members. Then, in February 2019, Senator Edward Markey and Representative Alexandria Ocasio-Cortez tabled in the House of Representatives a nonbinding resolution for the Green New Deal legislation calling for: the United States to shift to 100 percent renewable, zero-emission energy; an end to fossil fuel subsidies; a ban on crude oil exports; investment in electric cars and high-speed rail; a focus on clean air; and addressing social inequalities.[55] The plan draws its moral resonance from Franklin D. Roosevelt's New Deal created to bring 1930s America out of the Depression, but this time with a new focus on the climate alongside jobs and social change. A compelling case for a ten-year national mobilisation, it lays out a vision of the scale of changes that are needed for developed nations trapped in unequal, fossil fuel–based economies.

Seattle-based student Jamie Margolin, founder of the US group Zero-Hour, said, "The Green New Deal is not just about a specific piece of legislation or about a promise a politician makes. It's about finally ending the fairy tale. With the Green New Deal, we are calling to end the sacrificing of everything to protect that fairy-tale of eternal economic growth."[56]

At a Sunrise movement weeklong boot camp training climate activists on how to put climate justice into the heart of American politics, Emily LaShelle, twenty-one years old with blonde cropped hair, says, "When we were taught about the civil rights movement as kids, it was told to us as if a few big marches just happened and then the laws changed."[57] She continues, "But there was so much more work and effort by activists behind the scenes. And that's the kind of work we're teaching people to be involved in for this movement."

They are interested both in building people power—enabling young people to step into their power—and political power. Sunrise now actively supports those candidates it decides to endorse. The group, whose oldest staff member is thirty-three, is widely credited with becoming an influential force despite having minimal infrastructure. News website Politico says of Sunrise: "It's also undeniable that, whatever this earnest and improvisational organisation is doing, it's working. The national discussion around climate change has moved more in the past eight months than it did during the previous eight years."[58]

Benjamin Finegan, a twenty-two-year-old activist, told Politico that, while the group use their youth as a source of moral authority, they are not trying to reinvent progressive activism—just the politics of climate change, building off past movements. "We take a lot of guidance from slightly older to much older people in other movements," he said. Examples stretch from support in the early days from 350.org to a roster of volunteer mentors from movements like Black Lives Matter and Occupy Wall Street. Similarly, Sunrise's success with the Green New Deal is attracting attention from groups outside the United States, with others calling for a Global Green New Deal addressing climate justice not just within but also among countries.

Campaigners in Africa, Asia, and Latin America point out that the very people who have done the least to contribute to climate change, and have the fewest resources to cope with it, are paying the highest price—and that this needs addressing, from the macro level of structural global agreements all the way through to support for indigenous people on the frontlines and for the solutions they are nurturing. In Brazil's south-eastern Amazon, where rainforests act as a vital defence against the climate crisis, there's a history of intense clashes between the farmers and indigenous people. Women and young people have formed the Xingu Seed Network as a cooperative of seed collectors, who earn money by collecting seeds in the forest and selling them to local farmers, thus reducing tensions and reforesting 6,600 hectares of degraded rainforest. Understanding the importance of raising awareness to press for wider action, the Xingu network has connected with wider movements in Brazil and has welcomed school strikers from Belgium to visit and learn about the deep difficulties they face, the solutions they want, and the solidarity they need.

Too often, campaigners are taking huge risks. In many countries, people who speak up for the climate or stand in the way of oil and gas projects get murdered as the struggle for the environment becomes a struggle for human rights. According to Global Witness's chilling annual report, over three people were murdered each week in 2018, with countless more criminalised for defending their land and the environment against destructive industries like mining, logging, and agribusiness.[59] Harriet will never forget the visceral shock of that awful cold day, 10 November 1995, when news came through to the sparse vigil outside London's Nigerian Embassy, that the Nigerian government had hanged nine activists, including playwright and Nobel Peace Prize nominee Ken Saro Wiwa. The leader of the Ogoni people's battle against Shell's oil drilling in the Central Niger delta, Ken Saro Wiwa had founded a mass-based social movement. He accused Shell of waging "an ecological war" against the Ogoni people, destroying their farming and fishing livelihoods, their drinking water, and their health, leading to the abuse of their human rights. Today, the Ogoni people are still battling, still committed to nonviolence, still calling for their rights and for Shell to clean up the area despoiled by oil spills, and they have connected with the new climate movements. Justice rarely drives in the fast lane, it seems. But maybe, just maybe, the end of the world's love affair with oil is in sight.

## SOLUTIONS ARE THE WIND IN OUR SAILS

Engaging the public in global issues is never easy. The very words "climate change" sound abstract, and past campaigns mean they conjure images of far-away polar bears starving on melting icecaps. All of the research shows that most people care first about themselves and their families, then their neighbourhood and their nation, and only finally about global issues.

That is starting to change as countries lurch from forest fires and heat waves that kill to torrential downpours and floods. Of course, many people in developing countries have been on the frontlines for decades, as a Bangladeshi activist said years ago, referring to the rising sea levels bringing salt into the freshwater supplies in his low-lying country: "For us, climate change is happening now; we can already taste climate change."[60]

As the climate emergency bursts more and more into people's lives, they are increasingly ready to take action as individuals in their lifestyle choices, enthusiastically supporting NGO campaigns to eat less meat, buy fewer clothes, plant trees, use tote bags, stop using plastic straws, cycle or walk or take the bus, leave the car at home, don't fly. All of these steps are important in themselves, help engage people in the solutions, and so gradually shift the wider public consensus and build toward the next step. Individual actions also show governments the public support for the big, bold measures that they need to implement. Indeed, research keeps showing that people want and expect their governments to take more direct action on climate change.

But while concern is growing, most people, most of the time, are more preoccupied with keeping their jobs, paying their rent and fuel bills, and protecting their children's health. Organisations such as Ashden make sure they emphasise wider benefits that win and maintain public support for climate action. People can relate to practical examples of things that improve their lives and also speak to their values—such as ensuring jobs for the next generation or protecting green spaces and biodiversity.[61] Thus, local authorities seeking to close roads to cars emphasise the improved health for children and reduced incidence of asthma once pollution levels fall. Likewise, measures that improve social housing and reduce greenhouse gases—for example, insulation—also reduce people's fuel bills and give them warmer homes, making them healthier and even improving their mental health. By framing climate solutions in terms of other such benefits, local authorities can win wider support. Interestingly, in European public opinion research, almost eight in ten people across the EU agreed that taking action on climate change would lead to innovation and make EU companies more competitive.[62]

In response to public pressure, local authorities across the UK are declaring a climate emergency. The resolutions, tabled in grand, echoic town halls, are being passed with high rates of cross-party consensus. Now the challenge is for councillors and officers to implement climate action plans, despite their tight budgets and the pressures of electoral cycles that leave leaders reluctant to take unpopular measures in which the pain is immediate and the gains arrive after they have left office.

Globally, too, mayors are sharing best practices and taking inspiration from pioneers—such as Medellin, the Colombian city previously best known as the home of drug lord Pablo Escobar, whose story was dramatised in the series *Narcos*. Then it was the murder capital of the world. It also faced a new threat: rising temperatures in the city. So the local government planted thousands of trees and shrubs along its streets and public spaces, transforming rubbish dumps and dangerous back alleys previously frequented by gangs, and prioritising areas lacking green space. Local people from disadvantaged backgrounds were trained to become city gardeners to tend these new green corridors, which have encouraged cycling, and new public facilities such as playgrounds where mothers chat as their children run around. Birds and insects have returned to the city, and Mayor Federico Gutiérrez announced that the interventions cut temperatures in the area by over two degrees Celsius.

Clearly, local governments should not reinvent the wheel: they should instead steal with pride—from each other, from companies and social enterprises—scaling or replicating successful models as citizens work to pioneer and build the sustainable carbon-free alternatives. One such inspiring example is the inventive community energy group Repowering.

## REBELLION ON THE ROOFTOPS

In South London, Repowering was the brainchild of Afsheen Rashid and the fast-talking Agamemnon Otero, an American-Uruguayan with a wicked twinkle in his eye, who restored his houseboat floating on the Thames in the shadow of Vauxhall's shiny glass towers. Agamemnon is one of those infuriating people who have lived five lives while the rest of us struggle with one. Diagnosed with cancer as a teenager, he has trained as a doctor and been a dancer, a successful artist, a City banker and now leads the community energy revolution. Repowering uses renewable energy as a way to address injustice and give consumers power, illustrating how civil society can build the living alternative within the current system, motivating others to scale or replicate the model. All of us need these beacons on the hill to inspire us.

As dusk falls on the Styles Estate, near Brixton, the unofficial capital of Britain's Afro-Caribbean community, Harriet meets Agamemnon, jangling a jailor's collection of keys to get onto the roof through heavy security doors, into the elevator, powered of course by solar—though sadly, he remarks, the solar energy cannot clean off the elevator's urine and semen stains. The tidy rows of panels were England's first community-owned solar panels on social housing. It is quite a claim to fame. Founded in 2011, Repowering is a community-interest company with the "just transition"—ensuring that workers in a changing economy are reskilled to still earn a livelihood—in its DNA. The money made from selling solar energy to the national grid pays to train young people from the housing projects in everything from putting up solar panels to discussing energy policy with their MP.

Raised in alternative communities in the United States, Agamemnon says, "I grew up off-grid and I've been to the promised land. I grew up in communities where we made our own bread, we grew our own veg, would cook and eat together, young and old." Still living those values—he squeezes fresh aloe vera to use as face cream, with a warning not to kiss after using, given its bitterness—he says he would not stay there now. "It was amazing, but it was a little isolated community outside New York pretending that if we just did everything right in our own community, all would be OK. But you have to go to the heart of the problem, the cities, to the urban environments where most people live and you have to build systems that allow people to reconnect with their environment, in order to change the system."

In housing notorious for deprivation, drugs, and high rates of imprisonment, Agamemnon's secret to success is the "matriarchy theory of organizing." After struggling to interest people in solar energy, Agamemnon met local resident Fay Gordon who, forty years earlier, had visited Wales's Centre for Alternative Technology and tried to interest the council in solar and wind power. She knew everyone in the neighbourhood, and when she called a meeting, people turned up. Fay taught Aga that, to attract young people, they had to offer an accredited internship, pay properly, be strict, and support them for the long term.

So when Agamemnon went to the next neighborhood, and the next, he looked for the project matriarch, who advised him, and hinged off her to meet the younger women. He says, "These women will cook, clean, cry, yell, push troublesome men off the estate—these women push the policy and they talk about the real action on the ground. So, my job is to translate that huge emotional enthusiasm into a business case. Only those women can do what they do; and they need to focus. So, my job is to bring in the funds. The respect is profound." Of course, he laughs, "There's always a guy messing around, causing trouble, trying to take the credit, or embezzling the funds."

The schemes are cooperatively run, with a wide shareholder base. The solar panels generate power and save carbon, save people's fuel bills, and generate profits, returning 3 to 4 percent to investors and paying into funds that the co-ops have invested in, helping other energy co-ops, training youth, and supporting people in fuel poverty by installing energy-saving appliances. Agamemnon describes Kamillo Mehmet from Algeria, the first man he met on the estate:

> The wind was whipping through his flat; there was no insulation; it was full of rotted-out holes; he was freezing cold. For him, he was happy that the lights were on at all. He said he would love solar panels but he couldn't pay any more. So, for me he just clarified the energy system. He wanted the energy generated locally and through a co-operative—but only if was the right price. He could not pay more. So that has been my goal. He is dead and gone but his vision, his multi-colored thread, has been woven into the fabric.

For Agamemnon, the finance system obscures the true cost of carbon, with environmental costs left out of the equation, and the poorest people paying the most for their fuel while massive profits are skimmed off the top. He says people come to their sessions "for the food and music, because the local leader is there, because they want to see the young people make their lives better, because their energy comes from their own rooftops. That is the cooperative thinking. The moment you lose that cooperation, it's the death of everything because then you take out more than the world can stand."

He is inspired by Elinor Ostrom's writings on governance of the commons—that fishers should set fishing policies or farmers should decide farming policies. Ostrom, the first woman awarded the Nobel Prize in Economics, investigated how, from Switzerland to Kenya, communities have found ways to manage the commons—grazing land, forests, and irrigation waters—for today's needs and for future generations, issues at the heart of today's debates about managing the planet's shared resources. Community energy schemes encapsulate the rise in so-called place-based activism, which runs alongside calls for global changes to be driven by national and international players. US communities despairing of national leadership on climate have doubled down at the state level. As California governor Gavin Newsom loves to remind anyone, California would be the world's fifth largest country by GDP. He is among those declaring that they are "still in." (In contrast to President Trump pulling the United States out of the Paris Agreement.) Indeed, California and twenty-three other states sued to stop the Trump administration's legal reversal of states' authority to set their own rules on climate-warming tailpipe emissions.[63]

In a twist on the old phrase, people are saying, "Act local to solve global"—build at the neighbourhood level the solutions that need scaling up or replicating for wider impact. Community energy is a popular way to engage people and create energy that is "decarbonised, decentralised, and democratised," as organisers frame it. The UK's 350 community energy groups are generating energy equivalent to the demands of 100,000 homes. This is good. But it is not nearly good enough and was stalled by the government's withdrawing support in 2019. One report estimates that by 2030, with the right government policies, the impact of community energy could be twelve to twenty times larger than today, with beneficial impacts including generating more community support for the next phase of decarbonisation.[64]

Agamemnon, passionate about sustainable, business-focused solutions, bangs the roof- railings. "We don't want charity, we don't want a leg-up. We just want a level playing field to compete—and that is what we are not getting." Lifelong activist Giles Bristow, now program director at Ashden, believes we have to focus more on systemic local and national support for such community solutions so they can go to scale. He says:

> The environmental movement was slow to turn its firepower on systems that are the cause of global emissions—such as electricity and power generation, buildings, transport—and this hamstrung the larger organizations, while a small number of NGOs and small businesses were championing energy access as a systemic climate and poverty issue. Now that is changing as the movement realize we need systemic support for decentralized solutions.[65]

A self-styled green wolf of Wall Street, Agamemnon is restless. "Solar is a great gateway drug," he says, but he wants to go much further. He points across the stunning city skyline, lit by pinpricks of coloured lights breaking into the dusky sky, toward Repowering's second social housing project and then down to the previously neglected scrap of land where a cache of weapons and £50,000 in cash were once found—but which is now a community garden. Brixton, with its rich history, now finds itself in the riptide of gentrification, with such pieces of land holding the balance of cities' ecosystems. Here and across London's transport network, communities are planting "energy gardens," with solar panels, trees, and vegetables, creating biodiversity corridors, harvesting honey, and even growing hops to make their craft Energy Garden Ale, which, in a fitting symbol, just fizzes over. Agamemnon says every action you take can actively encourage the system you want to see:

> Just start right where you are, and think how right now, you can build change in your local area and link it to the larger narrative. Start with your electricity and your gas—because the choices are real when you are doing things where you live. You need to make your own personal shifts, and you need to shift

government policy. You need both at the same time—the chicken is sitting on the egg!

And then, in a blur of yellow Lycra, Agamemnon is pedalling off to fix another deal.

## GREEN JUSTICE

Campaigners are haunted by the coal mine closures of recent decades and the resonance today that seems to pitch tackling climate change against jobs and the working-class communities that depend on them. "Trump digs coal" banners at the president's 2016 election rallies, which decried Obama-era environmental laws, and conservative prime minister Scott Morrison's pledge to back Australia's coal mining industry against "reckless" and "job-destroying" cuts both hit home—although neither leader has in fact been able to stop the industry's decline. Nevertheless, campaigners are acutely aware of the importance of engaging with communities hit by the shift away from fossil fuels, and of managing this well.

In 1998, a Canadian union activist, Brian Kohler, published an article that attempted to reconcile the union movement's efforts to provide workers with decent jobs and the need to protect the environment—thus creating the idea of the "just transition."[66] This concept is seen as critical to ensuring that social and environmental policies reinforce each other and that the shift to a green economy creates jobs and livelihoods and addresses inequalities. It has been forged through new civil society alliances between trade unionists and green campaigners. But the need is great, with whole communities in, for example, South Africa depending on coal mining. The multinational companies can walk away; the residents cannot. Thus, the solutions must address their needs for alternative jobs and governments must invest in reskilling people and kick-starting the new industries of the future.

In India, the Centre for Science and Environment, among the longest-standing voices for social and environmental change, is now championing the just transition. In 2015, the Indian government passed legislation requiring each mining district to set up a District Mineral Foundation (DMF), an agency with a mandate to help communities living in mining areas by empowering them and improving their incomes. Chandra Bhushan of the Centre for Science and Environment explained:

> It took us about seven to eight years to convince the government. . . . The DMFs are responsible for collecting 10 to 30 percent of the royalty paid by mining companies and will also be responsible for using those funds to help the people living in those areas. . . . The funds are meant to be used for educating people, improving health services and improving nutrition. A part of

the money should also be kept as funds for the future. I think some of this money could be used for the just transition.

Indeed, a key recommendation of the Centre is that these funds be used "to revive the economy of the area when mining finishes, to avoid the issue of "ghost towns."[67]

In October 2019, Harriet was in Copenhagen for a gathering of the C40—the mayors of the world's largest cities—who signed up to the Global Green New Deal, reaffirming their "commitment to protecting the environment, strengthening our economy, and building a more equitable future by cutting emissions."[68] Faced with blocking actions at the United Nations by governments from Brazil to Russia, which are accused of "serving the interests of the fossil fuel industry," the mayors are seeking to create another momentum. Congresswoman Alexandria Ocasia-Cortez was given a rock-star welcome, saying, "It is unsustainable to continue to believe [in] our system of runaway, unaccountable, law-breaking pursuit of profit." Instead, she said, the world needed to adopt "a cooperative, collaborative" system, "whose economy . . . benefits the middle and lower classes and marginalised people." She continued, "Our current logic created this mess and operating in the same way will not get us out."[69]

The Global Green New Deal is a bold pitch for the total transformation of our economies—to take out carbon and take out inequalities, joining solutions to the two issues at the hip. Campaigners are, for the first time in years, confidently arguing with a steely determination for a wholly different values base that turns back to nature, that respects the wisdom of indigenous people, and that revives democratic participation and community solutions. They are pushing forward ambitious plans and policies to ensure that the next major climate change talks, COP26, do deliver fundamental changes—and to ensure that the day after COP, activists are back on the streets and in the fields nurturing the solutions.

Everyone was gearing up to push for major governmental commitments at those talks when Covid-19 swept all aside. Environmentalists fear that the rush for economic stimulus after the pandemic will be used to reverse fragile gains and see a dash for fossil fuels injecting old-fashioned growth—as when governments from India to the United States rolled back hard-won environmental protection laws in response to the pandemic.[70]

Environmentalists are arguing that as governments seek to recover from Covid-19, it must be a greener and fairer recovery, with solutions based in nature and transformational change across the whole of society. As UN leaders gathered virtually in September 2020, the Prince of Wales made his most impassioned plea yet, saying the environmental crisis: "has been with us for far too many years—decried, denigrated and denied. It is now rapidly becoming a comprehensive catastrophe that will dwarf the impact of the coronavirus pandemic." He continued: "Without swift and immediate action, at an unprecedented pace and scale, we will miss the window of opportunity to 'reset' for . . . a more sustainable and inclusive future."[71]

Giles Bristow at Ashden believes this is the moment to bring together the arguments around power, exclusions and justice:

> The environmental movement has become more systemic in its approach to climate change and the edge of activism is the increasing questioning of capitalism itself as people call for justice and a fundamental shift in the values which our systems reflect. Now is the time for us to bring together the protest movements with the positive solutions in a total reshaping of society and the economy.[72]

The clock is ticking. All of the science proves—and Covid-19 reminds us to listen to the science and respond at scale—that this decade is our last chance to pull the planet back from the brink of total climate breakdown. Bill McKibben of 350.org says: "Climate change isn't like other issues. It's a timed test. And so, the longer you delay action, the more dramatic that action has to be just to meet the math of climate change." Citizen movements are rising to the challenge of that test. With less than ten years to save our economies and societies, nature and the planet, even humanity, it will have to be global action unlike any we have seen before.

*Chapter Four*

# The Doves Take on the Drones

*Citizens are fighting the toughest battle of them all—for peace—by tackling conflict at its roots and pressing nations to turn their swords into solar panels.*

Born in Damascus, Syria, in 1973 to a ministry legal adviser and a housewife, Abir Haj Ibrahim dreamed of becoming a belly dancer. Years later, she laughs, "But I couldn't do belly-dancing. I tried—I took several courses, I watched TV shows. I longed to be able to move like that."[1]

Instead, Abir is moving and shaking in another way—building peace among the shattered ruins of her country's brutal civil war. It seems improbable. Can ordinary civilians take on the might of warring sides and steer them away from war? It calls to mind the unidentified young man in Tiananmen Square: a solitary figure in a white shirt holding a shopping bag in front of a column of tanks on 4 June 1989, as students demanded democratic reform in China.[2]

This is the most audacious of all citizen responses to our fractured world: to seek to prevent people from picking up deadly weapons by tackling the root causes of conflict, to stop those already at war from fighting, and to build lasting peace once the guns fall silent, helping people reach across bloody divides, forgive, and build new lives together. Conflict, where division has spiralled out of control, is surely the most intractable of all problems, where nation-states have failed, and the international community is struggling. Yet citizens and civil society groups are working at local, national, and global levels to stand against violence and build peace in an age where attacking the other—whether within or beyond their borders—is on the rise. They are fighting for peace through campaigns targeted at governments and business—from stopping the trade in deadly weapons fuelling war to remorselessly pressing governments to work together to stop conflicts. From the ground up, they are building peace, brick by brick, through alternative means to solve conflicts at the source and heal fractured societies. And they are defending and building up the values of community and collaboration in the teeth of the onslaught of ideologies that say that competition—whether between individuals, groups of people, or nations—is what drives societies to succeed, even as this lays the seedbed of conflict.

There was a time, after a spike in armed violence at the end of the Cold War, when the zone of peace was gradually expanding; it was a quiet good-news story with the number of conflicts falling between 1990 and 2007.[3] No more. Violence is on the march. Today, more people are dying in battle than at any time in the past twenty-five years. By 2014, people were embroiled in forty wars from Yemen and Somalia to Libya, with terrorism also reaching an all-time high. More people are displaced by conflict now than at any time in human history. Fifteen years ago, approximately 80 percent of humanitarian aid went to helping the victims of natural disasters. Today that ratio is reversed, with 80 percent of aid meeting the needs of victims of violent conflict. Conflict also fuels violent extremism and remains the main driver of terrorism, with over 95 percent of terrorism deaths occurring in countries already in conflict, such as Afghanistan and Nigeria.[4]

As conflict rises, at least 22 percent of the world's population—over 1.6 billion people—is paying the price.[5] It is predicted that, by 2030, over 60 percent of all poor people will be living in fragile and conflict-affected countries, as conflict both directly pushes people into poverty and prevents progress on enabling more people to live above the poverty line. The shape of conflict is changing: where once armies went into battle, with soldiers the victims, today, civilians are just as much in the firing line; 30 to 40 percent of political violence is directed against them.[6] In 2019 in Syria, 83 percent of deaths and injuries were among civilians.[7] Atrocities seem to have become the new norm,[8] so much so that the record number of civilians killed or injured by explosive weapons in worldwide conflicts last year prompted calls for UN member states to conduct an urgent review of military rules of engagement. Germany and Austria have urged states to prevent and reduce the "devastating harm" to civilians from airstrikes and bombs in urban areas—a call supported by the International Network on Explosive Weapons, a coalition including Human Rights Watch, Save the Children, and Action on Armed Violence.[9]

Civil society faces an uphill battle. If its effectiveness in addressing climate is at an unprecedented level, its role in tackling conflict is the most challenging. Its positive contribution is also the least recognised or understood; historians and the media focus on conflicts and on military solutions, ignoring civil society's quiet successes.

## BUILDING PEACE ACROSS SYRIA'S BATTLE LINES

Abir Haj Ibrahim took a roundabout route into being a peace builder. After college, she worked in trading flowers and then in accounting for oil company Total before stumbling across a British Council training course on civil society organizing that lit something inside her, just as the idea of being a belly dancer once had. It changed her life forever. She remembers, "I participated in a leadership in community development program and they had so many answers to the questions in my head about equality and justice, how decisions can be made in an empowering way, about participation." But then the war started.

Syria was at that time a middle-income country of twenty million people. The Assad family had ruled for a quarter of a century, with President Bashar al-Assad taking over from his father in 2000, keeping tight control through a brutal authoritarian regime. People suffered from high unemployment, corruption, and the lack of political freedom. Then the northeast, the country's breadbasket, was crippled for two years running by drought, widely attributed to global warming. Unable to survive, people moved into the towns, adding to the pressure on scarce resources.

In March 2011, demonstrations erupted in the southern city of Deraa. Young boys painted graffiti: "The regime must go." They were hunted down and shot as the government swept in with deadly force to crush the dissent. But protests demanding the president's resignation mushroomed nationwide. When repression of the protesters stepped up, some took up arms; then foreign-backed Islamist groups weighed in, spawning a fully fledged, many-sided civil war into which superpowers piled, with Russia, Iran, Turkey, the United States and Western countries all chasing their regional goals. During nearly a decade of war, chemical weapons have been used, doctors killed, all the red lines of the Geneva conventions on warfare crossed multiple times, and UN-backed peace and humanitarian efforts have struggled against the divisions of key member states. An estimated half a million people have been killed or gone missing in the war, while a staggering 12.6 million—over half the population—have had to flee their homes, displaced internally or as refugees in other countries.[10] According to the pro-opposition UK-based NGO Syrian Network for Human Rights, 29,257 children have been killed in the conflict,[11] and over 90,000 people have been "disappeared," mostly at the hands of the government.[12]

The human cost of the civilian casualties first crashed into our living rooms with the heartbreaking TV footage of a young boy, Omran Daqneesh, dusty, bloodied, dazed, sitting on an orange ambulance seat with his little legs dangling, after a bomb was dropped by the Russian-backed regime on a rebel-held area. In the photos, he does not seem to realise that he has a gash in his head. His brother Ali, hit in the same strike, later died. The footage captured the confused tragedy of the children in this relentless war.

Before the war, Abir and her friend Ghada had started a network, Moberadoon, to support people leading community activities. After they were forced to become refugees in Beirut, a new urgency propelled them to extend this approach, bringing young people from different sides of the conflict together. These groups help people to talk through the underlying causes of their differences, find out all they have in common, and, step by step, explore how they could live together in peace again. She reflects, "At the start it was so difficult. People just wanted to flame the revolution or have the regime win. People held positions in a very hard way. We helped them see that violence is not the way; to move from violence to nonviolence." They carefully worked through issues, exploring people's underlying beliefs and their feelings below the surface hostilities. They developed a whole curriculum on people's values, which underpin everything, learning techniques from the South Africans who had worked through the deep scars left by apartheid-era conflicts.

The Moberadoon network stretched at one time to four thousand committed social activists working to the same model across war-torn Syria, from Syrian government–controlled areas, the Free Syrian Army, ISIS, and multiple other fighting groups. They also connected Syrian refugees scattered across Europe, from the Netherlands to Scandinavia. Though entirely based on work in small groups, the cumulative effect spreads wider, as these bright young people tirelessly promote their mission to end the divisions behind the fighting through structured sessions to find common ground. Abir says, "They are peace ambassadors, doing initiatives in their local community, a movement for peace everywhere. In one instance, we were able to freeze a sectarian conflict." Such individuals feed Abir's dogged optimism. "Yes, the war drags on," she sighs. "But if we did not do our work, there would be even more violence and we would have less chance of bringing people together. We pave the way for a peace agreement to come."

When Harriet led peacebuilding organisation International Alert, they cooperated with the Moberadoon network, whose members Harriet first met on a sunny rooftop of a safe house in Lebanon. A balmy wind blew gently as people piled their plates with meze steaming with scents of mint and coriander. To get there, people had risked their lives, crammed for hours into tiny cars, smuggling themselves out of Aleppo, crossing checkpoints controlled by ISIS or the Syrian government. Their conversation flows easily as they share their struggles—until suddenly you know you have asked a question that crosses a line, that might endanger people by giving away where they live or which side they support, or how they organise under such an autocratic regime. Everyone goes quiet then starts talking loudly about the food.

One young woman came that morning from Aleppo, which was being pounded into dust. People she worked with were being killed; she was surrounded by death. Harriet knew that if she were in this woman's place, she would leave; she would be too scared. While Harriet was driven smoothly back to Beirut, this woman would begin her slow, tortuous, dangerous journey back from the sanctuary of Lebanon, where she could have stayed, to a city that was hell on earth. She believed that she had to return to this horror and danger to play her part in doing whatever she could with her fellow citizens to stop the flow of blood and hatred. Her quiet courage floored Harriet.

The young woman talks about a man who came to one of the group's dialogue and therapy sessions. He lived on one side of Aleppo's bloodstained line of control between the regime and the Free Syrian Army. From his window, a few floors up in a high-rise, he told her, "I lean on my balcony and I look down on people on the other side of the line—and I wonder how we will ever live together again." It was the moment of reflection that led him to approach Moberadoon to learn how to build reconciliation. This is the ragged heart of peacebuilding, which needs to take place both before and after the men in camouflage sit down to negotiate a deal. Pressure from communities forms part of the dynamic bringing leaders to the talks table. Even though formal agreements can end the fighting, for people to live together again, investment is needed in reconciliation and in addressing the root causes of the conflict. Civil society plays a critical role here, working at all levels.

In the Philippines, for example, Francisco Pancho Lara, as a young activist, organised against the Marcos dictatorship. A larger-than-life character famed for his "chicken dance" to liven up meetings, he recalls happily the excitement of the people's mass street protests that removed Marcos. More recently, working for International Alert, he has been dedicated to building peace in the Philippines, which is still riven by violence, including the world's longest-running civil war. For years, he has been part of secret "back-channel" talks between the communist guerrillas and the government, a stop-start ride of breakthroughs followed by setbacks. At the same time, the organisation has been lobbying parliamentarians to build support for laws that would address the causes of the conflict (for example, disputes over land), engaging the military and the police on moving toward settlement, tracking violent incidents so political debate is informed by data, not prejudice, and supporting indigenous communities negotiating with mining companies. This engagement at every level of society, Pancho argues, is the only way to end violence. It is difficult at the best of times. But peace builders are working at the worst of times.

## CITIZEN VOICES IN PEACE TALKS

Peace agreements run on different "tracks." On track one are the official talks by governments and the warring parties, usually brokered by an outside party—such as the UN, a superpower that can strong arm the parties to the table, or perceived neutral countries such as Norway and Cuba, which hosted the peace talks to end Colombia's fifty-year-old civil war in 2016.

To assist the formal talks, track two diplomacy involves players with influence beyond the warring parties, such as civil society, women's groups, and businesses—"non-state actors," in the jargon—who can contribute without the requirements of formal negotiations. Bringing in insights from the public, they can make progress when the formal talks are stalled. Moberadoon have participated in track two of the UN-brokered Geneva peace talks on Syria, putting forward the views of women's groups.

Track two includes back-channel talks, where citizen groups shuttle unofficially between warring parties—who officially deny talking to each other—for months and years before the parties will even come to the peace negotiations. Mostly, international NGOs undertaking such negotiations operate in strict secrecy and make great efforts to stay off social media or the web so that when they meet fighting parties, no one is worried about breaches of confidentiality.

Track three comprises people connecting directly at the grassroots, removed from the formal peace talks but creating the space to reshape attitudes. Shifting the public will for peace is in some ways the hardest task of all. You cannot legislate or sign agreements to change people's views. This is where civil society can help; for example, through enabling people to trade with each other to heal the divisions of war. This was, of course, the driver behind the establishment of the European Community, which brought together former enemies, after World War II.

In 2008, India and Pakistan agreed to allow limited trade across the Line of Control, one of the most heavily militarised zones in the world, separating the two parts of the disputed region of Kashmir, after seven decades of conflict. NGO Conciliation Resources worked with others to help use this small opening to build peace.[13] They helped develop the civic bodies and practical mechanics to enable trade to happen, including by setting up the Jammu and Kashmir Joint Chamber of Commerce and Industry (JCCI) as the first-ever organisation with members from both sides of the Line of Control. As former JCCI president Y. V. Sharma said, "More than actual GDP, what the trade process has brought to fruition is emotional GDP. . . . I believe that this has immense potential to make borders irrelevant." The initiative started to soften the barrier between the two sides, give ex-fighters new livelihoods, and deter the Indian and Pakistani armies from firing in the areas where trade and travel took place across the line. Said ex-combatant turned small-scale trader Majid Khan, "The LoC [Line of Control] trade not only dramatically improved my livelihood but also reconnected me with my family and homeland, without compromising my political views."

Tragically, a large proportion of peace deals hammered out between warring parties fall apart within five years—usually because they do not address the underlying causes of the conflict and have not involved all of the affected parties adequately in the negotiations. That is why, for the Colombian peace process, the government led by President Santos had first studied other peace deals around the world—and decided to include victims' groups and women's groups, for example.

Between 1992 and 2011, fewer than 4 percent of signatories and fewer than 10 percent of negotiators at peace-talk tables were women. Yet research shows that, when women participate in peace processes, the agreement is 35 percent more likely to last at least fifteen years.[14] So having women feeding into talks makes total sense. Abir says of the Syrian talks, "Sometimes they are listening. Women are there but it's structured in a checklist or a showcase kind of way as opposed to taking our ideas seriously. It's always consultation, consultation. We need to see action."

Civil society has made vital contributions to rebuilding community cohesion—in Northern Ireland, or South Africa, in Nepal after the end of the civil war and in Rwanda after the genocide. When the guns finally fall silent—what professionals call "negative peace"—efforts must be redoubled to embed "positive peace" so people have access to justice, jobs and a voice in governance: all the tangible gains that will enable them to believe in and support peace because their lives are getting better and they have something to lose if they go back to fighting. That takes a myriad of initiatives at all levels of society, from reform of the legal system and provision of local governance and services, to trade unions organising in workplaces and community schemes embedding normal relations between previously warring sides. Critical to that process is transforming the role of security services, which are often part of the problem, so some civil society groups are reaching out to work with them and weave strands of social cohesion.

## RETHINKING SECURITY AND STABILITY IN MALI

The small town of Mopti in central Mali once had direct flights bringing French tourists to marvel at the ancient heritage sites before moving up to romantic Timbuktu. Today, the only planes are painted camouflage colours or sport the UN's white and blue symbol, while sandbags and barbed-wire protect military bases. Mali has been plagued by violence since 2012, when an armed rebellion by Tuareg-led jihadists with links to al-Qaeda broke out in the north, before fighting also began in the central belt. The UN's peacekeeping mission MINUSMA, established in 2013, has the highest casualty rate of such missions in the world.[15]

Mali has long struggled with weak governance, poverty, youth unemployment, droughts, and hunger, with ethnic tensions exacerbated by lawlessness and marginalisation. Around Mopti, schools have been closed by jihadists, and children face an uncertain future. Porous borders over which arms, drugs, and people are trafficked create a major security headache in the region, and global powers have piled in. As well as UN troops, there are soldiers in Mali from France, the UK, the United States, and four neighbouring countries. Many citizens blame the ongoing violence on the state's inability to provide security and services such as healthcare and education and believe that human rights abuses by governments and corruption with impunity drive some young people to join armed groups.[16] In June 2018, for example, the UN reported that Malian troops from the regional force G5 Sahel had "executed 12 civilians" at a market after a soldier was killed.[17] Violent extremist groups use incidents like this to promote their ideology, promising protection and alternative rules of law. Research by International Alert based on interviews in local communities found a complete lack of trust in the security forces, running across all sections of society, both feeding off and exacerbating ethnic tensions.

In 2018, Harriet was a fly on the wall at a community forum in Mopti that, for the first time, brought people together with some of those they feared the most: the Malian military. Around the table, in a dusty, empty school, farmers, foresters, and different religious communities gathered together with men in fatigues—the police, army, and forest guards. A journalist animatedly explained how after his Fulani friend was killed by security forces, he was so angry that he joined the armed groups—but in the end, turned away, realising that their vision did not represent the Islam he believed in. This journalist is now one of a brave group of community leaders who regularly discuss local issues with the security forces and try to improve the situation. A shy young teacher, who was unable to work after jihadist threats to kill teachers closed down five hundred schools in Mopti region, told Harriet she had never sat in a room with the military before. "This has transformed my opinion of them and their role in protecting us. I now understand that they have problems too," she said. Another public forum under the same initiative brought people together to discuss how to improve the justice system, which is a major area of resentment. As next steps, they planned to bring those who have joined armed groups into the dialogue sessions. This kind of trust-building work needs to be rolled out across the nation, argued group members.

The UN peacekeeping force MINUSMA has a mandate to stabilise the region, reduce intercommunal violence, reopen schools, and restore the presence of state and public services. But to succeed in these objectives in the long term, these forces need to win such communities' support, taking an approach to security that starts with addressing people's concerns and building from the grassroots up. It also means much more investment in addressing the root causes of the conflict. The international community needs to support Mali's government to improve access to justice, reduce inequality, address conflicts over access to land, and create job opportunities for young people. Without these long-term solutions, peace will prove elusive.

The challenge is how the ripples from civil society's islands of change can spread out—how to reach enough people to create the groundswell for transformation. Otherwise, pockets of progress are drowned out by the surrounding violence. All civil society initiatives wrestle with this conundrum. In peacebuilding, it is a constant struggle to address both the needs of individuals—to grieve, to forgive, to repent—and the structural reforms to tackle the root causes of conflict, such as scarcity of jobs, inequality, land reform, and changes to the justice system. All levels are needed for a society to rebuild out of the rubble of violence. That is why peace builders need to live in skyscrapers, not bungalows. Like Pancho in the Philippines, they need to work at all levels—from providing psychosocial support for individuals to lobbying governments on policy changes. The conundrum about where to focus is also faced by civil society countering violence in the West. Of course, it is not the same as in all-out "hot wars," but peace builders are also seeking to counter other types of violence and division.

## TAKE YOUR KNIVES OUT OF TOWN

Jamaican-born Neville Staple was the original Rude Boy, once famous for the slim line suits and pork-pie hats he wore as legendary vocalist for The Specials while bending his skinny legs to the infectious brass beats of two-tone hits such as "Rudy, A Message to You," later sung with Amy Winehouse. Two-tone, the ska-fused-with-punk soundtrack of the culture counter to Margaret Thatcher's 1980s Britain, was part of a wider stance by artists against the rise of the neo-Nazi National Front through initiatives like Rock Against Racism. Having moved to the UK as a child, Neville remains a celebrated son of Coventry, the Midlands city best known for the devastation caused by German bombing. There, Coventry Cathedral, which was kept deliberately as a forlorn ruin, a memorial to conflict, now hosts a thriving network fostering reconciliation.

At its annual conference, the hubbub rises as peace activists from Syria to Nigeria share tactics with people tackling knife crime and violent extremism in Australia or New Zealand. As with every global issue, there are strong connections between people countering violence overseas and at home. Sometimes, people assume that peacebuilding is only about ending all-out wars like Syria. But, in fact, it can equally help to address violence in countries that are not at war. While each context is different, peace builders everywhere can share principles and examples of what has and has not worked.

Neville and his wife Christine "Sugary" Staple are speaking about their grandson, Fidel Glasgow, their daughter's only son, who was just twenty-one when he was stabbed to death outside Club M—its third reported stabbing: "One night, we were in bed and the phone went and then we were pulling on our clothes and rushing to get out the door. When we got to the hospital, our daughter was telling us that he was going to pull through, that they could save him. We could see that he was already dead."[18]

As a young man before he found a new life with the band, Neville Staple had slipped into a life of crime, eventually being convicted for burglary and serving a spell in a prison for young offenders. Sugary, who confides that Neville was her pinup boy, also had a tough youth growing up in Hackney, North London. "We both know what it's like for today's young people—we've been where they are so we can talk to them—to try to stop the knife crime running riot across Britain's streets."

The rise in violent crime has pushed the search for solutions up the agenda, with city leaders reaching out to engage civil society in holistic approaches. Everyone looks to the methods successfully implemented in Glasgow. Named the murder capital of Europe in 2005, Glasgow initiated a holistic public-health approach to violence, treating it like a disease and dealing with the causes rather than the symptoms. A wide range of local agencies collaborated, from social workers and schools to hospitals and local communities, building a culture of early intervention, ensuring tougher enforcement alongside support in finding jobs. And, over time, it worked. Knife crime dropped, and the murder rate was almost halved.[19] Now campaigners are pushing for the model to be adopted across the country.

Meanwhile, Neville and Sugary have rereleased "Rudy" with new lyrics: "Stop your running about. Take your knives out of town." They tour with the video to talk with young people, helping them to see another future away from gangs and knives. The Specials' lead singer Terry Hall said of the rerelease: "It's a cry to respect each other and show each other love. Because that's all we've got."

## #NEVERAGAIN

It is 14 February 2018. Children, friends, teachers from the Marjory Stoneman Douglas High School in Parkland, Florida, will never come home again. Seventeen people gunned down. Another terrible day, another terrible mass shooting in the United States. Students vowed #NeverAgain and launched a movement for gun-law reform. "We will not just be another statistic. We will not stop until we see change," said eighteen-year-old Sabrina Fernandez, president of the student body. [20]

Stoneman Douglas senior Emma Gonzalez said, "If all our government and president can do is send thoughts and prayers, then it's time for victims to be the change that we need to see." The grieving students travelled to Washington, DC, and addressed rallies, debated on news channels, wrote opinion articles, raised money, and organised the nationwide March for Our Lives. Their efforts culminated in the biggest protest for gun control in the modern era, to petition for stricter gun controls including a ban on assault weapons like the one used in the Parkland shooting. As in the climate school strikes, here again were young people showing leadership and swinging into action, catapulting the long-running, divisive issue of gun violence and control into a new political space, opening possibilities of change long thought impossible.[21] It is the role of civil society to shift what people think is acceptable or achievable, to change laws, and also to change norms and culture—and these young people were showing how.

One of the exciting features of the campaign was the way that more established, bigger groups came in behind the youth-led quick-response Parkland campaign and were prepared to do so without pushing their brands. Michael Silberman of campaign-advisory group MobLab notes: "Following the Parkland mass shooting . . . large national groups like Everytown provided background support such as logistics and travel funding to support the student-led March for Our Lives—without any presence on stage. To prepare for advantageous 'movement moments' like this, NGOs need to work out what they're willing to risk for the sake of their greater goals."[22]

But #NeverAgain was up against it. The National Rifle Association (NRA), which ranks among the United States' most powerful lobbying groups, has repeatedly blocked national moves to regulate gun ownership. The Parkland survivors realised that they had little time to lose. All too frequently, in the aftermath of killings, people respond with an outpouring of public sorrow, but then the gun-rights narrative kicks in. Conscious of this, the students were quick to take to Facebook, using social media to multiply and amplify their message, garnering legions of support. Other groups collaborated to help build power and political pressure. For example, there was a voter registration drive led by groups such as Everytown for Gun Safety so high school students could vote on gun issues, as a follow-up to marches for gun safety, especially in areas where Republican representatives were receiving campaign contributions from the NRA.[23]

There is no official count on guns in the United States. According to the Pew Research Center, four in ten Americans say they own a gun or live in a household with a firearm, and the rate of manslaughter by firearms is the highest in the developed world.[24] The Gun Violence Archive (an organisation tracking the numbers) records 39,438 gun-related deaths including suicides in 2019.[25]

The protests following Parkland notched up some gains. Oregon tightened up some gun restrictions, while Florida looked to impose higher age limits and a longer waiting period for buying semi-automatic rifles like the one used at Parkland. Some companies—Delta Air Lines, United Airlines, and car-rental firm Enterprise—swiftly ended NRA-member discounts. In late 2018, US shipping group FedEx confirmed it, too, was ending ties, saying NRA no longer brought in enough business.[26] Reuters reported at the time: "It suggests the NRA no longer has the economic clout to inspire fear in the corporate world." Back in 2000, the NRA had nearly put gun maker Smith &Wesson out of business when it branded the company a "sell-out" for agreeing to back stronger gun controls.

As every campaigner knows, every step forward is followed by another back. Young Americans have questioned the old taboos about possessing firearms and are shifting the calculus. But holding the powerful gun lobby to account and overcoming a culture where, for many, the gun is synonymous with personal freedom and seen as a guaranteed civil right still presents a huge challenge. It will take a concerted effort by civil society to further shift the cultural and political debates. Two years before Parkland, President Obama said, in his tearful January 2016 speech on the continuing scourge of school shootings:

> Every time I think about those kids it gets me mad. . . . So, all of us need to demand a Congress brave enough to stand up to the gun lobby's lies . . . all of us need to demand governors and legislators and businesses do their part to make our community safer. We need the wide majority of responsible gun owners . . . to join with us to demand something better.[27]

But even he failed to make headway. Currently, the energy and organising sense of young people seem like the best hope to deliver the necessary shift in values.

## BLACK LIVES MATTER

In the post–civil rights movement era, the violent racism that persists on the streets of the United States—including from police and other state actors—has come up against a new generation of activist responses. Most influential is Black Lives Matter (BLM), the racial justice movement originally started by Patrisse Khan-Cullors, Alicia Garza, and Opal Tometti following the fatal shooting of unarmed seventeen-year-old African American Trayvon Martin by George Zimmerman, a neighbourhood watch coordinator, who was cleared of his murder.

In the summer of 2013, labour organiser Alicia Garza responded to Zimmerman's acquittal on her Facebook page, sparking a national debate over racial justice, gun violence, and civil rights.[28] People flocked to mass protests and #BlackLivesMatter went viral, with the deaths of African Americans at the hands of the police and racial injustice at the forefront of the movement. The iconic name became both an organisation—a decentralised network of chapters where members organise and "build local power to intervene in violence inflicted on Black communities by the state and vigilantes"—and the banner under which thousands of organisations and individuals press for change in the United States and beyond.[29]

Then, on 25 May 2020, a video captured the slow suffocation of unarmed forty-six-year-old father George Floyd—pinned to the ground by police in Minnesota, an officer's knee continually pushed into his neck despite his increasingly desperate plea: "I can't breathe." The horrific footage flew around the world, provoking outpourings of grief, anger, and solidarity on a scale rarely, if ever, seen before. Millions took to the streets to protest in support of Black Lives Matter throughout the United States and far beyond.

The momentum created by what has been described as the largest civil rights movement in US history continues building toward longed-for change on structural racism, way beyond the issue of police violence alone.[30] The principles espoused and resources published by the Black Lives Matter Global Network are based on nonviolent, nurturing approaches to "healing justice," but the movement is clear that without addressing the roots of racial inequality, it will be impossible to end the violence and the conflict it fuels. As the slogan on the streets goes, "No justice, no peace."

Direct action is only one part of the toolkit. "You move in the ways that are strategic," said BLM cofounder Patrisse Khan-Cullors, also an artist and Fulbright scholar, before the 2020 eruptions kicked off.[31] "We actually have to have all of it. We have to be in the streets. We have to be working with elected officials. We have to be moving ballot initiatives. We have to be fighting for the elected officials that we want to see in office. It's not one or the other."

It has not been easy, she said. "We were called terrorists, and not only . . . by right-wing pundits, we were called terrorists by former elected officials, current elected officials, appointed officials. . . . We were sued. They didn't win, but we were sued."

Activist and lecturer Frank Leon Roberts credits the organisation and the wider movement with notching up concrete victories as well as "the myriad ways that #blacklivesmatter has influenced our contemporary moment and given us a framework for imagining what democracy in action really looks like . . . the BLM movement has succeeded in transforming how Americans talk about, think about, and organize for freedom."

He also credits the movement with "popularizing what has now become an indispensable tool in 21st-century organising efforts: the phenomenon that scholars refer to as 'mediated mobilisation.'" He credits BLM with pioneering the use of social media as a mass mobilisation device, which was followed by successes such as #MeToo, #NeverAgain, and #TimesUp.[32] Between them, they figured out how to marshal today's tools and on the back of that spread decentralised movements—coordinated but without a top-down institutional structure. The BLM movement has spread beyond the specific issue that set it alight, and beyond the borders of the United States where it began, snowballing into an international movement calling for a once-and-for-all decisive shift away from the blight of racism in all its shapes across different countries and contexts—including an honest reckoning with the deep shadow cast by histories of colonialism and global exploitation, including within civil society itself.

## PEACE TECH PIONEERS

Mass mobilisation aside, social media and tech can support limitless initiatives, of course, including the prevention of violence. Harriet was inspired by one fairly modest-sounding example in Ettadhamen, a deprived suburb of the Tunisian capital, Tunis, which turned out to have had an extraordinary impact. Disaffected young people came together to map their area on OpenStreetMap (a collaborative digital tool)—and found a stronger sense of belonging in the process. As an enthusiastic young student, his long hair pulled back in a ponytail, told Harriet during her visit, "Here we have drug problems, we have terrorism, but we want young people to change their minds, and to change people's lives." At that time, in 2016, more ISIS foreign fighters came from Tunisia than any other country.[33]

After the revolution that toppled Tunisia's dictator Ben Ali, civil society turned its attention to building a more democratic society and addressing the chronic social and economic challenges that were stoking anger. Young people in particular were disillusioned that, following their leading role in changing the regime, their prospects looked no better, least of all in a neighbourhood like Ettadhamen—marked by poverty and high youth unemployment, and branded as a hotbed of drugs and radicalism. For young people facing discrimination at every turn, joining a group like ISIS seemed to offer status and a way out. The trick was to provide another option.

Research revealed that while young people were stigmatised for coming from Ettadhamen, it was also at the heart of their sense of identity. So a group of students used OpenStreetMap to map out their neighbourhood on their phones, adding street names and details previously only marked in affluent areas. After their studies, they went street by street, mapping every grocer and mosque, the barbers and the schools. It was so tiring, they complained laughingly to Harriet, as it was Ramadan—they were longing to eat, drink, and rest, and the elders scoffed at them for "playing on their phones again." But the data they collected also identified areas in need of basic services, which so impressed the initially sceptical local authorities that they were asked to help determine a phenomenal one-third of local government spending in the area. They organised public meetings and facilitated discussions for this participatory budgeting process, proposing repairs for roads and streetlights, rubbish collection points, and playgrounds.

They also addressed relations between young people and the police. One participant said, "As a young man of Ettadhamen, you have this negative relationship of mistrust between the youth and the police—in fact, that is the main cause of people joining ISIS." Some told Harriet how their "friend" or "cousin" had considered joining ISIS but now, empowered and engaged in society, had changed their mind. Others have gone on to stand for local government office, founded their own organisation, I-change, and inspired others to follow their model. As the young man from the OpenStreetMap project said, smiling disarmingly before dashing off to a university class: "Of course we are not *the* answer for Tunisia. But we are part of the answer."

In 2015, the UN Security Council's resolution on "youth, peace and security" marked a historic change in acknowledging young people's leadership in innovative peacebuilding. As in climate discussions, it seems that older generations are finally waking up to the power of youth. Another example is the Ushahidi (meaning "testimony" in Swahili) app in Kenya begun by young activists using phone calls and text messaging to monitor and map political violence following the 2008 election crisis as a way to help contain it. The tool is now used in different countries for humanitarian relief, election monitoring, and other purposes.

## INVESTING IN PEACE

"We the people of the United Nations determined to save succeeding generations from the scourge of war" opens the Preamble to the United Nations Charter of 1945. These lofty ideals of international cooperation stand mute before the conflicts and divisions of our time as today's governments pursue an inward politics of self-interest that is actively undermining multilateralism. The UN is struggling to uphold peace or to stretch its budgets to meet refugee needs; countries are withdrawing from or renouncing international human rights treaties; fewer multilateral agreements are being signed while in the UN Security Council, vetoes are rising. People often point the finger of blame at the United Nations, but it is no more than the sum of its nation-state members. When collective challenges get tougher, it is time to redouble, not walk away from, global cooperation. When, at the height of the Covid-19 disaster, President Trump announced that he would halt US funding and membership of the World Health Organization, he inflicted a major blow to global collaboration to bring the pandemic under control, resulting in damage to international relationships.

The multilateral institutions have not helped their own case, often being out of touch and pushing one particular worldview. The International Criminal Court, for example, has been accused of entrenched bias against Africa while the World Trade Organization seems to many to favour only wealthy nations, thereby institutionalising global inequalities. Reform of these multilateral institutions is vital, and civil society must continually remind governments that self-interest is in nobody's interest.

In contrast, true public interest is tied to foreign policies that foster peace and address effective global solutions. That means adopting smarter tactics and engaging the public in the defence of multilateral solutions—an approach that has worked well in Sweden, Norway, and Germany, where civil society and political leaders make the case for global citizenship, winning support for global solutions at the national level.

To address the challenges of this decade, the global community needs to find new ways of working together; we must invest more—far more—in movements and actions for change on the ground and far less in selling the weapons of war. As well as working away from the bottom up to build peace, civil society presses from the top down for a fundamental shift in thinking, strategy, and resources—and to tip the grotesque imbalance between the billions spent on training and equipping the military, so that we can "win" wars, and the amount invested in averting conflict and in winning and sustaining peace. That struggle has become all the more critical in our era of inflammatory, nationalist rhetoric, which can flip into fighting when international collaboration is denigrated as an approach to solving shared problems. The Covid-19 pandemic has laid bare the dangerous consequences of nationalist populism in many countries. Some leaders tried to downplay the threat of the virus, others to pretend a ring-fenced national solution was possible—often with deadly results. But overall, people and politicians have faced up to the inescapable global interconnectedness of the pandemic and its solutions. Anxious publics have seen the benefits of cross-border efforts in science and medicine, and they want to see more; most also understand that winning this battle will involve ensuring that vaccines, for example, are shared fairly among the global family.

We are familiar with many of the practical tools to resolve conflicts without violence and to build peace: diplomacy and mediation, more effective justice and democratic systems, civil society speaking out against human rights abuses, and maintaining the—often narrowing—space for dialogue and disagreement. Huge citizen movements have mobilised at moments of crisis, from the Vietnam War to the Iraq War. Today, the energy that fuelled such movements needs to be channelled into pushing for longer-term structural changes, and to protect multilateral approaches.

Civil society needs to build a more effective collective voice for investment in multilateral peacebuilding. Despite spiralling conflict, peacebuilding remains underused and underfunded compared to other interventions. By one estimate, annual expenditure on peacebuilding in 2016 was equivalent to just over 0.5 percent of the US$1.72 trillion global military expenditure.[34] In fact, in 2018, total world military expenditure rose by 2.6 percent from 2017, according to the Stockholm International Peace Research Institute (SIPRI) with the top spenders being the United States, China, Saudi Arabia, India, and France, which together accounted for 60 percent of global military spending.[35]

The peacebuilding community is tiny—much smaller than those tackling poverty or climate change, for example—and has not been as politically astute nor as effective at collaborating to win political support. NGOs have tended, understandably, to focus on conflicts where they are working, leaving little time to forge alliances that could shift political perspectives. As some peacebuilding is dangerous, people have also become used to a low-profile culture. But this culture of keeping quiet has spilled across the whole sector, preventing peacebuilding from rising up the global priority list. It is strange that, in this era, the peace movement is not on the streets or in our newspapers. Indeed, most people do not even know that peacebuilding as undertaken by civil society is an activity, as distinct from the peacekeeping done by the UN blue-helmeted soldiers who use military force to prevent violence. Peace, it seems, has a PR problem.

As Martin Luther King Jr. said: "Those who love peace must learn to organize as effectively as those who love war." That is why, in 2018, leading international NGOs formed the +Peace coalition to campaign for more support for peacebuilding. Madeline Rose, the dynamic then coordinator said, "The fates of communities and nations have never been so intertwined. Today's problems—acts of violence and extremism, growing inequality, climate disruption, and restricted civic space—cannot be solved by any one nation or through outdated and ineffective approaches. It needs a strong coalition."

The coalition is putting to governments the hardnosed argument that peacebuilding is effective and a good value for money. It points to the figures. For example, the Global Peace Index estimates that for every US dollar invested in prevention, sixteen dollars is saved in the cost of conflict.[36] As Madeline tweeted, "Global military spending should not be rising when none of our greatest security threats have military solutions. Climate emergency = no military solution; grievances and inequities that drive violent extremism = no military solution; great power competition = no military solution."

Previously at US NGO Mercy Corps, Madeline had a proud track record, having masterminded passage of a bipartisan congressional bill to reduce violence globally by committing the US government, across departments, to devise and implement a ten-year strategy, with funds, to tackle the long-term causes of violence and fragility for ten years in ten countries.

"Every national security strategy keeps saying we need conflict prevention, yet the numbers were not changing and we were frustrated," she explains. Three figures—of rising conflict, rising homicides, and rising costs of violence—were at tipping points. Thus, she developed the idea of this bill and built a 75-strong NGO coalition that pooled resources for lobbying. Then, most impressively of all, she won crucial cross-party support—a huge feat in today's deeply partisan US politics and itself a demonstration of the need to work across divisions to achieve change—so that four and a half years later, the Global Fragility Act of 2019 was passed.

Representatives Michael McCaul (R) and Eliot Engel (D), both of the House Foreign Affairs Committee, led the bill process, with Engel commenting:

> We have learned a great deal about what drives violence and instability in what are called fragile states. We know it takes goals and strategies. We know it takes strong sustained investment over the long-term. We know it takes serious research and analysis and that it takes agencies across government working together towards the same goals. This bill takes all that knowledge and establishes an overarching policy framework for the United States government. It will help ensure that our government is working in lockstep to prevent violence and extremism and that we are working closely with civil society groups to assess internal and extend external drivers of instability to implement these initiatives on the ground and to monitor and evaluate the work.[37]

Leaving no stone unturned, and in a bid to engage individual concerned citizens, the +Peace coalition is also running a drive to get the term "peacebuilding" in the dictionary. Words matter, and shaping the narrative is a key civil society tactic. Climate activists for example, have successfully pushed people to use terms such as "climate crisis" or "climate emergency," which articulate urgency.

Lexicographers monitor which words are joining our everyday lingo. So it was significant that "climate strike" was named 2019 word of the year by *Collins Dictionary*, following earlier winners such as "fake news," "populism," and "austerity."

Words recently entering our vocabularies include "instagrammable," "adorbs," and "hangry" (being so hungry that you are angry).[38] But *peacebuilding* had yet to be accepted despite a forty-year track record. Since the +Peace coalition's first action—putting a giant dictionary outside Shakespeare's Globe Theatre on the River Thames—Collins, Macmillan, and Cambridge dictionaries have all responded, adding the word to their online versions. The others have yet to agree, but the peacebuilders will keep asking, seeing this as one tiny step forward in their wider campaign for support and funding at scale. Meanwhile, civil society continues striving for another leap of progress: to stop the flow of weapons that fuel conflict.

## FOLLOW THE ARMS

This time, Harriet realised, she had gone too far. Butterflies were multiplying in her stomach. Sweating in the murky, dark belly of a Challenger army tank, she clutched her invitation to the Midland Bank annual general meeting in one hand and held tight to her seat with the other. Would she end up in prison? Just how badly had she messed up?

It was May 1995, and Harriet had bought a one pound share in Midland Bank (now part of HSBC) so she could attend this annual general meeting. She wanted to ask the chairman why the bank was providing finances for sales of Hawk fighter jets to Indonesia, which was bombing the people of occupied East Timor as they struggled to regain independence.

The tank's long—albeit empty—gun barrel protruded as it rumbled slowly through the heart of the City of London before halting in a side alley by the concrete complex of the Barbican. Harriet opened the tank hatch and emerged, blinking into the sunlight. Photographers snapped and cameras whirred, putting the World Development Movement's (WDM) call to stop financing arms sales to repressive regimes all over the news. Harriet asked her question and was not arrested. Bear in mind that this was before 9/11; you surely could not drive a tank into the City today.

It was a short-term tactical success among the long-running, ongoing civil society campaigns to stop the arms sales to repressive regimes that fuel conflict. We both spent a lot of time at WDM targeting the banks that provided the finances and shining a light on the government's shadowy Export Credit Guarantee Department (ECGD), which was underwriting the loans. To upend the usual argument thrown against us that arms sales were a boost to the UK economy, our painstaking research exposed the extent to which the taxpayer subsidised the industry (including through the millions of pounds written off by the British government) as underwriters for weapons delivered by British companies but not paid for—by customers including one Saddam Hussein who had been sold British tanks before the UK went to war with him. We will never forget the shock on officials' faces as our members deluged them with campaign letters. "The public *never* write letters to us," one distressed official told us. By targeting this weak link in the chain, the campaign won a government ban on ECGD support for arms sales to the poorest countries—even if it did not go as far as we wanted.

Having won the High Court case over the arms sales–linked Pergau dam, WDM took another case to the High Court to prevent sales of the fighter jets to Indonesia—and we lost. We lobbied, successfully, for tighter controls on arms sales to be part of a promised new "ethical foreign policy" and a European Code of Conduct to rule out arms sales to repressive regimes. While many similar efforts by civil society have hammered away over the ensuing decades, lethal weapons still flow to authoritarian regimes and regions at war. Worse still, weapons sales are rising: in 2014–2018, increasing 7.8 percent over 2009–2013 and 23 percent over 2004–2008.[39] At the top of the arms export list is the United States, its share rising from 30 percent to 36 percent of world sales, with over half (52 percent) of US arms exports going to the Middle East in 2014–2018. In the same period, British arms exports increased by 5.9 percent, with 59 percent of exports in the period 2014–2018 going to the Middle East, the vast majority being combat aircraft to Saudi Arabia and Oman.[40]

The long-running, single-minded Campaign Against the Arms Trade (CAAT) is a tiny, dogged outfit hidden away in London's backstreets, remorselessly pressing the world's superpowers and most powerful companies. Their research exposed UK weapons being used by Saudi Arabia in its indiscriminate strikes on Yemen, which have killed thousands of civilians and created a humanitarian disaster, to shore up the government against the rebels. CAAT highlighted that the UK has licensed over £4.7 billion (US$5.7 billion) worth of arms to Saudi Arabia since the bombing of Yemen began in March 2015, including for aircraft, helicopters, drones, grenades, bombs, and missiles. This, said the group, is despite overwhelming evidence of repeated breaches of international humanitarian law. The campaigners were convinced that the UK government was breaking its own rules governing arms exports and took the case to the court. They lost.

Knocked back but not knocked out, they decided to appeal. Not an easy decision for a small organisation with a small bank balance. On 20 June 2019, the Court of Appeal ruled that UK arms sales to Saudi Arabia for use in Yemen were unlawful, concluding that it was "irrational and therefore unlawful" for the secretary of state for international trade to have granted licenses without assessing whether violations of international humanitarian law had taken place. A landmark decision, it was a huge victory. As a result, the government must retake all decisions to export arms to Saudi Arabia in accordance with the law. It stopped issuing new arms-export licences to Saudi Arabia and its coalition partners, the UAE, Bahrain, Kuwait, and Egypt, for use in Yemen. Paul Murphy, director of Saferworld, who supported the court case, said:

> The Court of Appeal has finally confirmed what has been obvious for years: Saudi Arabia is guilty of committing repeated, serious violations of interna-

tional law in Yemen, and the UK Government has been wilfully ignoring this in its decisions to sell weapons. With the UK providing humanitarian assistance to Yemen and claiming to be leading efforts to establish a peace process, it's time to end the contradictory policy of arming the conflict.[41]

## CONFLICTS COSTING THE EARTH

Weapons can never deal with the root causes of war and are especially powerless against climate change—which is, increasingly, a contributing factor to conflict. CAAT argue for jobs to move from weapons production and into sectors solving climate problems. It is an "ecosystem" point of view, connecting the crises in climate, conflict, refugees, and inequality and seeking equally connected solutions. This is just the rounded thinking and acting that is needed in the 2020s as we search for whole-system solutions.

The same systems approach is demanded by the deep connections between mining and conflict. According to the World Bank, 40 to 60 percent of civil wars over the past 60 years have been triggered, funded, or sustained by the extraction of natural resources.[42] From the Democratic Republic of the Congo to Myanmar, such conflicts have centred on, and been sustained by, the allure of timber, gold, and gems—while the struggle over resources such as oil has been a central driver of international conflicts, such in the Middle East.

Ben got drawn into the opaque world of the diamond trade and its links to fuelling conflict in Africa, made famous by the film *Blood Diamonds*, when he was running the successor to the Anti-Apartheid Movement, Action for Southern Africa. He worked with other NGOs to try and stem the flow of diamonds funding bloody civil wars in countries like Angola and Sierra Leone. He took part in the first uneasy negotiations in Kimberley, South Africa, in 2000, between NGO representatives; industry executives from the global giant De Beers and the trading centres in London, Antwerp, and New York; and diplomats from countries such as Botswana, which were reliant on the legitimate diamond trade for half of their income. The parties started to thrash out an agreement to stop conflict diamonds from reaching the global marketplace.

A year later, they met again in the conference centre of the Twickenham rugby stadium, convenient to London's Heathrow Airport. In the middle of the meeting, diplomats' phones started buzzing with unbelievable messages. The only TV to be found was a tiny one in the security guard's office. Ben craned his neck alongside the other delegates to see the news footage of the Twin Towers attack, everyone united across nations in their shared horror. Their meeting was abandoned, the venue evacuated, with Ben out on the street while London airspace went into lockdown. The so-called Kimberley Process talks resumed and did pin down a deal—but the NGOs later withdrew, frustrated at the industry's lack of commitment to fully cutting off the supply of conflict diamonds once the heat was off.

Other conflicts have centred on scarce natural resources such as water, where increased pressure, exacerbated by climate change, is often a trigger for violence. In Mali or Nigeria's central belt, for example, herders moving across farmers' lands in search of water or grazing add to the cocktail of causes for the conflict. Concern is rising that, as the climate changes, pressure on food, land, and water will intensify, sparking conflicts, especially as people move in search of resources.[43] What is more, according to the United Nations Environment Programme, conflicts in which resource scarcity is at play are more than twice as likely to start up again in the first five years after a peace deal has been signed because these root causes are rarely properly addressed. Wealth sharing and the management of natural resources are make-or-break issues.

Many organisations support local communities in managing natural resources and ensure that governments and businesses respect human rights. Others, such as Global Witness, expose companies' most heinous abuses. Such activities underscore, yet again, the need to connect civil society's strands of engagement in response to the intertwined problems. Economic liberalisation and the single-minded pursuit of profits, including by the giant oil multinationals, has contributed to global conflict. If, in a managed way, oil companies stopped exploring, drilling, and extracting, one cause of conflict would be removed—while simultaneously reducing climate change and its own destabilising effects. We can turn the connecting vicious cycles of violence into virtuous cycles of peace. And we can take inspiration from so many on the frontlines, including the bravest and humblest man Harriet ever met—Dr Abuelaish.

On 16 January 2009, Dr Izzeldin Abuelaish's three eldest daughters and his niece were killed when their bedroom in Gaza was ripped apart by Israeli tank shells. In his book, *I Shall Not Hate,* Dr Abuelaish tells his life story, from an impoverished childhood in a Palestinian refugee camp to becoming a leading infertility expert, famously treating patients on both sides of the conflict.[44] When the shell hit his family home, Dr Abuelaish was live on Israeli television talking by phone to the reporter; a heartrending clip is on YouTube. His response to this tragedy was to redouble his efforts for reconciliation and peace, including through founding the charity Daughters for Life to help Middle Eastern women continue their studies abroad.

"What makes evil flourish is for good people to do nothing, to sit there thinking they're protected," he says. "I say, no, you need to take action, you need to be proactive and do more. Hope is not a word. It's an action."[45]

*Chapter Five*

# Seeds of Hope among Displaced Lives

*With more people than ever forced to flee their homes, citizens are stepping up to show common humanity.*

Alf Dubs arrived in Britain through the mass Kindertransport rescue mission as a child fleeing Nazi-occupied Czechoslovakia in 1939. Today he serves in the House of Lords. A lifelong champion of refugees' rights, including running the Refugee Council, when Harriet worked with him, he still finds himself having to defend the rights of lone refugee children seeking safety in Britain.[1] In January 2020, he called for legislation to ensure that unaccompanied children could join their families, writing, "The way we treat the most vulnerable is a test of the kind of country we aspire to be. When I arrived here as a refugee child, with 10,000 others, I never thought that 81 years later I'd be fighting for a few hundred to be allowed to find their families here."[2]

He is concerned about how anti-foreigner and anti-refugee feeling is being stoked across Europe, with too few people prepared to speak out: "Refugees are people who are fleeing from war, from torture, from fear of death and therefore we owe them a responsibility over and above that which we owe anyone else. It is the highest level of responsibility."[3]

Many people have felt that responsibility viscerally, volunteering on the US border, at the French port of Calais, and across the Mediterranean: people like Louisa Waugh, a lively, straight-talking nurse-turned-writer-turned-peacebuilder with silver rings on her fingers and a loud laugh. In 2018, she returned to the Greek Island of Samos, close to Turkey, for a second stint with Samos Volunteers—one of the many groups that have sprung up as volunteers across Europe spontaneously seek to fill the gap left by reluctant or overwhelmed governments. What she had encountered two years before was bad enough, but things had gotten worse. "Then there were around 1,300 refugees in a camp with a capacity for 500 people. Now there are more than 3,500," she told Harriet when back home in Cambridge.[4] "It is so overcrowded, families are sleeping outside the camp, in tents, under the trees. They have no running water, toilets or electricity, and no one is collecting the rubbish, so rats are inside the tents, and snakes on the ground."

Louisa has worked in hot spots such as Mali and the Central African Republic, where she was once pinned in her car as prisoners broke out of the central jail and went on a rampage. She has seen refugee camps in the poorest countries, and nothing—she pauses, looking Harriet in the eye—nothing is as bad as Samos, here in the centre of Europe. "At the camp, refugees are queuing three to four hours for their meals; on certain days, the camp has run completely out of food." People turned up at the centre saying they had not eaten anything for several days. "The refugees, all people like us but stranded throughout the Greek islands, have dropped off the news agenda, but they have nowhere else to go."

She has photos on her phone of the faces crowding at wire fences, photos that encapsulate much of the past decade of forced displacement and detention affecting millions. Blinking back tears, she remembers an elegant Syrian violin player who left the camp carrying his tiny daughter on his shoulders—hoping to make it through to mainland Europe and a better future somewhere else, always somewhere else.

After World War II, the United Nations High Commission for Refugees (UNHCR) was formed to support the millions of refugees across Europe. It was one building block of the new international order, constructed by governments reeling from the Holocaust, the war, and then the Iron Curtain, determined that we would "never again" face such tragedies. Governments signed the UN Convention on Refugees, committing to accept people "unable or unwilling to return to their country of origin owing to a well-founded fear of being persecuted for reasons of race, religion, nationality, membership of a particular social group, or political opinion."

In 2020, the numbers of people forced to move exceeded those displaced by World War II, becoming a defining issue of our age. The UNHCR estimated that nearly eighty million people were forcibly displaced worldwide, of whom twenty-six million were refugees abroad, half of them children.[5] They come from Afghanistan, Syria, Myanmar, South Sudan, Somalia, Yemen, Iraq, the Democratic Republic of the Congo, Venezuela—and they seek shelter overwhelmingly in neighbouring countries, such as Turkey, Pakistan, Colombia, Uganda, and Sudan, with Germany the only wealthy country among the top ten recipients. The other 45.7 million are displaced within their own country—such as those living in flimsy shacks in northeast Nigeria.[6]

Every two seconds, someone else is forced to flee. So, in the past hour, another 1,541 people have packed their bags and set off on a perilous journey in search of safety.[7] Most are fleeing conflict, making it hard to return as the fighting drags on, so that now, on average, people's time as a refugee stretches out over seventeen years.

Yet just at the very time that we need collective global action to cope with the worst refugee crisis in history, the rise of xenophobia and populist authoritarianism threatens our ability either to engage internationally or to build social cohesion at home. Jan Egeland, secretary-general of the Norwegian Refugee Council and former UN lead on humanitarian affairs, encapsulates it: "The mood is the worst I have seen in 40 years of humanitarian work . . . We have more closed borders, less resettlement and a bigger funding gap than ever."[8]

At the first-ever World Refugee Forum in December 2019, the *Financial Times* commented:

> While the actions of the rich industrialised countries have long contributed to forced migration—from regional conflicts to climate change—some also undermine the response. Mr Trump's calls for a reinforced wall on the US-Mexican border and his policy of punishing and returning migrants have legitimised similar actions in parts of the EU and Turkey.[9]

Initially, as people fleeing war streamed across Europe's borders and refugees suffered in squalid camps, as in Calais, the international NGOs were caught unprepared. We were not ready to mobilise a humanitarian response in our own backyard, failing to grasp the scale of the crisis, and did not show the boldness required as events profoundly reshaped political realities around us. We seemed flatfooted and cowed, worried about our international mandate crossing into "domestic" issues. It was a moment that underlined just how much we need to rethink NGO approaches—as well as how much some members of the public are ready to get involved when they see governments walking away.

## COMMUNITIES WELCOME REFUGEES

Photographs of Alan Kurdi's little three-year-old body lying lifeless on a beach in Turkey on 2 September 2015 reverberated around the globe. He had drowned with his mother, five-year-old brother, and at least nine other refugees from the war in Syria, his family having made a desperate bid to cross the Mediterranean for the Greek islands, in the hope of ultimately reaching relatives in Canada. For Debbie Rix, as for many Canadians who went on to take action, this was a turning point: "In my store, the front page of our national newspaper had that picture above the fold. People kept coming in and turning the newspaper over, saying 'I don't want to see that.' I kept turning it back over and saying: 'We *have* to look at this—we can't look away.'"[10]

She put out a Facebook call and was soon leading a community group to sponsor a refugee family. Her initiative got an amazing response of human solidarity from ordinary Canadians to a crisis happening thousands of miles away in Europe. Over 14,000 Syrians reached safety in Canada between November 2015 and January 2017 after being sponsored by similar local groups. The surge in support came as part of a longer tradition of community-based refugee resettlement. Canada had a tight immigration policy until the late 1970s, when it brought in the sponsorship approach in response to the "boat people" fleeing the war in Vietnam; a total of 327,000 refugees have since settled there in this way, supported by many thousands of Canadians.[11]

"The amazing thing is that it actually became an election issue," says Gloria Nafziger from Amnesty International Canada. "There was such a demand on the part of Canadians to respond to a crisis. The government we currently have [led by Prime Minister Justin Trudeau] was elected in part because it made its promise to the Canadian people to respond to the demand."[12] As in the 1970s, people have demanded that their government do more for refugees, while showing they are prepared to take practical action at the community level to this effect. It can be a perfect dance: civil society prepares the way for government commitments and then ensures their success.

Now community sponsorship is spreading internationally, including in Britain, where following well-organised pressure from the NGO Citizens UK and others, the government agreed to support a similar initiative. Under the scheme, community groups take responsibility for a refugee family for two years, along with the tasks normally shouldered by local authorities, such as finding schools and a home. The government allows these refugees, selected by the UNHCR as the most vulnerable, often from Jordan or Lebanon, to enter with full rights.

The Welsh town of Narberth was among the first in Britain to host a family. When the town swimming pool faced closure, the community took it over. When the library was in trouble, they decided to help. Now they have stepped in to welcome Syrian refugees, sponsoring the town's first Muslim family. Locals found a house, helped the family settle in, and bought pigeons for Mr. Batak to keep in his garden, as he used to do in Damascus, so also connecting with the old Welsh tradition of pigeon fancying.[13]

Pioneers like Narberth were an inspiration for people in Harriet's corner of South London where the Herne Hill Welcomes Refugees committee cram into one another's front rooms, sitting on the floors or standing, but always with time to get to know each other before settling down to the agenda. It is a movement fuelled by tea and homemade buttery biscuits—which were even once raised under Any Other Business. It can be hard work, but most groups are enthusiastic about the benefits of getting to know their local community, make friends, and have fun while coming together to help people in difficulty. Being honest about how much you yourself gain is fundamental to community action as it is never pure altruism—and is all the stronger for that. Harriet has met new neighbours, discovered the local fish and chippy's commitment to local initiatives, relished falafels donated for the fundraiser, and went all mushy when Elaine the flower lady staggered in carrying window boxes for the refugee family.

The first three committee members met in the home of Rachel Griffiths, a bubbly actress who was talking nonstop about her Myers-Briggs-tested tendency to love shiny new things more than completing and finishing things—a personality trait that the British government's Home Office would push to the limit. Harriet was making a fuss over the labradoodle, while leaning back was lanky, chilled Nick Jeyarajah, whose Tamil grandparents left Sri Lanka in the early 1960s amid mounting tensions. Just home from the university, he was searching for work in international development "somehow," while on a zero-hours contract in London's trendy Pop-Up Brixton (a collection of containers bursting with local beers and street food). Frustrated that the government was accepting so few refugees, the group placed down their tiny counterweight. They realised that it was just one family. But for that one family, it would make all the difference. Nick says:

> Refugees are the victims of world politics: wars, political strife, a changing climate. It always seemed wrong that a group of people who are by definition in need of help are so routinely left behind and even vilified in our country....
> I am so angry that Britain is not being more generous, is not doing more to help with the refugee crisis. This is such a practical way that we can help one family. And send a message to the government that the people of Britain do care and so we should accept more refugees.

Opening Rachel's laptop, the trio plodded through the daunting Home Office criteria, brows creasing with worry. Realising they would need a whole team with a range of skills, they set about arranging their first public meeting. Leaflets made, they trudged down the streets, pushing them through bristly letterboxes, past yapping dogs—for local action, good old-fashioned leaflets, with public meetings and an occasional market stall, cannot be beaten. They raised money, found a landlord willing to rent at below-market prices, and recruited volunteers. Of course, they also shamelessly promoted their cause on social media and in the press, inspiring others to join the movement, which now ranges from a Syrian refugee community organisation to a West Midlands business.

The positive response to the first callout blew them away. The group members have suffered multiple setbacks and torn their hair out over government welfare benefit payments that took months to arrive. But each time, people popped up to help—people like Peter, the decorator who picked up a leaflet as the group froze at a winter market stall and duly painted the house ready for the family's arrival.

Nick sees community involvement as, "a powerful mechanism toward both helping refugees, and creating a more tolerant, open society." He says:

> It goes further than helping an individual family—an amazing thing in itself. There is something special about people actively welcoming others, especially vulnerable refugees, into their community. It is a demonstrable expression of empathy and intent, performed by a collective group. I like to think of it as a form of political communication.

Furthermore, for Nick, "The sense of empowerment and enfranchisement is something that seems to be quite rare in society at the moment." It is an example in microcosm of how civil society can shift a culture—and start to build a different world between the cracks of the old.

Finally, the Home Office sent word that an Iraqi single mother, Dalya, with her three children, would be arriving in December. Having fled Iraq, they had been struggling to survive in Lebanon in terrible conditions for five years. A flurry of activity was sparked and then, eighteen months after the group started, a small welcoming party set off to Heathrow Airport.[14]

Dalya had heard that London was busy and the British cold and unfriendly. "Sorry about that!" she laughs now. "I was nervous, but also very excited because this was such an important step. It changed my whole life. . . . Some nice people were waiting for me at the airport. I cried and they cried. I felt like I was in a dream."

As the children ran into their new home, the girls started arguing about which room to have. The littlest immediately settled at the child's desk and started drawing. The skinny boy beamed from ear to ear as he took in his room, complete with books and a football. Just one month later, the five-year-old was grinning a gappy grin and holding up a sparkly card: "Pupil of the Week." Dalya is proud that her children never stop talking about how they want to take personal action to stop climate change—a sense of empowerment, she remarks, that they learned in Britain: that with good ideas and good thinking you can care for your society.

Now, a year later, Dalya feels totally at home and is helping the group to sponsor a second family. She says, "I want to help somebody I don't know. I have lived with difficult things and I know what people are coping with. So, I want to give refugees a new chance, a new life." She concludes, "Governments should be very proud of their communities who do sponsorship. If this world had more such people, then society would be better."

## CITIZEN ORGANISING

Rachel has now become involved with the national organisation with which Herne Hill Welcomes Refugees is affiliated, Citizens UK. It was the brainchild of Neil Jameson, considered the godfather to community organising in the UK, who was inspired by the original founder of the movement, Saul Alinsky (see chapter 8). For Neil, civil society plays an equal role alongside the state and the market, which it can support and challenge. Citizens UK's focus is not on becoming experts and following the "single-issue" model of campaigning. Rather, it is about equipping people with leadership and skills, enabling them to determine the priority issues to tackle in their community, breaking big problems down into winnable chunks, and engaging positively with people whose minds they want to change. Citizens UK even established a "Guild of Organisers," turning community organising into a profession, and has trained over three thousand grassroots leaders in "the art of broad-based community organising to help their neighbourhoods and cities be more powerful."[15]

One key tool adopted from the United States was the hosting of citizens' assemblies, to strengthen democracy as people hold those in power to account. Herne Hill Welcomes Refugees participated in a citizens' assembly in the run-up to local elections. Hundreds of people, genuinely diverse, packed into a cavernous student hall. Tightly choreographed, every group had a few minutes to inspire political candidates by showing what they had achieved already and asking for practical support from the candidate, if elected.

Like everyone, Rachel has multiple impulses to action. Having a deep Christian faith, she is passionate about living the church's values; she is also committed in her acting work to Freire and Boal's techniques, in which the audience participates in theatre, themselves creating political and social change.[16] She was performing in Calais when the conditions for refugees hit home: "I was angry to see women refugees not being able to wash their clothes. Anger is a catalyst. Community sponsorship felt like a doable response." In Citizens UK, they talk about using your anger a lot. For Rachel:

> The desire to make change comes from a place of anger. Citizens UK think about the world as it is—and then the world as it should be; the anger comes from the world as it is. It gives you fire in the belly. In church, we are told that anger is only OK if it is righteous; everyone tells you that anger is negative, but the emotion itself is not the problem—it's the outpouring and what you do with it. It is about how you channel your anger. It is new to really look at anger, not to dress it up . . . we need to just own it and feel free to stand up against injustice.

In many countries, faith communities—in mosques, temples, gurdwaras, synagogues—are the backbone of movements for social change, whether sustaining "traditional" or "liberal" values, because they have an established group of people meeting regularly, with a mandate and a building. Organisers have often tapped into existing networks like those based on faith or trade unions, a skill that the new wave of activist campaigns are relearning as part of a wider renaissance in grassroots organising. Rachel says, "The church must be a place of sanctuary. Society takes more notice of a church that is active—otherwise what do we say that we are standing up for? It's not about people coming to church . . . but the church joining in with what is already taking place."

In Western democracies, declining participation in collective institutions such as faith groups, trade unions, or political parties, has affected citizens' engagement in the big debates of our time. These are institutions where people learn to argue out different views, to feel represented in wider debates, to think through problems together with others in a way that social media can never replicate. Without them, older people, especially, feel in retreat, left behind by wider societal shifts, no longer part of bodies that are shaping and representing their values. Of course, people have fashioned alternatives, building new networks and new ways of communicating, especially through tech. But institutions and local organising will always play a critical role, and, increasingly, civil society groups are returning again to these more direct, relationship-based ways of making change—even if also strongly supported by digital networking.

For Rachel, theatre and the arts can also be pivotal, especially on big global issues that require a leap of imagination: "Theatre is very dynamic; you are emotionally engaged and creating connection is what creates change. It is on a heart level." For the refugee crisis, as on climate change, the arts help us imagine a different world, to dream of how the world could be different, to see things we cannot see every day, to create a community of people. It is this imagining, connecting, and hoping that is at the heart of what drives all transformative social change.

## A WIDE ENOUGH IMPACT?

One dilemma playing on the minds of community-sponsorship groups is the imbalance in people's time and energy to support one family. They worry about all those refugees who risk their lives to reach safety and wait interminably to know if they can stay, sometimes in detention, and the millions trapped for years in terrible camps. Could they do more for them? And what about people already struggling in the deprived public housing of Manchester or Philadelphia? Is help to one new refugee family misplaced when there is so much social injustice at home? Groups may feel uneasy about whether community sponsorship is a privatisation of care that should be shouldered by the state.

In response, advocates argue that one small action in one small place can have a wider impact. In fact, it almost always does. For example, the community group in Wales has inspired others to follow suit while the strength of community support sends a signal to government and is a platform to press for policy changes. One critical link in creating local bottom-up alternatives is to join up and multiply them through networks and links—in person and online. In recent years, as trust in traditional institutions has imploded, people's horizons for trust have come back down to their street, their workplace, and those they know personally. So that is where civil society is rebuilding, articulating a local-to-global vision that helps build a more welcoming culture. That is why organisations like Amnesty International, the Red Cross, or Avaaz have, alongside more traditional and hard-hitting policy-focused campaigns, celebrated how communities are welcoming refugees, showcasing the power of kindness in order to shift the overall culture and, ultimately, policies.

To amplify Herne Hill Welcomes Refugees' message, the group joined Citizens UK's campaign #ExtendTheWelcome pressing for refugees resettled via community sponsorship to be additional to government goals on refugee numbers. Group members engaged with their MPs, who held debates in Parliament. And in the summer of 2019, the government announced that from 2020 onward, refugees sponsored by communities would be additional to those coming via government schemes. It was a small but significant success.

Community sponsorship is still tiny in the UK: 90 groups had welcomed 424 refugees by December 2019. Ayham Alsuleman, himself a Syrian refugee, was one of the first to join the Herne Hill group, quickly going on to work professionally in supporting refugee resettlement, most recently for the Greater London Authority. While stressing that it is still early days for community sponsorship in the UK, he says, "The scheme can never replace the role of local authorities and government, but the role of civil society is very important in supporting refugees—it changed my life! I would hope the scheme becomes a permanent part of the British culture of welcoming strangers."[17]

As Ayham says, sponsorship's personal nature helps shift attitudes in society. In one village in Kent, in southern England, community sponsorship kicked off a storm of local opposition to refugees coming until, that is, they met the family. Once they saw the disabled boy struggling to get on the bus and the young mother rushed into hospital with complications in childbirth, the village dropped their hostility and joined the support team.

In Canada, the inspiration for community sponsorship, an estimated two million people have been involved in welcoming Syrians, and one-third of the population has had some contact with a refugee family. The racism and xenophobia of the far right have not taken root in that country. There may be no causal connection; or there just may be.

And there is the argument that, while you can always belittle community efforts as too much effort for too little reward, efficiency is the wrong yardstick. Many countryside villages still have pubs and shops, for example, only because of communities organising hours of volunteer time. These places are wildly inefficient—better by far to drive to the nearest supermarket or chain of pubs. But that's not the point: people need a local shop, especially overstretched parents with crying babies, those who cannot afford cars, the elderly, and the sick. As Covid-19 swept in, local village shops saved people from venturing into town and kept the community together. People enjoy volunteering, keeping a local service going, chatting with each other, checking up on the sick or sad. That is the heart of community life and it far outweighs the balance sheet.

Wrestling with such problems is also part of the process. Innovative forums such as citizens' assemblies or online engagement allow democracy to move to a more decentralised, deliberative model for the 2020s, which includes ensuring groups marginalised as racial or religious minorities are at the heart of debates.[18] In particular, the very process builds bridges across political and cultural divides; this is so-called contact democracy, which brings people together to discuss issues, in contrast to the polarising stances of party politics. In the United States, E-Democracy, an organisation committed to expanding participatory democracy through online technology, believes that online community forums can help involve marginalised groups including immigrants. Their founder, Steven Clift, stresses that forums work best when they are focused on a locality as opposed to being citywide, and when they mix general information with politics. As Clift says: "The key is real relevancy in people's lives."[19]

Civil society keeps innovating, searching for new ways to build societies strong and compassionate enough to support refugees while addressing community tensions.

## FEAR STOKES HOSTILITY

While the crisis is obviously first and foremost felt by refugees themselves, its reverberations are shaping politics and community relations in societies that have accepted huge numbers of refugees, as well as in those that have not. In the United States and in some European countries accepting relatively small numbers, people still feel unsettled and threatened. Debates about refugees have turned into discussions about migration more broadly and have, in turn, bled into wider issues of identity, community, and race, with a terrifying escalation of openly xenophobic and racist positions from governments—and rising attacks on ethnic minorities. Civil society has a vital role in both countering this narrative directly and addressing the underlying causes of people having to flee their homes.

Right-wing populists have used the refugee crisis as potent rocket fuel. They have pitted host communities against refugees and migrants as "the other," building a hostile nationalist narrative, playing to people's loss of identity and fears of their way of life being overwhelmed. Studies by the University of Maryland found that, among Americans, Republicans estimate that 18 percent—and Democrats 13 percent—of the population is in the country illegally. The actual figure is just 3 percent.[20]

As President Trump made hard-line immigration policies the centrepiece of his first election campaign and his administration, citizen groups swung into action. Activists have marched against the wall along the Mexican border; ignited an outcry when children were separated and held in concrete-floored cages; crowded into airports when the government banned the entry of people from seven Muslim-majority countries; and declared their own "sanctuary cities." When the administration announced a record-low annual quota of 18,000 asylum seekers would be admitted in 2020—down from 30,000 in 2019 and from a 1980 peak of 200,000[21] —the American Civil Liberties Union (ACLU) took to the internet, calling on their 1.5 million members to lobby against such historically low numbers.

The ACLU also files legal case after case challenging each of the government's crackdowns on immigration and defending migrants. One of these is that of Jessica Colotl, the face of the Dreamers—the 800,000 undocumented children brought to the United States mainly from Latin America—who came from Mexico at age eleven and was among the first to go public about her undocumented status in 2010. Her story helped rally the campaign that won successes in the Obama era, giving the Dreamers the temporary right to live, study, and work. Groups had to mobilise to defend those rights, as they came under threat from the Trump administration, as did Jessica's own status in the United States. People have taken to the streets, protesting, picketing, and petitioning, from sit-ins to hunger strikes. United We Dream, which says it is the country's largest youth-led immigrant movement, works with the mantra that "an informed community is a powerful community."

In Britain, the new government of Boris Johnson, elected with a thumping eighty-seat parliamentary majority in December 2019 on a "Get Brexit Done" ticket, lost no time in staking out a hard line on keeping out and returning as many asylum seekers as possible. The government saw it as red meat to the new voters who had helped them sweep to power—and to keep hold of hard-Brexit right-wingers among their supporters. The realities facing desperate people seeking sanctuary were expendable in this battle. Among the public, however, the context became more complex.

The Covid-19 crisis showed people how much they depended on migrants as health workers, care-home assistants, and delivery drivers for shopping. Underlying public support for migrants was rising, polls showed. At the same time, the numbers seeking asylum in Britain had dropped once the Covid-19 travel and lockdown restrictions hit. In the face of the emergency, the government quietly cut the numbers being held in detention and housed asylum seekers—who were destitute due to government rules forbidding them from working or receiving public funds—in hotels, along with other homeless people. As lockdown eased the immigration minister reassured Parliament there would be a return to "business as usual": asylum seekers began being evicted back onto the streets just as a second wave of the virus mounted, with no one but charities to turn to for help.

But when new images emerged of desperate people making the dangerous journey in overcrowded rubber boats across the English Channel to seek sanctuary in Britain, the far right jumped on the opportunity to restoke hostility—protesting at the ports and making videos of themselves as "citizen journalists" gleefully banging on the doors of terrified asylum seekers in hostels. Mainstream tabloid newspapers ran hysterical headlines about a migrant invasion. Just as campaigners were finally forcing the government to admit the manifold injustices caused to the post-war Windrush generation of Caribbean migrants—increasingly denied legal rights such as jobs or health care from 2013 on, and many later wrongly deported under its "hostile environment" policy after decades of living in Britain—it reached for the very same playbook to promise ever more draconian clampdowns on people whose only crime was fleeing fear, war, and persecution. Civil society was reeling in the face of the renewed onslaught, but also regrouping, reorganising and uniting as never before. Ben took up a new role behind the scenes helping build a new campaigning coalition to press for root and branch change in the asylum system. It aimed to mobilise both the committed activists and the many more people who, all the polling shows, support decent treatment for asylum seekers and refugees.

## CRIMINALISING COMPASSION

As governments worldwide crack down on compassion, they are making it harder not just for formal NGOs, but even for individuals and community groups, to extend the hand of friendship. In Hungary, for example, a new law in 2019 made it criminal to assist asylum seekers with their applications.[22] In the French Alps, mountain guide Pierre Mumber, who offered hot tea and warm clothes to four West African asylum seekers, was convicted of "facilitating irregular entry" and sentenced to a three-month suspended sentence, though this was overturned on appeal in November 2019. Rym Khadhraoui, research fellow at Amnesty International, said, "Pierre is unfortunately one of many people facing harassment, intimidation and attacks at the hands of authorities for supporting migrants and refugees."[23]

Amnesty International has documented how the US government used the criminal justice system to threaten and punish those defending the human rights of migrants and asylum seekers at the Mexican border.[24] Dr Scott Warren was charged with harbouring two migrants after providing them with water, food, and medical assistance in Ajo, Arizona, although he too was ultimately acquitted in court. He had had the temerity to lend his support to No More Deaths, No Mas Muertes, whose mission is "to end death and suffering in the Mexico–US borderlands through civil initiative" by providing direct aid, witnessing to abuses of migrants, raising awareness, and pressing for more humane immigration policies.

A similar battle is being fought in the Mediterranean, where the UN estimates that in 2018, six people died every day trying to reach safety across its deep waters.[25] Citizens from all walks of life have leapt into the breach, helping to rescue drowning migrants, but they face growing hostility and aggression from governments. The motley crew of the German boat *1958 Seefuchs* has included: Peter, a North American Cambridge postgraduate student in ancient history; Hans, a taxi driver from Munich and an excellent cook; Henry, a retired baker; and Martin, the second engineer, who worked for decades at General Motors in Detroit, and of whom Peter says, "He was quiet and never spoke badly of anyone—it has to also be said he didn't know ship engines very well."[26] During two weeks in June 2017, the *Seefuchs* rescued over three hundred migrants. But in 2018, the crew found themselves at loggerheads with an anti-immigrant Italian government determined to stop the boats. First, ports were closed, then Deputy Prime Minister Matteo Salvini of the right-wing populist League Party sensationally called for rescue boats to be sunk and the *Seefuchs* crew—among others—to be arrested. Seeking to thwart the rescue missions, the government raised problems ranging from issues with the minutia of ships' registrations to—in the case of the *Aquarius*, operated by Doctors Without Borders—"illegal waste disposal."[27]

It worked; the *Seefuchs* crew became afraid. One night, they heard of a boat carrying 120 people but felt they could not go to help. Peter agonised:

> How is it that a rescue boat was fleeing from, instead of going towards, a boat in need? I think we feared we would become like the Aquarius, stranded at sea, or the Iuventa, impounded. If we rescued these people, what harbour would let us in? Would we be accused of people smuggling? Would our NGO be banned? The campaign to criminalise NGOs has worked. We were a rescue boat afraid of rescue work. We were intimidated. And so, we motored away as 120 people likely drowned.[28]

While NGOs threw down legal challenges to the Italian government's actions, Peter was considering his next moves. Most people, of course, cannot take to the high seas. But all citizens have a role to play in challenging callous attitudes and fostering caring ones, whether in discussions with friends or family or through civil society activism.

## IN THE FACE OF XENOPHOBIA

Gemma Mortensen, a long-time leader of campaign coalitions on global conflict, including as former CEO of Crisis Action, where Ben worked with her, was moved to cofound a new organisation, More in Common, by the scale of the challenge posed by the refugee crisis and rising xenophobia. She was shaken to her core by the murder of her friend, British MP and former Oxfam worker Jo Cox, at the hands of a far-right extremist in 2016. She was also profoundly shocked by the forces unleashed following the rise of President Trump when she was working for Change.org in the United States and the backlash to the refugee crisis in Europe, with advanced democracies failing to respond effectively. To Gemma, all of this amounted to "a severe threat to our values and our future" and prompted deep personal reflection.

She believes civil society must understand better what is happening beneath the surface and listen more carefully to the full spectrum of voices, way beyond the liberal, activist bubble. More in Common took its name from Jo Cox's maiden speech to the House of Commons when she declared: "We are far more united and have far more in common with each other than things that divide us."[29] The group takes analysis of people's opinions, values, and sense of identity and then distils this to inform strategy, innovative models, and messaging for civil society action.

Gemma told us, "I came to believe that society is like an iceberg. We're too much focused on the daily discussions and opinions back and forth above the surface—but hidden underneath the sea is the much bigger business of people's core values. We in civil society don't do nearly enough to address that."

More in Common's US report *Hidden Tribes* identified two highly antagonistic "wing groups" of vocal conservative and progressive activists slogging it out on big issues such as immigration megaphone-style, often on social media. But two-thirds of people are in the "exhausted middle," put off by polarising debates. Gemma says these people do not get heard enough—and that civil society should do more to engage with them and help give them voice in shaping public debate and government policy.[30]

She believes that NGOs, which can come across as arrogant about the moral rectitude of their worldview, will need to move away from talking mainly to, and mobilising, people who think like them. Instead they need to go back to the basics of good campaigning by really listening to a much wider spectrum of groups of people, including this "hidden middle." That would broaden the base for change—even if it could represent a challenge to committed activists who do not easily depart from their own particular language or assumptions.

More in Common also undertook research in Germany, which has accepted more refugees than any other European country—over a million at the height of the Syrian war. In towns and villages, people rallied to teach German, provide clothes and blankets, and help refugees settle. They continued their support even when difficulties arose, such as the attack by a group of refugee men on women in Cologne's train station on New Year's Eve 2015. In 2017, More in Common found that, despite mixed views and a polarised debate around Germany's response to the refugee crisis, Germans remain generally supportive, with a strong sense of responsibility to people seeking protection from conflict and persecution—and that this is tied to their self-identity as Germans.[31] Nevertheless, even the most liberal are apprehensive about the prospects for successful integration of Germany's newcomers, and the far right is picking up strength, too.

## HOPE OFF THE MAP

Despite the anti-refugee rhetoric of populist movements in Western politics, most refugees do not even touch the hems of wealthy nations. Over eight out of ten refugees live in developing countries, with over 3.6 million in Turkey, huge numbers of Afghans in Pakistan, and the largest African refugee communities in Uganda and Ethiopia.[32]

In Lebanon, at least one in four people is a refugee, overwhelmingly from neighbouring Syria; that would be like Britain hosting nineteen million refugees or the United States accepting 81 million. Schools run double shifts and queues snake out of health centres. There, as in so many places, the challenge is to meet people's immediate needs while also creating the conditions for long-term change.

Shatila, in Beirut, Lebanon's capital, is a refugee camp. But don't think *tents*. Think a tiny corner of the city into which nine thousand Palestinians crammed, fleeing the *nakba* (disaster) that displaced them when Israel was created in 1948. Fast-forward to the Syrian civil war, and thousands of fleeing Palestinians, already forced from their homeland to Syria, now had to move again; they had squeezed in here, pushing the numbers to over twenty-two thousand. Given the precarious security situation, Shatila remains off the map of the big aid agencies, and people lack basic services. Beneath a chaotic canopy of electric wires, it is a ramshackle, living image of official neglect, impossibly crowded, overwhelmed and under-served, but jingling with life. The main arteries are muddy potholes over which little kids jump as they run off on errands, and young men do wheelies on their slimline motorbikes; older men trudge home from building sites, covered in white dust.

Equally crammed is the half-finished concrete home of NGO Basmeh & Zeitooneh, which translates as Smiles and Olives, symbolising peace and nourishment and resonant of the call over a century ago by American working women for "bread and roses"—both the basics and those life-enhancing extras such as love and laughter.

Women's groups were the starting point for Basmeh & Zeitooneh, founded in 2012 by five Syrian refugees including Fadi Hallisso, whose background spans IT, engineering, and the Jesuit priesthood, and who sports a large black beard along with his deeply reflective, quiet manner. Basmeh & Zeitooneh believe in serving and empowering individuals, creating community centres as focal points around which people come together and organise themselves. Today they run seven centres in Lebanon and two in Turkey. Like many civil society organisations, they provide services to meet people's immediate needs but always with an eye on the bigger strategic prize of longer-term change.

Visiting their Shatila centre, Harriet squeezes up the staircase past children rushing to class and women on their way to an income-generating cushion-embroidery workshop or a small business course; past ashen-faced elderly women waiting to see a doctor and glamorous young people learning about making videos. On the top floor, they are running peace education classes, developing a whole new curriculum based around psychological support to traumatised refugee children, many of whom have known only war their entire, tiny, fractured lives. Having all their services in one place, bang in the centre of the community, is part of their strategy—they had seen other women's centres flounder because they were hard to reach or did not have childcare.[33]

International Alert worked with Basmeh & Zeitooneh and an inspirational young Syrian, Elio, who leads their peace education program and who told Harriet, "Peace is about being able to play. The world can never be as peaceful as these two hours the children have here, this little moment."

In his gentle, soft-spoken way, Elio explains that the children have often seen blood and killing. They have watched people holding a gun to a family member's head. They are angry and confused, and many feel guilty about surviving. Gradually, they learn to play together again, to express their waves of sadness through painting or dance, to find calm.

These children have tough lives. One boy works in a bakery so arrives covered in flour. Another little girl wakes at two every morning to do the chores at home—her mother is sick, her father not around—so that she can come to her peace education classes. "I'm only a kid here," she says. After singing and dancing, the children settle down to draw, surrounded by pots of paint. They paint solid houses, often by the sea. The little girl explains that her picture is of her home in Syria and her father, still in Syria, whom she wants to see again.

Basmeh & Zeitooneh's work is slow and painfully underfunded, yet urgently needed if Syrians are to recover from the war and rebuild their country afterward. Study after study highlights the scale of mental trauma among Syrian refugees, their suffering worsened by lack of treatment. According to the UNHCR, "The most prevalent and most significant clinical problems among Syrians are emotional disorders, such as: depression, prolonged grief disorder, post-traumatic stress disorder and various forms of anxiety disorders."[34]

## DIRECTING FUNDS SOUTH

Let's be frank: across all countries and issues, much of the time, raising enough funds preoccupies NGO minds. For those on the frontlines of the refugee crisis, securing funds is a constant struggle, dominating their daily operations. Some global organisations, such as Save the Children, are household names that receive donations from the public and can win major contracts from governments and international agencies. Oxfam has shops and huge lists of generous individual givers who provide part of its income; others get support from the Catholic Church or the Muslim faithful. But, globally, only a fraction of funds reach NGOs from the refugee-affected countries themselves, prompting repeated calls for "localisation."

UN data shows that 85 percent of government humanitarian funding for NGOs in 2016 went to international NGOs, with over half (53 percent) going to just ten organisations. National and local NGOs fared less well, together receiving just 1.5 percent.[35] At the 2016 World Humanitarian Summit, all players agreed that by 2020, at least a quarter of humanitarian funding should go to local and national actors "as directly as possible"—but the reality lags far behind.

It is part of a wider criticism—especially scathing from international civil society network CIVICUS—of the handful of major international NGOs that dominate humanitarian responses, having become adept at winning government contracts to deliver services.[36] They stand accused of monopolising the funds, being too focused on protecting and promoting their brands, poaching the best staff by paying Western salaries, paying lip-service to partnerships while expecting local groups to take all the risks, especially in conflict areas.

Danny Sriskandarajah, now wrestling with these issues hands-on as chief executive of Oxfam GB, commented while previously secretary-general of CIVICUS, that the normal way of working "has served to magnify and entrench capacity imbalances. Trapped in a vicious cycle of underinvestment, many southern and smaller organisations cannot pitch for the big money."

Of course, even their fiercest critics acknowledge the good they have done and that many international NGOs channel funding to local partners. Their public fundraising was also hit hard by the pandemic restrictions, from their shops to sponsored runs and events, and NGOs for international causes were largely excluded from the support provided to charities by the UK government. It hit their programs and capacity hard at a time when the need for global solidarity was even greater. Nevertheless, the call is growing for them to adapt to 2020 realities, putting local civil society first, ensuring that funds go directly to local groups, listening better to their partners and learning more from them. As Danny said, "Many INGOs boast a remarkable record in global activism and social change, something which they can and should be proud of. But it is also becoming increasingly clear that their organisational model needs to undergo radical transformation to keep pace with changing needs, new technologies and a shifting global landscape."

Despite outperforming on every key performance indicator, despite impressive monitoring and evaluation, Basmeh & Zeitooneh lurches from one funding crises to another. As the Syrian war grinds on, compassion has faded. Says founder Fadi Hallisso, "We're trying to prepare people to rebuild Syria in the future, but we don't know what we'll be able to continue doing next month."

Think tank Century Foundation fellow Thanassis Cambanis has noted, "The group has done everything right — rising out of the community it serves, responding quickly to new local needs, delivering help with minimum funds wasted on costly overheads—yet it faces a worse funding shortfall than its bigger, more lumbering counterparts. . . . When Basmeh & Zeitooneh staffers approached the United Nations for grants, they were told to pitch projects bigger than US$5 million. If they proposed a US$5 million project . . . they were told they didn't have the capacity."[37]

In response to such obstacles, three hundred Syrian organisations formed the Syria Campaign to fan waning Western interest in the nine-year emergency, urging people to support civil society in Syria, for example by backing the White Helmets' rescue work amid the bombing or lobbying the United Nations to take action on breaches of human rights. "This agenda shouldn't be defined by Western NGOs or westerners. It should be defined by Syrians," said CEO James Sadri. "If we're serious about putting Syrians at the heart of what Western NGOs do, then we have to listen to them."

In the meantime, like so many struggling NGOs and citizen groups working to support refugees in conflict-affected countries around the globe, Basmeh & Zeitooneh continues its critical programs—just as forcibly displaced individuals continue stepping forward, often without group structures or resources of any kind, doing what they can to bring their neighbours together in the camps they have to call home.

## STITCHING SOCIETY BACK TOGETHER

The day Harriet reaches northeast Nigeria, the young Nigerian soldiers have gone on strike. Worn down by fighting an elusive terrorist army in the forests, they are refusing to go back to the frontlines. She is visiting people trapped in cramped camps who have had to flee the fighting in their villages. A woman and man—once a teacher and a shop owner leading comfortable lives—show her around their meticulously organised one-room home, patched together using old food-aid sacks, the UN logos turning into a kind of wallpaper. They are the lucky ones. Others wait days to be registered, huddling in a huge, unfinished concrete warehouse. An old woman gingerly lifts a blanket off her leg—it is swollen, black and blue, pussing; but there is no doctor to help her. The school, boasting its UNICEF—UN Children's Fund—stamp on a grimy wall, is empty. The teachers have not been paid; no one is learning anymore.

This is the region notorious for the abduction of the 276 Chibok schoolgirls, snatched from their boarding school by Boko Haram. Their parents have tenaciously carried on demonstrating every day at a fountain in the capital Abuja and every week in Lagos, for the 112 girls still missing. An early hashtag campaign, #BringBackOurGirls, swept through social media with a grim-faced Michelle Obama holding the slogan card, grabbing the attention of the media, governments, and aid donors.

But thousands more men and women have been abducted by Boko Haram in northeast Nigeria. Fatima, at eighteen years old, has scars running down her face and neck from trying—three times in three years—to escape. On the fourth attempt, the insurgents tied her and another girl up, dragged them behind motorcycles, and left them for dead. Regaining consciousness, she struggled with her baby, the son of a militant, to a village where people cared for them.

Now she is in a camp for internally displaced people, with others from her village. Far from being welcomed back, she was rejected by her own community. They feared that those abducted had been infected with the "bad blood" of Boko Haram and rejected their children. This is where civil society steps in to support victims, help stitch back the social fabric, and rebuild the bonds of trust and empathy that are the very foundation of all communities.[38]

At first, you think you have stumbled on a mother and toddler group. Young women with brightly coloured headscarves chat idly while children clamber over their legs and babies nurse. One young girl stares ahead, blank, dead to the world. Then, coached by a facilitator, women begin to tell each other stories, of the horrors seen and lived, sharing nightmares and shattered dreams, their inability to sleep, eat, or love their children. They put words to their pain. Such dialogue cannot feed their hungry child or bring back the dead, but it can help women, girls, men, and boys recover from the psychological and social devastation of war. Faith leaders have joined dialogue sessions encouraging the community to accept the returning victims, and now their children play together again.

A young volunteer in one camp, Yusuf, tells Harriet how his parents were abducted when Boko Haram attacked his home in Bama.[39] His father died in captivity. "Now I am the head of the household. I used to be a carpenter but now I have no tools, no work, no home. I have lost everything," he tells her. "Initially I was angry and eager for revenge. I thought I would kill Boko Haram fighters." Joining the camp discussions, however, Yusuf soon became an active proponent of dialogue. When he saw the man who had taken his parents, he was ready to kill him. But instead, he says, "I went up to him. And then I held out my hand to him. Because, if we don't learn to forgive, we will never have peace. Now I spread the message in the camp. Because without raising awareness about building peace, even if the military defeat Boko Haram, we won't have peace for a thousand years." It is a message about reconciliation across divides that resonates across the continents.

## TOWARD A GLOBAL COMPACT

Throughout the world, organisations are empowering citizens to win policy changes on migration and refugees from governments and the UN. Digital campaign group Avaaz, for example, ran a campaign under the banner #The-World♥Refugees, focused on opening our hearts to refugees. In 2013, they flipped the model of government "match-funding" for every dollar an NGO fundraises. They raised US$1 million from their members for a "challenge fund" to donor governments, asking them to invest in Syrian refugee children's education; governments matched this at a ratio of 100 to 1. Avaaz organised for Tima, the aunt of Syrian toddler Alan Kurdi, to deliver a 1.2 million signature petition to European ministers and parliamentarians in Brussels, calling for a humane twenty-first-century refugee policy in his memory. Former British prime minister Gordon Brown said, "Avaaz has driven forward the idealism of the world. Do not underestimate your impact on world leaders."

Any new international vision has to grapple with the transformation of numbers of people on the move and the conflicts, inequalities, and climate at the root of those movements. Myriad civil society organisations have been heads down at their computers, typing away on concrete policy proposals and lobbying hard for new global rules, new approaches to the issue. And they are having some success. Against the odds, 2018 ended in a rare win for multilateral collaboration, when a new UN Global Compact on Migration was signed—even if without the United States, Hungary, Poland, or Australia—and endorsed by the United Nations General Assembly. Despite the inevitable UN fudges, it was a remarkable statement of international commitment on refugees and was underpinned by strong civil society campaigning; a pushback in the global-level battle against intolerance. German chancellor Angela Merkel received a standing ovation after her speech reminding nations why the UN was founded after World War II and the "incredible suffering on humankind" caused by the Nazi regime, saying the new compact was about "nothing less than the foundation of our international co-operation."[40]

By contrast, the US government condemned the agreement as "an effort by the United Nations to advance global governance at the expense of the sovereign right of states."[41] The stance of the two governments shows how the refugee crisis distils out perhaps more than any other issue the diverging routes humanity faces in dealing with our global challenges: a retreat behind ever higher walls or seeking to fashion collaborative international solutions. Which route lies ahead over the long term depends on how citizens act on this defining issue.

In 2019, delivering one of its commitments, the compact was followed by the first World Refugee Forum, a mechanism to review progress against concrete objectives. With strong refugee representation, even if a poor showing from the leaders of major countries, the forum agreed on commitments on how a new global consensus could work in practice. Then, on 24 January 2020, in a landmark ruling, the United Nations Human Rights Committee determined that people who flee the effects of climate change and natural disasters should not be returned to their country of origin if essential human rights, including the right to life, would be at risk.[42] It was another breakthrough for civil society organisations with far-reaching implications for the international protection of people displaced by climate change. The World Bank predicts that climate change, resulting in problems from water shortages to natural disasters, could force some 143 million people in sub-Saharan Africa, South Asia, and Latin America to move by 2050.[43] For the first time, they may now have valid claims for refugee status under the 1951 Refugee Convention.

Civil society was the lynchpin in ensuring that these new policy commitments were proposed, agreed on, and supported. Building a new international vision to meet refugees' growing and complex needs calls for a creative transformation in civil society's responses, too. In the coming decade, citizens will seek to turn the tide on the hostile measures of nationalist populism by both pressing national and international governments for better measures to respond to refugees and working from the ground up to win public support. Achieving this will take the full panoply of strategies, from the scale and reach of major organisations able to challenge governments in court to individuals ready to extend the hand of friendship. Governments cannot legislate for public support; only civil society can build that, street by street, city by city, nation by nation. If you can judge a community by how it treats its most vulnerable, the same is true of our global society. How we serve refugees is a yardstick of our values and, if we have seen the worst of humanity in our responses to the refugee crisis, we have also seen the best.

Pope Francis, in his Christmas message from the Vatican balcony, in December 2019, described people struggling across the desert and the seas only to arrive at "walls of indifference." Instead, said the pontiff, we should lead our lives as a gift to others—this "is the best way to change the world."

*Chapter Six*

# The 99 Percent Fights Back

*As the global wealth gap yawns, citizens are building a fairer economy from below, pulling back the curtain on corporate abuses and battling for new global rules on tax and trade.*

August 1997, and we were bumping along the Kent roads in southern England before swinging into the headquarters of multinational banana company Del Monte. A small team from the World Development Movement (WDM), we were cramped into our small, distinctly dodgy and very hot white van. In the back: some banana skins. Well, a ton actually, donated by the Body Shop, which used the bananas to make shampoo. For anyone who has not spent time with a ton of banana skins—it gets a little smelly. Having parked up in the loading bay, the hit squad leaped out of the van and started desperately shovelling the skins into a pile on the tarmac, shooting nervous glances at the security guards. Harriet squished up the slimy pile and planted a placard reading: "Stop Del Monte Dumping on Banana Workers." The tipped-off camera crews got their pictures, and management agreed to talk.

That night, the footage ran on the TV news along with that of planes spraying pesticides on plantations in Costa Rica and a report on the conditions suffered by workers growing bananas for our supermarkets. WDM's demand that multinational banana companies recognise trade unions and stop using dangerous chemicals had been launched with a bang. It was a classic, multipronged campaign. We had collaborated with the trade unions in Costa Rica and with NGO experts Banana Link; identified our demands and the right company to target; secured media coverage; and mobilised our thousands of grassroots members to send their bright-yellow banana postcards to Del Monte with whom we were now negotiating. We won some gains—one step in a deeper, hard-fought struggle by trade unions on Latin American banana plantations. We were also contributing to wider moves to make companies clean up their own act, while being part of long-burn pressure for international regulation of multinationals—an idea still so badly needed but still struggling to get past square one.[1]

For Harriet, that campaign set her life's path.[2] Because, strange to say, she became addicted to the politics of bananas. Doing the research, she went to Costa Rica where handlebar-moustached trade union leader Carlos Arguedas drove her through mile after mile of eerily quiet banana plantations. Not a sound. That, sighed Carlos, is because they are sprayed with so many chemicals that no creature stands a chance; chemicals like DBCP, known to be so dangerous to the human reproductive system, it was banned in the United States but still at that time made there, exported, and sprayed on banana plantations. Carlos himself was one of the tens of thousands of "burnt ones" left sterile by using DBCP. He was taking Harriet to meet a couple that was not so lucky.

Juan also sprayed chemicals. When his wife Maria gave birth, it was the shock of their lives. The head of their baby boy was four times bigger than his body. His eyes and nose were joined together. He had no proper eyelids. His skin was a sickly green. Parts of his brain were missing. On the little table covered with a white crocheted doily, Maria showed Harriet her photos. Her eyes filling, she explained how he cried all the time, in pain his whole short life, unable even to sleep. The worst thing, she said, was, "I couldn't hold him because it seemed to make him cry more. So I just talked to him and cried with him. It's the worst thing that can ever happen to anyone. There are no words to explain what life is like." Harriet knew then, as still today, that we have to change the way global trade is run.

So when the chance came to help create the alternative, she grabbed it. At WDM, we had been one of the founding mothers of Fairtrade, with Ben on the board even before any products reached the shelves. Harriet now had the opportunity to make the bright new idea of fair trade bananas happen with the global organisation behind the Fairtrade International stamp based in Bonn, Germany.

She had no idea of the multi-headed battle she had got herself into. Fairtrade International set the common standards needed to get the Fairtrade stamp—in particular the fair price paid to farmers and decent working conditions—and certified the producers and traders who were meeting these standards, while working with everyone in the supply chain from farm to shop with their wildly competing interests. Even within each group in the chain, there were constant tussles. Harriet naively assumed that the Fairtrade banana producers—at first in Costa Rica, Ecuador, and Ghana—would be in solidarity with one another. Dream on. The phone rang with producers having a go at each other almost more than they complained about the traders—

who also phoned to criticise other traders, as well as the producers, not to mention the retailers, who in turn laid every problem at the consumer's door. The crazy determination to compete head to head with some of the world's largest multinationals to get Fairtrade bananas on Europe's supermarket shelves meant everything was constantly in crisis, from missing banana shipping containers to securing that vital supermarket shelf space. But, against all the odds and all the forecasts of expert economists, Fairtrade succeeded, flourishing—including in bananas—into a powerful solidarity movement between farmers' and consumers' movements. Producers and campaigners are at the beating heart of a fairer way of doing trade.

## A FAIR, LIVING ALTERNATIVE

"You'll never make it work," said the chocolate buyer at Tesco as he turned down the chance to stock the new Maya Gold chocolate from Green & Blacks, the first UK product to have the Fairtrade stamp. Within weeks, he was on the phone: "You'd better get over here. We're being bombarded by phone calls. From vicars."

"You'll never make it work," said the UK Department for International Trade's highbrow economist, declaring Fairtrade bananas would always remain a niche. The very next week, leading supermarkets Sainsbury's and Waitrose announced they were switching all their bananas to Fairtrade.

Today, 1.7 million smallholder farmers and workers are organised into 1,707 Fairtrade-certified producer organisations across 73 developing countries. In 2018, they sold produce worth US$10 billion, clocking up significant market shares in some cases involving over 6,000 companies.[3]

Oscar Wilde said: "An idea that is not dangerous is unworthy of being called an idea at all." Fairtrade today seems just a part of our everyday shopping baskets; indeed, that is the hallmark of its success. But when it started, it was an audacious move: that right in the belly of the capitalist beast, campaigners would prove that consumers were ready to pay more for products ensuring a fair price to disadvantaged farmers and workers. Harriet worked for fifteen years leading the building of Fairtrade in the UK and internationally. The movement aimed to create that small bubble within global trade showing how a fairer economy and society could look—but the vision was always to change the mainstream, while inflating the bubble of change puff by puff.

Fairtrade seeks to redress the deep structural inequalities in trade by working on the oldest principle for change: organise. Often, the smallholder groups, many of them cooperatives such as those of Latin American coffee farmers, were born from a long-held radical vision of organising for social change—in their community and their country. Through Fairtrade, they found the global partners they needed. Indeed, it was the coffee farmers of Mexico who first came up with the idea of Fairtrade. Facing starvation with the collapse of coffee prices in 1989 following the tearing up of the International Coffee Agreement—which left free market liberalisation to sweep away government regulation of trade—they reached out to Dutch NGO Solidaridad, and the idea of the Fairtrade mark was born. Behind the mark would lie standards that set the rules for producers, who would have to be democratically organised into cooperatives or groups because lone smallholders have no hope of negotiating with powerful traders.

Traders who sign up to the Fairtrade scheme can buy only from certified producer groups and must pay the guaranteed minimum price, calculated to cover the costs of sustainable production; if the market price goes higher, they receive that, but the minimum price is a safety net. The premium—worth on average 10 percent of the price—is paid on top to the producer group. Producer groups decide democratically how to use the premium, whether by investing in processing their crops or training the next generation of farmers. From coffee, Fairtrade went on to open markets with producers of tea, cocoa, sugar, bananas, and other fresh fruit, flowers, nuts, wine, cotton, even with gold miners. Indeed, now there are a dizzying thirty-five thousand Fairtrade products you can buy across the world. In the past five years, producers earned more than US$780 million in premiums, on top of the minimum price.[4]

Trying to put justice into mainstream markets is not for the fainthearted. Named among the "10 women who rule in the world of food" at the Milan Expo 2015, Marike de Pena has been a tenacious leader of Fairtrade, chairing the Latin American producers' network and Fairtrade International, which, long a key feature of its democratic structure, is part owned by the three continent-wide networks of producers. But Marike always remains deeply rooted with the Fairtrade organisation she heads, the Asociacíon Bananos Ecológicos de la Línea Noroeste (Banelino), based near the border with Haiti in one of the poorest areas of the Dominican Republic. In 1996, 369 farmers, after gaining small plots through land reform, joined forces. Through Fairtrade, they found international markets paying a fair price. But it was tough. To win orders and prove to hard-headed banana buyers that smallholders could meet their strict quality requirements, the cooperative managers had to reject 60 percent of the farmers' fruit at first. But that won them loyal customers. Decades later, they are still selling their Fairtrade bananas, when many smallholders have gone to the wall, unable to compete with cheap fruit from the vast plantations.

Banelino is earning a million dollars a year in premiums, which over twenty years has transformed a very poor community, says Marike. She reels off a long list of how the farmers have used the premium to build up their skills, buy equipment, and invest in environmental improvements and the wider community. For example, the premium pays for schools, including for children with special needs, a dispensary, and a rural health centre as well as medical services to migrant families from Haiti, caring for twelve thousand patients a year.

For Marike, this is the heart of Fairtrade, unlocking the power of producers: "Over all this time in Banelino we have seen so much progress. Here are poor producers and their communities taking responsibility for a topic as complicated as development, delivering above what the state is doing. We are the change-makers."

These changes have included converting from conventional to organic, to be in tune with nature and add value to their bananas without the terrible side effects of high chemical use. More recently, they stopped monoculture and began diversifying into honey and cocoa; the focus is now on biodiversity. Marike says, "It's a way that we as family farmers can be the best in class, and different from the big plantations." But all this has been possible only through the global solidarity of consumers buying Fairtrade products and campaigning relentlessly for shops to stock them and fellow citizens to buy them.

## A MARKET FOR CHANGE

Success, they say, has many parents. Certainly, Fairtrade was an idea nurtured by visionaries right across the world, but if anyone can claim the parentage in Britain, it is the sprightly Richard Adams, a serial social entrepreneur. In 1975, he sent out the first catalogue from pioneering fair trade company Traidcraft, later helping establish the Fairtrade Foundation, inspired by the Dutch labelling scheme. His focus was always on shifting the whole market, using Fairtrade to change the attitudes of consumers and companies. At his cosy Northumberland home, he leaps up to show Harriet early Traidcraft catalogues full of jute handcrafts, describing it as a "seedbed" where ideas were tested. The move to the Fairtrade mark was the next logical step to bigger change: "We were using the market to change the basis of the market. Getting into the mainstream is what we were playing for."

It was also about engaging many more people beyond committed campaigners through daily positive action, not just words: "For me, Fairtrade was a way of changing the thinking of people in the developed world." It succeeded, he says, because it had physical objects—Fairtrade coffee and tea—and a route for people-powered practical action for social justice.

"Fairtrade brought people together to do something that felt more useful than just handing over their money to charity. . . . It was good at enabling people with little money to engage as it was only 10 pence more for a pack of tea. They could live in a way that was only slightly different but together do something significant."

Fairtrade grew in the market because seasoned campaigners, often supporters of charities such as Oxfam or Christian Aid, got organised, firing off letters to shops and brands asking them to offer Fairtrade goods. Fairtrade breaks a big global problem (unfair trade) down into bite-sized chunks (get your shop to stock Fairtrade bananas); it's concrete—and it's winnable. It brings global and local action together. As soon as one shop or brand agreed to offer a Fairtrade product, campaigners were on to the next one. Success breeds success—and local groups felt constantly empowered by seeing more Fairtrade goodies appear on more shop shelves. The 100 percent Fairtrade-committed companies, such as Equal Exchange, Cafédirect, or Divine chocolate, were in the vanguard, but major brands piled in behind their lead, such as Starbucks coffee or Ben & Jerry's ice cream, not to mention supermarkets' store-brand Fairtrade ranges. All thanks to the dogged determination of the local groups.

Soon after taking the helm of Fairtrade in the UK, Harriet was scratching her head about how to build awareness with no funds, when Bruce Crowther, a vet from the northern Lancashire town of Garstang, came bouncing in to meet her tiny team with a bright idea: he wanted to set up Fairtrade Towns. The team laughed. Fairtrade was still proving itself as a serious system for certifying packets of coffee or tea. How could a town possibly be called Fairtrade? But gradually, Bruce won the argument. It was a brilliant move, teaching Harriet always to be open to left-field ideas. Setting up Fairtrade Towns gave local campaigners a way to connect the big idea of trade to their locality, their village or city. You need to get a certain proportion of local shops, restaurants, and employers to offer Fairtrade products, have the local council on board, secure stories in the local press, and create a steering group: then you can call yourself a Fairtrade Town.

Volunteer supporters piled in, enjoying healthy rivalries as towns raced to beat each other. People have paraded around the main street in banana suits, bribed the public with chocolate samples, held Fairtrade wine tastings and school assemblies. They have talked to shop managers and written to companies, collected signatures to lobby the government for fairer trade deals and organised thousands of public meetings where visiting Fairtrade producers chat directly with the public. You cannot beat having fun as a way to engage people. There are now over two thousand Fairtrade Towns, including cities like San Francisco and Rome, in thirty countries from Canada to New Zealand. And Fairtrade Schools have enthusiastically taken up the idea. Another learning point chalked up: you have to go where the energy is—because energy for campaigns will shift to different groups at different times.

Today, 92 percent of British people recognise the Fairtrade mark. Grassroots success has been complemented by companies and retailers promoting fair trade and media coverage. As the leader of a Mexican coffee cooperative told Harriet, quoting an ancient Indian saying: "Many little raindrops falling in the mountains make the mighty rivers flow." But you can never take such hard-won gains for granted. Fairtrade campaigners are now having to fight back again as companies test their own "ethical" schemes, consider dropping Fairtrade altogether, or turn to certification labels with less demanding standards.

Back at Banelino, Marike says, "In producer countries, we have achieved so much with Fairtrade; that is why we fight for it. But we risk losing relevance and being just another NGO—that's not why we built Fairtrade." She has turned her attention to developing exciting plans on combatting climate change, tackling human rights, and engaging women and the young. "The future will be about being part of the public debate again," she says, "being more of a campaigning organisation, going back to how we started. So now we need to build strong global leadership to push for change in the next decade." More immediately, however, she is concerned about members of the cooperative who have Covid-19, and indeed the Fairtrade network is finding ways to support producers as they struggle with the impact of Covid on community life, workers' safety and market sales.[5]

## SHIFTING THE MAINSTREAM

There's no doubt that Fairtrade has played its part in the wider movement pushing companies to address their responsibilities to their global suppliers. As Raul d'Aguila, leader of the Latin American producers, told Harriet, "Don't judge Fairtrade's success just by market shares; it's also about changing agendas when we negotiate with companies."

Richard Adams was also always interested in the wider ripples from throwing the Fairtrade stone into the market pond:

> Fairtrade was a leader in proving that you can set up a system to look at issues regarded as unquantifiable—such as ethics or labor rights. Fairtrade created a cadre of people in other businesses, with a conscience and some social sense, who could reference Fairtrade and try and influence their companies. Once Fairtrade got going, it showed that people are buying this in their billions, there are processes, systems and a market—that could be used by other people to start to lever open their corporates and sectors.

So Richard believes that Fairtrade fostered mainstream companies' interests, first in corporate responsibility and now in environmental, social, and governance (ESG) criteria, which have blossomed over the past forty years. Laughing, Richard is flicking through his books again, searching for a quote to prove just how much the corporate world has changed. He finds one.

Nestlé chief executive Helmut Maucher, saying back in 1990, "Of course, I am not against culture and ethics, but we cannot live on that. The 'fighting spirit' should have priority, and not this ethical and social drivel that is so fashionable."[6]

Influenced by the work in the United States of Alice Teppermarlin, who established a methodology to rate companies—including SA8000 as the accountability standard for workers' rights in factories—Richard believes that if you want to be a new consumer, you need to know which companies are disclosing information, recognising trade unions, narrowing pay differentials, and promoting industrial democracy.

Now the chair of the Fairtrade Advocacy Office, based in Brussels, Richard sees the influence Fairtrade has had on governments across Europe, such as in France, where the state has endorsed Fairtrade criteria, and on the European Union itself. One breakthrough was when the European Parliament agreed that public authorities could make a deliberate choice for Fairtrade and consider other social and environmental concerns when they put contracts out, not just be bound by price and the narrow laws of the conventional market. This followed a similar ruling in the Dutch courts, following a challenge from companies.[7] It illustrates how the direct change citizens can create through bottom-up alternatives can then push the state and mainstream business to back such alternatives at scale. In turn, governments can create a framework of rules that allow the alternatives to flourish more.

Richard can reel off Fairtrade's gains, but is clear eyed about the scale of the challenges: "Civil society has been the prime mover in this debate—it has moved governments and businesses. Yes, concerns about what we are consuming are still a minority sport, but you don't need the whole of society to flip, you need to reach a tipping point." In his well-known book *The Tipping Point: How Little Things Can Make a Big Difference*, Malcolm Gladwell argues that, to shift society's behaviour, you need only 10 percent of people to make a change.[8]

Now Richard stresses the need for a new macroeconomic approach, which moves away from the fixation on constant growth and GDP, changing the framework of market priorities. "We're a lot closer to that being recognised now," he says, "but we still don't have a different economic model. We are further on, but still some way away from that alternative."

## SWEET JUSTICE IN THE CHOCOLATE TRADE?

Fairtrade has often played tag with campaigns to highlight the human and environmental consequences of company behaviour, especially along the international supply chains that bring goods to Europe and North America. Major NGO exposés have revealed child labour, and even slavery, on cocoa and coffee farms; low wages and inhumane conditions in Asian factories making clothes for main street fashion labels; and even how the ultimate symbols of status and glamor—diamonds and gold—fuel brutal conflicts in Africa and leave people in dire poverty (see chapter 4). They have pulled back the curtain on the environmental costs of poisonous chemicals and industrial methods used in modern farming, and the devastation caused to both people and local environments by the mining of raw materials that go into our daily products, from mobile phones to plastic bags. Subverting carefully crafted brands through shareholder action and consumer pressure, these campaigns have forced whole sectors to respond.

For example, civil society groups are putting the spotlight on the inequalities in the chocolate trade—and pressing the sector to commit to ensure that all cocoa farmers receive a decent living income. The global chocolate business is worth a sweet US$100 billion,[9] with Swiss-based Barry Callebaut, the world's biggest supplier of chocolate and cocoa products, posting a 12 percent jump in net profit of US$648 million in 2019—even if pandemic lockdowns saw takings dip in 2020.[10]

However, the majority of the five million small farmers who grow the world's cocoa were already living in dire poverty before the Covid-19 downturn was the latest hit to send the market tumbling—on top of the 40 percent crash in world cocoa prices in 2016. Most companies are simply not paying fair prices, often paying less proportionately than in previous decades. When cocoa prices were high in the 1970s, cocoa accounted for up to 50 percent of the value of a chocolate bar. Today this has plummeted to 6 percent. By contrast, the industry and retailers who feed our chocolate habit make creamy profits, taking 35 percent and 45 percent shares respectively of the global value chain.[11]

Half of the members of cocoa-farming families in the world's biggest producer, Côte d'Ivoire, live below the internationally agreed-to extreme poverty line of US$1.90 a day. Low prices mean that children work the farms. A 2015 US government–commissioned study estimated that over 2 million children labour in West Africa's cocoa fields.[12] Worse still, the US State Department estimates that 10,000 to 12,000 children in Côte d'Ivoire's sector are victims of trafficking and enslavement.[13] Little wonder many people are now quitting cocoa farming in search of a better life in the cities or overseas.[14] "Every young person looks up to migration, either internal or international, as an ultimate goal," says Delali Margaret Badasu, director at the Centre for Migration Studies at the University of Ghana, in the world's second biggest cocoa producer.[15]

Sindou Bamba, general coordinator of the Coalition of Ivorian Human Rights Actors (RAIDH) also underscores the environmental costs:

> The cocoa industry continues to exploit both forests and communities of West Africa for large quantities of cheap, environmentally unsustainable cocoa beans. . . . The low price of cocoa is costing us dearly here . . . in terms of deforestation and abuses of human rights. It is high time for the industry to start paying growers a living income and to implement sustainable production practices to ensure the resilience of local ecosystems, because without forests we will all suffer and pay sooner or later.[16]

Years ago, Harriet attended Chocovision, a gathering of cocoa players in the Swiss mountains. Proceedings got off to a flying start with Sir Bob Geldof giving the assembled guests his characteristic two barrels as he berated them about child and forced labour in cocoa. The audience revelled in being challenged by a rock star, but the moment he left, discussions returned to how companies would sort everything out themselves. When the government of Cote d'Ivoire pushed the case for minimum prices, the cocoa bosses invoked competition law, tut-tutting loudly that discussions on price would be illegal.

As the poverty crisis of cocoa farmers has mounted, chocolate companies have come up with a plethora of their own schemes and badges on their bars to try and show they are responding, although these mostly sidle away from the central issue of increasing the price farmers get paid. Pressure is growing for more far-reaching industry-wide change, including from NGOs and trade unions, which are beginning to make inroads in pressing for guaranteed decent incomes. One sign of the impact of this was the main global gathering of governments, NGOs, and industry and the World Cocoa Conference, conceding in 2018 that "the cocoa sector will not be sustainable if farmers are not able to earn a living income. . . . A sustainable cocoa sector is a collective responsibility of all stakeholders, and we should work together to achieve this ambitious goal."[17]

Civil society coalitions such as the Global Living Wage Campaign have pioneered how such levels could be set in a way that is grounded in local economic realities but consistent across countries and industries.[18] And this is now being extended to those such as cocoa farmers, who do not earn a wage but live off what they grow. Fairtrade International commissioned a study to establish what the living income would be for cocoa farmers in the world's top exporter Côte d'Ivoire.[19] It calculated that the income a typical cocoa-farming family of eight people would need to provide for a basic but decent livelihood was US$7,318 per year. And yet, on average, they found cocoa-farming households earn just a fraction of this—US$2,707.

Campaigners are now pushing chocolate companies and governments in manufacturing countries to use the living income in trade arrangements with cocoa-exporting countries. Things are so bad in the chocolate trade that, without action soon, there may be no farmers left prepared to grow a poverty crop; so maybe—just maybe—this is the global industry where a shift to the living income could make a breakthrough. In previous decades, such "meddling in the market" would have been rejected out of hand. But, with the post–2008 crash and Covid-19 economic crises, the appetite for a renewed role for governments in managing trade may be greater. Instead of the trade wars of nationalist populists, which try to pit the workers and farmers of one country against those of another, or the hands-off approach of the free market purists who say price and profit alone must reign supreme, civil society is seeking to pioneer an approach where global trade is managed to spread its benefits more widely. Governments such as Germany's are starting to back the idea and bring other chocolate-manufacturing countries together, so campaigners are gearing up for a long push.[20]

## CONFRONTING THE GROWING GLOBAL GULF

The grotesquely unfair share of wealth received by producers in our global supply chains is just one aspect of the global fire of inequality raging ever stronger. With the long-term economic impact of the coronavirus pandemic predicted to deepen yawning income gaps, the need for far-reaching action on the issue is even more pressing. Covid-19 plunged most countries into a recession in 2020, with income per head falling in more nations across the world at the same time than at any time since 1870. The World Bank concludes: "These downturns are expected to reverse years of progress toward development goals and tip tens of millions of people back into extreme poverty."[21]

Inequality is at the heart of the citizen uprisings that have swept our world. It would be wrong to boil this all down to simple economics. One driver is the many people feeling that they have a less than equal share of voice, of being disempowered against a political elite that maintains control no matter what. They believe "politicians are all the same," whether they're in the Washington swamp, the Westminster bubble or the intertwined state-business kleptocracies of Middle Eastern capitals. This is seen in the battle of rural areas and small towns versus the metropolitan elite, such as in the "France périphérique" of the gilets jaunes movement versus privileged Parisians.[22]

That said, economics still poses the core challenge. And Covid-19 has seen every marker of inequality deepen as the poorest have been hardest hit: the lowest earners in any country are the most likely to have lost their jobs to the pandemic—in millions of cases overnight and without any right of recompense; to have had unprotected direct exposure to the virus; to have missed out on remote working and schooling, or indeed any schooling at all; and to have a pre-existing health condition making them more vulnerable to severe Covid disease. In Western countries, where black and minority ethnic communities have been far more likely than white people to suffer these effects, their often lower economic status is a core driver of this divergence. At the international level, poorer countries have suffered from inadequate health services and infrastructure and the protective equipment and treatments that go with them. Their more fragile economies will find it much harder to "bounce back" from drastic downturns and will be left further behind by a growing digital divide, where wealthy countries that have relied on technology to overcome restrictions on meeting in person are doing more and more business remotely and virtually.

These stark inequities must be tackled as the global community struggles to learn and recover from the pandemic. For everyone's sake, the world we rebuild must be one where knowledge, good sense, and fairness are seen as smart economic attributes and where we are focused on people's livelihoods, not on growth for its own sake. Joseph Stiglitz, winner of the Nobel Prize in Economics, says:

> The pandemic won't be controlled until it is controlled everywhere, and the economic downturn won't be tamed until there is a robust global recovery. That's why it's a matter of self-interest—as well as a humanitarian concern—for the developed economies to provide the assistance the developing economies and emerging markets need. Without it, the global pandemic will persist longer than it otherwise would, global inequalities will grow, and there will be global divergence.[23]

Even before the pandemic, two-thirds of the world's people lived in countries that have had increased income inequality over the last thirty years.[24] The gap in incomes has widened in most developed countries, but also in better-off developing countries, especially those seeing fast growth, such as China and India.[25] One of the starkest trends has been accumulation of wealth at the very top. Between 1980 and 2016, in North America and Western Europe, the top 1 percent of people captured 28 percent of the average increase in real incomes while the entire bottom 50 percent captured just 9 percent of it.[26] Increasingly, overall economic growth tells us little about how the majority of the population in a country is doing because it is so unequally shared out. Modern-day inequality is also characterised by a huge transfer of national wealth from public to private hands, with this doubling since 1970 in developed nations as state assets have been privatised.[27]

Beyond even the top 1 percent, the very richest have taken by far the largest slice. As Oxfam point out today, 2,153 billionaires hold more wealth than the 4.6 billion people who make up 60 percent of the planet's population, while the 22 richest men in the world have more wealth than all the women in Africa.[28] And what is more, the very richest have increasingly become a globalised group, accumulating their wealth across borders and holding it offshore in tax havens to avoid paying their fair share into still national-based tax systems, while spending it fluidly across the borders.

Thanks in part to NGOs' canny use of such "factoids," the recognition of the problem of inequality has spread—including to unlikely institutions such as the IMF and the World Bank and economists of both the left and the right. Even billionaire fund managers such as Ray Dalio and Paul Tudor Jones are now saying that something should be done. In 2019, Dalio called on US politicians to declare the growing wealth gap a national emergency and take urgent steps to address it or face the prospect of a violent revolution.[29]

Burgeoning inequality has been powered by the shift to sweeping liberalisation of recent decades. But it has been felt more starkly since the 2008 global crash, and, as mentioned, we can expect it to rocket further in the long economic tail of the coronavirus pandemic.[30] With the overall economic pie no longer growing, those nearer the bottom are seeing their living standards squeezed. The two financial crises have also exposed deep flaws in the current economic model, especially in the Anglo-American sphere, where a deregulated finance sector has dominated a shrinking industrial base. Here, whole areas have lost industries, jobs, and the communities that went with them, from the American rust belt to the old industrial heartlands of the North and Midlands of England or the former coal mining South Wales Valleys.

While inequality among people is growing, the gap between countries has been falling as many developing countries put on fast growth. Countries such as South Korea have been transformed from one of the poorest after the Korean War, with an annual income per head of US$67 in the early 1950s, to US$ 30,600 per head today—much of it based on an export-led model of economic development.[31] This global trend has been dubbed the "the great convergence," reversing the period when Western nations pulled away from the rest of world in the nineteenth and twentieth centuries.[32] As a result, there has been significant progress in cutting poverty and improving life chances. According to the UN, the proportion of the world's people living in extreme poverty fell from 36 percent in 1990 to 9 percent in 2018.[33] We have seen some startling improvements in life chances, too. For example, the numbers of children dying before their fifth birthday fell from 34,000 a day in 1990 to 15,000 in 2017.[34] That said, stark gaps between rich and poor nations remain, with the average income of North Americans, for example, 16 times higher than that of Africans.[35] The UNDP says 1.3 billion people still live in extreme poverty right at the bottom of the global ladder.[36]

The surge in growth has enabled many millions of very poor people to get jobs and better incomes—including women who had no paid work of any kind—although too many have also been subject to exploitation. All this has happened while the incomes of people in the "global middle," between the poorest half of people across the world and the top 1 percent at the other end, have been squeezed, including incomes of many low- and middle-income earners in North America and Europe. Populists have fashioned a successful narrative from merging these two trends by saying that the economic rise of developing countries and a sellout by the elite through "bad" trade deals have been the main cause of falling living standards in the left-behind parts of rich nations. They have lashed out in trade wars against China or called for Brexit in order to "take back control." They have been adept at shifting the focus away from the richest people accumulating wealth at the top to what economist of inequality Thomas Piketty calls "the frontier": blaming poor people coming across the US southern border or into Europe on boats and trucks, or workers in factories in China and Mexico.[37]

Beyond street protest movements and populism, mainstream civil society has been grappling with these shifts in the global economic order and patterns of inequality. When we both started out campaigning on global development, things seemed dire—in the 1980s, people in Africa were getting poorer each year on average—but also more cut-and-dried. At that time, one part of civil society in rich Western countries was mobilising public support to press governments for more aid, fairer trade policies, and cutting poor countries' international debts. Meanwhile, another part of civil society worked for greater fairness at home. For example, when Ben led campaigning at the British homelessness NGO Shelter, the desperate shortage of affordable housing in London was a key focus of campaigning. But despite its reputation for in-depth policy research, the charity focused little attention on the money flowing into the London property market from the wealthy global elite buying up homes, then leaving them empty while they waited for their value to grow, leaving thousands of homeless Londoners in crowded temporary accommodation. This was seen as a separate "international" issue.

When we both worked in international development NGOs, they focused largely on poverty in developing countries even though the issues—such as who controlled and benefited from international trade and finance—were just as relevant to poverty at home. Today, the challenge of global inequality remains as profound as ever, just in new clothes. Civil society is needed to fight the changing shape of global inequality set to accelerate in the decade ahead, across its interlinked global, national, and local levels. The strategies that win will break through previous lines separating work on "international" and "national" poverty and focus on the causes of inequality across borders. This will be a defining battle of the next decade.

One part of this will be mobilising against the danger that escalating economic nationalism and trade wars could turn into a spiral of beggar-my-neighbour competition—and possibly worse, as they did in the 1930s. Citizens will need to defend the mechanisms through which countries collaborate on addressing international challenges across borders, from the European Union to the World Trade Organization, for all their faults. But a proactive citizens' agenda will also focus on a major refashioning of the global and national rules and the practices of business to ensure that the benefits of global economic interaction can be shared in a radically fairer, greener way. This is a tall order. But organised citizens are winning the campaign breakthroughs that work toward the big-scale change needed. The sweeping economic measures deployed to tackle the Covid-19 crisis will have to give way to just as radical new frameworks to deal with its long-term impact; and this cannot just mean a return to business as usual, as was the case in 2008.

## TAXING TIMES

One front in citizen action against inequality is, at first, a less-than-attractive-sounding proposition: campaigning for more tax. Growing out of the aftermath of the last financial crisis, as severe public spending cuts came down after the banks were bailed out, civil society started to shift more attention to the other side of the equation: Were companies paying their fair share of taxes into government coffers? In Britain, this burst into the public consciousness when Occupy-inspired group UK Uncut mounted noisy disruptions of tax-dodging companies on the main street with sit-ins in shops such as mobile phone giant Vodaphone.[38] Behind the scenes, groups had been building up evidence of a growing epidemic of tax avoidance by large companies and wealthy individuals; the protests, beginning in 2011, took that information to the streets. NGOs had long criticised the use by multinational companies of transfer pricing—trade between their subsidiaries in different countries, which is estimated to make up a third of the value of international trade—to minimise declaring sales and profits in developing countries, thus depriving those countries of badly needed tax revenues.[39]

Now, wider strategies of profit shifting, as it is known, have become rife—companies push profits through complex legal and accounting chains to end up in hard-to-trace shell companies set up in low- or no-tax havens, simply to avoid paying tax anywhere. Corporate tax dodging is estimated to cost US$500 to 600 billion in lost tax across the world every year, with poor countries losing US$200 billion, according to the Tax Justice Network.[40] Oxfam America president Raymond C. Offenheiser says, "Tax havens are at the core of a global system that allows large corporations and wealthy individuals to avoid paying their fair share, depriving governments, rich and poor, of the resources they need to provide vital public services and tackle rising inequality."[41]

John Christensen is one of the cofounders of the Tax Justice Network, which has become the analytical nerve centre of the wider movement. Originally from the island of Jersey, a leading tax haven, he knows the system from the inside as a trained forensic auditor and economic adviser to the island's government for eleven years. He felt that the booming financial-services industry based on tax avoidance was distorting the life of the small island in the English Channel and damaging its native inhabitants. But his attempts to raise such concerns fell on deaf ears, and he eventually returned to the mainland to look into the issues further. In particular, he discovered more about the damage caused by tax avoidance to developing countries. He was initially, in his own words, part of "a sad and lonely group, who, whilst we understood the issues reasonably well, had no political momentum behind us, and no clear vision of how to gather that political momentum."[42] UK Uncut's protests against Vodafone, Boots, and Fortnum & Mason were "like a turbo-charge for us," he says.

Further momentum was added to the growing tax-justice movement when international development NGOs such as Christian Aid and Action Aid began to champion the issue alongside groups focused on UK inequality, as part of a growing international movement. This issue demonstrates why civil society needs to organise at local, national, and global levels to tackle inequality. It highlights local impact—for example, collapsing local economies where small businesses paying local and national taxes are outgunned by internet-based giants who get away with paying far less tax. NGOs also target those with financial power who exploit the gaps between national tax rules and a global system allowing money to be moved around to tax havens. Some groups link across countries to shine a light on what is happening; Finance Uncovered, for example, trains journalists across the world, especially in developing countries, in the techniques of uncovering tax dodging, as well as corrupt financial dealings by politicians and companies. Other NGOs fight for the international rules that are ultimately what's needed to control the problem, while also applying pressure over national tax regulation on governments such as Britain's, which enable tax havens such as the Channel Islands or the British Virgin Islands to facilitate vast levels of tax avoidance.

Ben helped lead the campaign coalition of international NGOs that pressed for the G8 Summit hosted by Britain in 2013 at the Lough Erne golf resort in Northern Ireland to take action on tax avoidance. As protest Viking ships with sails demanding "End Tax Dodging!" sailed up and down the waters near the summit venue, NGO lobbyists pressed the case. On the evening before the summit, Ben was called by an official with a request to attend a meeting within the security zone early the next morning—inside a ferocious ring of security apparatus, some of it inherited from the era of Northern Ireland's troubles. He was to chair a roundtable discussion among NGOs, pupils from schools in the province's nationalist and unionist communities, and the British prime minister David Cameron, the host of the summit. In the bizarre surroundings of the security-enclosed clubhouse, the school children did an able job of engaging around the key issues, including tax avoidance, with the meeting duly fed out by the government press briefings for the day.

In the end, the pressure squeezed out some commitments to further international collaboration, especially on clamping down on the shell companies that facilitate much tax avoidance. But it was well short of the big action on tax justice that campaigners hoped for. As so often happens, securing change is a long road with incessant ups and downs. One boost came in the revelations by a group of newspapers across the world of the 2016 Panama Papers, uncovering vast quantities of data and internal emails from Panamanian law firm Mossack Fonseca about money laundering and tax evasion and the details of how offshore companies had worked to help large companies and leading politicians avoid taxes and hide their dealings.

Step by step, civil society is inching forward. Britain and France have both announced plans to introduce a new tax on tech companies in their countries—despite bitter opposition from President Trump. The OECD club of developed countries is drawing up proposals for a more coordinated common international approach that, for the first time, includes the idea of a so-called unitary tax solution, which NGOs have been pushing for, where companies' profits are split across countries in relation to their real economic activity so that each country can tax this fairly.[43] Then–IMF head Christine Lagarde, now head of the European Central Bank, said the established ways of managing tax were "outdated" and "especially harmful to low-income countries." In 2018, tax campaigners collaborated with cross-party MPs to secure new rules forcing British tax havens to stop hiding ownership of shell companies used for tax dodging and money laundering; attempts to take this further were stymied in 2019 when, faced with defeat at the hands of MPs, the government pulled an entire finance bill. Another major British tax haven, the Cayman Islands, was put on the EU's blacklist in 2020 immediately after Britain left the EU. While the edifice of tax dodging is under sustained attack from civil society, and crumbling in places, it holds out for now. But civil society continues to push for the necessary new global regulation—which would also strike a major blow in the wider battle against inequality.

## PRECARIAT PROTESTS

Harriet has never forgotten the many lessons she learned working in the Kentish Town McDonalds in North London in the late 1980s. She learned that the best way to wash a floor is with boiling water, as it kills more germs and dries faster. She also learned about the low pay and poor working conditions for staff in a major multinational company, her research used in the booklet "Working for Big Mac," produced by the Transnational Information

Centre—an organisation dedicated to connecting workers within the same companies across the world—which was covered in the *Guardian* newspaper. And she learned that you should always check with a libel lawyer. McDonalds sued—they sued all their critics at that time and always won, able to outspend everyone. The booklet was pulped; the *Guardian* apologised and settled out of court, with McDonalds donating the fine to Save the Children. It's one way to fundraise.

But Harriet did eventually discuss the research findings in court, giving evidence in the defence of the "McDonald's Two" who gave up years of their lives to defending themselves against libel claims from the multinational. As part of a radical offshoot, London Greenpeace, community gardener Helen Steel and unemployed postal worker David Morris had distributed on The Strand in central London a photocopied, crudely typed-up leaflet: "What's Wrong with McDonald's: Everything They Don't Want You to Know"—with a range of criticisms from poor pay to cutting down the rainforest. As usual, McDonald's sued for libel, a decision they must have regretted. The "McLibel" court cases dragged on for ten years, the longest in British legal history, the pair receiving some legal help along the way from Queen's Counsel Keir Starmer (now leader of the Labour Party). The judges found that the pair were right on some points and wrong on others, but all the while, the court cases fed a constant stream of media stories about the company's practices.

The redoubtable pair went on to take the UK government to the European Court of Human Rights, which, on 15 February 2005, ruled that the original case had breached article 6 (right to a fair trial) and article 10 (right to freedom of expression) of the European Convention on Human Rights. The court held that UK law did not protect the public right to criticise corporations, saying:

> In a democratic society even small and informal campaign groups, such as London Greenpeace, must be able to carry on their activities effectively and that there exists a strong public interest in enabling such groups and individuals outside the mainstream to contribute to the public debate. [44]

Meanwhile, in the broader economy, the shift to insecure work and low pay, resulting in the working poor, has been accelerating, as constantly underscored by the trade union movement. They highlight that workers are notionally "self-employed" or on continuous temporary contracts, outside of the, albeit diminished, rights and protections that permanent workers have held onto. From internet-shopping warehouse and delivery van workers to the Uber drivers of the "gig" economy, to low-paid agency care workers rushing between home visits to care for elderly or disabled people on slashed state budgets, a new "precariat" has soared and now accounts for one in ten—or 3.2 million—workers in Britain, according the Trades Union Congress.[45] Their vulnerable status across the world was starkly exposed when government lockdowns in the face of the coronavirus left many of these workers high and dry, beyond the welfare benefits or salary subsidies brought in to tide people over the crisis.

The number of workers in Britain at risk of missing out on key employment protections has nearly doubled in a decade, according to the Trades Union Congress, which lobbied hard for government support to shield them from the economic fallout of Covid-19.[46] While each country has its own local dynamic, there are strong global dimensions at play that cross old boundaries between labour markets in developed and developing countries. Big international gig economy companies such as Amazon, Uber, and Deliveroo use common strategies across countries where, in the words of one union organiser, "technology creates an on-demand working culture dominated by their smart phone, of precarious work, low paid, zero hours, tiny hours, agency, self-employed jobs."[47] In addition, many in the most precarious and badly paid roles are migrant workers.

In response, new unions for precarious workers have sprung up outside the traditional organising model based on employer and workplace. For example, the Independent Workers Union of Great Britain (IWGB), was set up in 2012 to organise couriers, cleaners, electricians, and others working on zero hours, on demand. They and other new unions such as United Voices of the World have helped win pay increases for cleaners in London universities and pressed for services to be brought back in-house with proper staff contracts. They have won legal cases from fast food delivery company Deliveroo and courier Hermes, forcing them to pay the minimum wage and holiday pay, as well as to repay unlawful deductions from workers' wages.

IWGB general secretary Jason Moyer-Lee is an American who was studying for a doctorate at the University of London when he first volunteered as a fluent Spanish speaker to support Latin American cleaners being shortchanged in the pay they were due. In 2011, cleaners and porters, with students' support, protested against services conglomerate Balfour Beatty WorkPlace being used by the university. Gradually, they became more organised, using both traditional union tactics and civil society campaign methods. Says Moyer-Lee, "For us, it's about disruptive surprise protests, direct action, mini-occupations and exerting as much public pressure as possible until it becomes better for the university to give in rather than risk continuing reputational damage."[48]

The workers won back pay, then the London Living Wage, and finally their "3Cosas" ("Three Things") to secure more alignment with in-house staff on sick pay, pensions, and holidays. Liliana, from Colombia, a cleaner at the University of London, was earning not much more than £6 an hour and was bullied by her supervisor. Now, she is on the London Living Wage of

£10.75 an hour. "I am not alone," she says. "We have solidarity. They cannot make injustices against us because we stand together."[49]

Community organising techniques have also been deployed to pressure employers into improving low-paid workers' wages through the campaign of Citizens UK, now focused through their Living Wage Foundation. This persistent, high-profile campaign has persuaded over 4,500 employers to pay a "Living Wage," independently calculated based on an essential basket of goods and services for a basic but decent living above the government's statutory living wage.[50] It has particular resonance for women, given that 62 percent of those earning less than the living wage are women, and nearly a third of all working women in the UK do not earn a wage they can properly live on, according to the Living Wage Foundation.[51] The fight for the living wage is therefore also often a fight for gender and racial equality.

While the campaign focused on pushing employers to take action directly, it may also have helped a Conservative government to shift on statutory minimum wage levels; in 2016 it announced the introduction of a "national living wage" as a higher legal minimum wage with the aim of getting this to 60 percent of median earnings by 2020. Harriet remembers, when working at the Northern Region Low Pay Unit, the implacable previous opposition of Conservative governments to minimum wages at all, which they argued would cause mass unemployment. Thus, these developments demonstrate how civil society action over many years secured a radical shift to cross-party support for the principle of a minimum wage, and then for increasing it, even if debate continues on levels. Living wage campaigns have also made important inroads in other countries such as the United States, Canada, Australia, and New Zealand.[52]

In the United States, the Fight for $15 campaign for a US$15-an-hour federal minimum wage has used creative hybrid approaches to great effect since being launched in 2012. Strikes by low-paid workers across gas stations, fast food, social care and supermarkets have helped win advances on pay and union recognition, with over 20 states and a string of cities across the United States implementing new laws endorsing the US$15-an-hour minimum wage—also forcing corporate giants like McDonald's and Walmart to increase pay. From small walkouts, the movement quickly gathered pace so that, in April 2015, tens of thousands of fast food workers in more than two hundred cities took to the streets in what labour organisers said was the largest protest by low-wage workers in US history. The movement also forged international links so that, in May 2014, fast food workers went on strike in 230 cities from the United States to Japan and Brazil. During his election campaign, President Biden pledged to increase the federal minimum wage to $15 an hour.

The campaign adopted a "directed-network" approach that blends a core of central organisation on big aims, strategy, and milestones, such as the big national-level strike, with decentralised action determined by local groups and alliances. It has convened a national-level supporting coalition across labour unions, churches, and economic- and racial-justice groups, as well as ensuring financial and administrative discipline. At the same time, says Tom Liacas of NetChange, it has empowered self-starting grassroots action:

> Opening to grassroots power, the Fight for $15 uses a distributed model to spark local worker-led protests and strikes all across the country. These self-starting events are supported by resources such as "how to start a local strike" guides and support staff who train local leaders. The result is a vast constellation of city and state-based Fight for $15 groups across the US and several other countries, each with its own local branding and messaging. The voices of local organisers and worker-activists are heavily favored over those of union bosses in movement communications and press work.[53]

This approach made it easier for other movements and campaigners to pile in with support where they saw a connection with their own agendas, such as local Occupy Wall Street sympathisers and Black Lives Matter activists. While the Service Employees International Union (SEIU) is behind the movement, it took the bold decision to break with the usual pattern of working only with union members, risking a pushback from membership-fee-paying rank-and-file members as their union invested resources in the campaign. But it paid off as Liacas reports:

> A Fight for $15 leader we spoke with off the record reports that the campaign has led to unprecedented gains in union negotiations with major employers nationwide. Wage justice has become a national conversation as cities and states across the country have raised the minimum wage. . . . During a recent international SEIU conference, a large majority of union members expressed their satisfaction with this progress and voted to renew their support for the campaign.[54]

## REAL UTOPIAS: THE SOCIAL ECONOMY

As well as contesting how the powerful set the economic rules, to drive down inequality, citizens have been building bottom-up alternatives that can be both bubbles of change expanding within the old order and beacons lighting the way to fairer, more sustainable economic futures. In fact, the two strategies help reinforce each other. Fairtrade is one such alternative, but there are many others spreading and growing.

Alternative propositions to market capitalism are almost as old as capitalism itself. It was in 1844 that weavers and workers in Rochdale in the North of England set up the first cooperative as a shop to supply one another with provisions at reasonable prices and escape the stranglehold of factory owners on supplies and prices.[55] While co-ops and other alternative economic models have remained in play ever since, they were pushed out of the limelight in the decades after World War II as many focused on the role of the state in driving equality via tax, welfare benefits, and access to public services or by intervening to manage how goods and services were produced and traded at national and international levels. But, recently, there has been a resurgence in this "social" or "solidarity economy" as the lurch to globalised market fundamentalism stripped back the role of the state. The idea that ethics, social justice, and environmental sustainability should be core concerns for business and investors has moved from the margins to the mainstream—so much so that it is easy to forget how citizen action has propelled this fundamental shift in thinking.

The social economy sits in a space amid the household, the market, the state, and conventional grant-based charities, using a range of hybrid models to provide goods and services. Social businesses put social and environmental well-being, equality, profit sharing, cooperation, and solidarity at the centre of their aims and ways of working, where conventional businesses prioritise maximising profits, shareholder returns, and competitive advantage—even when they might have an add-on social or green purpose.

Robin Murray, a pioneering economist of the social economy—as well as a former tutor and hero of Harriet's and another founding father of Fairtrade—explained: "The goals of these diverse organisations may be different, but what is shared is that they are driven by top-line social or institutional goals, not bottom-line financial ones."[56] They provide a route to democratise the economy through active citizen involvement beyond being simply passive consumers or workers. At the same time, the social economy does not rely on state subsidies or charitable grants, cherishing its financial sustainability and ability to forge its own path.

Out of the spotlight, this social economy has been flourishing globally and is much bigger than many realise. To take just one of its forms, cooperatives have a worldwide turnover of US$3 trillion with 12 percent of humanity being a member of a co-op[57] and they provide jobs for 100 million people.[58] In Italy, Switzerland, and the UK, for example, the Co-op supermarkets compete alongside the major capitalist retailers. Or to take another example, mutual benefit societies provide health and social protection services to 170 million people worldwide.[59] The social economy represents 10 percent of European businesses and employs over 14 million employees across the continent.[60] In Africa, nearly 100 million people use community-based savings schemes to save and make small loans for outlays such as house building or to buy seed or animals—usually with a very high repayment record.[61]

The growth of the social economy is partly a defence by communities in the face of crisis in the conventional capitalist economy. As Ed Mayo, then–secretary general of Co-operatives UK told Ben: "Cooperatives have a long tradition as havens in crisis. They focus on participation as a way to act. They often start as a tool for self-help, but then they move on to mutual aid, to mutuality where people increasingly identify with a collective aim."[62] An example is the spread of the credit union movement in areas where industries have closed, banks withdrawn, and loan sharks moved in to prey on those on low incomes. Instead, citizens can join a non-profit credit union, depositing money as in a normal bank, which is then loaned to members at reasonable interest rates. According to one UN study, there are more than 51,000 credit unions in 100 countries, with almost 200 million members and more than US$1,500 billion in assets.[63]

In Argentina, the "recovered factory" movement saw over 300 factories that had been closed during an economic crisis taken over by their workers and run collaboratively as a way to retain their jobs. Mutual associations providing insurance and financial services have grown—especially providing services to poor communities in both developed and developing countries that have been seen as "unbankable." Alongside financial cooperatives, ethical banks have been investing savers' money in sustainable initiatives such as Vancity in Canada, Triodos in Europe and Alternative Bank Schweiz in Switzerland. All kinds of alternative food networks, connecting producers and consumers locally and globally, have also blossomed.

People are searching for alternatives to an economic system shown not only to be generating profound inequalities, but also to be unstable and dysfunctional—and not fit to address the great social and environmental challenges of our times, such as social care for an aging population, or climate change. As Robin Murray observed, "The current crisis, like that of the 1930s, is the hinge between an old world and a new. . . . What is needed is a programme of more profound structural change, of a radical transformation of infrastructures and institutions that will be the precondition for a new, qualitatively different period of growth."[64]

As the world restarts its economy, shattered now by Covid-19, the need is profound to rebuild upon these social-economy foundations, forging new ways of doing business globally for a new collaborative, low-carbon era. What's more, the millennial generation is powering forward this upsurge in interest in social and environmental purpose. Conventional business schools are struggling to keep up with the demand from this generation seeking purpose for business. "Social entrepreneurship has gone mainstream and global," argues Peter Drobac, director of the Skoll Centre for Social Entrepreneurship at Oxford University's Saïd Business School.[65] "Younger generations in my experience are much more deeply connected to the world and to societal challenges. They want careers that allow them to create positive change."

# Chapter 6
# TECH FOR CHANGE

While big business has been quick to move in to capture the value of "collaborative capitalism," those possibilities are still being harnessed by alternative social economy models, which do not put profit first. Cooperative platforms are being developed to allow freelance workers or social businesses to connect without the proceeds going to the for-profit tech giants.[66] A platform cooperative is a democratically run member- or user-owned online platform or mobile app. Many are start-ups from communities of people—such as workers or users—to meet their needs or solve a problem by networking people and assets.[67] Examples include the brilliantly named Fairbnb.coop, a co-op that shares earnings between tourist-hosting homes and a community project in the place visited, or the Green Taxi Cooperative, the largest taxi company in the Denver metro area with eight hundred drivers, billed as the "people's Uber."[68] Many more are under development covering everything from freelancers offering services to photo libraries.

Web-based, non-profit initiatives are proliferating, based on citizens sharing and collaborating across borders for the common good—whether creating high-quality open-source software from the Linux operating system or Wikipedia's extraordinary 46 million articles in 300 languages accessed by 1.4 billion unique devices every month.[69] The content is provided and mediated by 200,000 editors and contributors, all on a voluntary basis. This shift toward treating information as a common good also opens up huge potential for innovation and problem solving through crowdsourcing ideas rather than the old idea of profit-based companies competitively developing new innovations in secret. Robin Murray argues that the social economy is a principal driver of social innovation:

> This is the case not just for particular methods and services—like the hospice movement or micro credit—but for whole systems of production. The revolution in information and communication technology has opened up strikingly different ways of organising things. Energy, for example, can be produced on a twentieth century model by giant power stations or by a distributed system composed of a multitude of local and household generators (like solar panels or even the batteries of hybrid cars) linked by smart grids. Centralised versus distributed: this is a battleground even more profound than that between public and private. It is being fought out in food and farming, in health care, water, education, the media, retailing, and not least finance.[70]

As disquiet grows over tech giants' power over our personal data (the information we receive, the prices we pay, and how we work), campaigns are driving for greater control, transparency, and accountability. This in turn is further driving the search for alternatives that are more democratic, are less driven solely by profit, and address the other, connected burning fires—such as a group of women in conflict-riven Yemen who formed an enterprise selling energy from solar panels.

A key step for this surging social economy will be to find ways to build impact at greater scale—and to ensure greater synergy between building the alternatives, social movement mobilisation and campaigning to change the rules. Activist-academic Professor John Gaventa led the Tennessee Highlander Center, in the hard-hit former coal mining Appalachian Mountains—a social justice leadership training school that played a key role supporting labour movement and civil rights activists including Martin Luther King Jr. and Rosa Parks. Now based at the UK's Institute of Development Studies at Sussex University, he has studied civil society strategies to challenge power and wrestle change in poor communities across the world.[71]

He strokes his beard as he weighs his words, telling Ben with energy and conviction about this vital link between organising to challenge power holders and building bottom-up alternatives:

> Building these alternatives is vital for movements too. But they need to meet two challenges. First, they need to link up to create system-level impact. All the small initiatives are good. They give people hope and different ways for citizens to engage. They build different skills and capacities for change. They show there is another path. But they don't add up unless they also connect up. The next step after letting these thousand flowers bloom is building horizontal networks. And then, next, if they grow in size—they will encounter power. The power structures are spongy enough to absorb quite a few small initiatives which run counter to their way of doing things. But if they get too big, then they challenge the power structures. That's when you need to ensure there are the rules and polices that can protect and develop them.

As well as expecting confrontation from mainstream power holders, civil society needs to guard against the dangers of being co-opted by them. Mayo, then at Co-operatives UK, told Ben:

> It's not so much that all businesses have to be cooperatives but that all businesses become more cooperative. I've always been in favour of engaging with business—of being open to learning from all other sectors. There are people in the belly of the beast who really want to change things—to find ways to adopt approaches from civil society. The risk is that in the process they become stripped of their value. Like when companies adopted environmental reporting from civil society models in the 1990s—but it became hollowed out of meaning. We've developed a range of tools to help us prevent this. I think we've learned that if the social movements maintain the essence of quality control as it goes into the mainstream, then it usually works better. We found that with Fairtrade—or with the Soil Association being the guardian of organic certification in the UK—whereas it has splintered a bit in other countries.... It's like a seesaw—with the world as it is on one side, and the world as we want it to be on the other. We need to focus on tools that can be the fulcrum, that tips us

from where we are today into that imagined better world of tomorrow. And it's not just about practical change—it's the shift in possibilities and values. What the philosopher Ivan Ilych called "tools of conviviality."

## PARMESAN AND SARDINES

In northern Italy's Emilia Romagna, the social economy is an established part of everyday life and the economy. Two out of every three people in this region of 4.5 million people are members of co-ops, which account for about 30 percent of the GDP of the region, one of Italy's most prosperous.[72] From restaurants to factories making advanced industrial products, from fashion houses to supermarkets, there is a highly developed ecosystem of worker, consumer, and service-provision cooperatives. And this regional base reaches out wider. For example, the Co-op supermarket based in the region is now the biggest retail chain in Italy, accounting for nearly a fifth of the national market, still owned by its 7.4 million members. It built this position by raising investment funds by crowdfunding from its members before crowdfunding even existed.

The cooperative model is also highly successful in the social sector, providing nurseries and care homes, reaching 85 percent of social services in the regional capital. Seen as community institutions, these ecosystems have benefited from wider support such as from the Catholic Church and the left-wing parties that have been in regional power for long periods. A supportive legal framework at regional and national level has also helped to provide a nurturing environment—for example, making it easier for co-ops to access investment funds or giving workers laid off by a business closure the right to seek to salvage it through a cooperative route.

The sector was central to revitalising the region left devastated and impoverished after World War II, with co-ops showing greater resilience in the face of external economic shocks. In Italy more widely, 87 percent of co-ops managed to come through the severe shocks after the 2008 financial crash, compared to just 48 percent of all businesses. What is more, the sector has helped keep down inequality, not only with smaller gaps between the highest and lowest paid within cooperative enterprises, but also helping to ensure Emilia Romagna as a whole has lower income inequality than in the wider economy—and higher rates of women in jobs.[73]

Iconic regional products such as balsamic vinegar and Parmesan cheese come from cooperatives. Members agree to protect traditional methods: cows fed on a specified diet of grass and hay, special copper vats in the cheesemaking dairies, and vast wheels of cheese sitting on shelves in a carefully regulated environment, finally to be sold as officially stamped "Parmigiano-Reggiano." Using these traditional methods and ensuring that the benefits of the lucrative trade are spread fairly does not mean the co-ops are not also savvy operators, their best-selling product being globally renowned. The 4 Madonne Parmesan-making cooperative, using milk from forty co-op dairy farms, wanted to promote its product in the United States against the widespread low-quality imitations. To do this, it raised €6 million (nearly US$7 million) by issuing special cheese bonds, guaranteed against its stash of thousands of wheels of maturing Parmesan cheese, where much value was tied up. Investors were happy to lend, knowing that if ultimately things went wrong, they would be able to recoup their money in the shape of the huge wheels of hard cheese in the vaults.[74]

The deep reservoirs of citizen collaboration in Emilia Romagna seem not only to provide fair incomes and a unique cheese but also an antidote to right-wing populism, beating off a strong push by Matteo Salvini and his anti-immigrant League party to win control of the region in the January 2020 elections, which ultimately returned the left to power. Salvini had been riding high in the polls when the grassroots "Sardines" movement changed the dynamic, with their online-organised anti-fascist flash-mob rallies tightly packing large numbers into city squares. The deeply engrained collective values reflected and nurtured by the strong social economy provided an underpinning for the social movement—the wheels of shared vision, lived alternative, and campaigning drive were turning together. As northern Italy were in the grip of the Covid-19 pandemic, the co-ops again played a central role in organising free deliveries of food to the old and vulnerable, taxis for transport to and from medical facilities including in isolated rural areas, and community-based care via the network of social co-ops.[75]

*Chapter Seven*

# A Tale of Two Pandemics

*The extraordinary story of how good campaigning and good science turned around the last global pandemic—and why this gives hope for the struggle against Covid-19.*

A group of protesters starts to jog on the spot, building momentum. Some lift their arms, raising a mimed spear in one hand, an air shield in the other—rocking their bodies to and fro. A deep-throated, stabbing "hoo, hoo-hoo" rises, in time with the stamping feet. Whistles puncture through. A woman takes up the lead chant in Xhosa and then, all around, comes the answering call in defiant harmony. Toyi-toyi was a hallmark of demonstrators in townships facing lines of heavily armed police during the struggle against apartheid in South Africa. But this demonstration was echoing around London's Whitehall on a spring morning in March 2001, seven years after Nelson Mandela had become president of the non-racial, democratic South Africa. The neoclassical grandeur of the South African High Commission, so often the target of anti-apartheid protests, could be glimpsed down the road. This protest, however, was focused on the anonymous-looking offices of the Association of the British Pharmaceutical Industry (APBI).

Organised by Action for Southern Africa (ACTSA), the successor to the Anti-Apartheid Movement, where Ben was director, it brought together anti-apartheid veterans and the next generation of activists, united against another type of apartheid: the five hundred South Africans dying every day from HIV/AIDS, who were priced out of the medicines saving lives in richer countries.[1] International drug companies were taking the South African government to court to block a new law that could slash the cost of essential medicines, especially antiretroviral drugs (ARVs) that impeded the HIV virus from multiplying in the body, and others tackling the secondary infections killing people with AIDS. The medicines were transforming people's life prospects in rich countries, where previously an HIV diagnosis had been a certain death sentence. But in South Africa—at the very centre of a pandemic that was becoming an existential threat to countries across Africa, causing life expectancy to plummet and destroying the fabric of whole societies—few could afford the medicines at the prices companies were charging.

"Long live the people's right to medicine!" called out one protester. "Long *liiive*!" came the chorus of reply. An ABPI official beckoned a delegation of campaigners inside to discuss their concerns. ACTSA had taken up the call for international pressure from the Treatment Action Campaign (TAC) in South Africa, which was building a formidable movement to win access to the life-saving medicines, working with others such as Médecins Sans Frontières and Oxfam, campaigning on essential medicines at a global level. As Ben and his colleagues sat across from the representatives of British drug companies such as GlaxoSmithKline (GSK), which were among those due to start court action, they echoed TAC's ambitious demand for the companies to drop the case.

The drug companies had lobbied hard during the law's passage through the South African Parliament, but in 1997, President Nelson Mandela finally signed off the Medicines Act. It empowered the government to use measures such as parallel importing (sourcing a drug in another country where the company already sold it cheaper) or bringing in generic versions. Having failed there, the companies then lodged a court case, effectively preventing the law coming into force pending the case's outcome. They claimed the law would undermine patents that protected their intellectual property—and so their profits and, they argued, their ability to undertake research to develop such drugs. Citizen groups countered that this was scaremongering and, while a reasonable return was fair enough, protecting them as a monopoly supplier of the drugs with prohibitively high prices, was not.

## FROM MOURNING TO MOBILISING

By the time of the 2001 trial, TAC was already a force and a long way from its messy, tentative beginnings. It was launched in December 1998 with a fifteen-person protest on the steps of St. George's Cathedral in Cape Town. Two deaths had sparked the move: that of Simon Nkoli, a Soweto-born anti-apartheid, gay rights and AIDS activist who had narrowly escaped the death sentence for treason, but whom AIDS killed that November—at his funeral, TAC cofounder Zackie Achmat called for people to "cry, rage, mobilize, don't only mourn." The second death was that of murdered thirty-seven-year-old single mother Gugu Dlamini, from KwaMashu township in Durban, who had dared to disclose her HIV-positive status on a local radio program for World AIDS Day.[2] A group of local men stoned and beat her to death, pushing her body over a cliff. Afterward they told her neighbours, "Come and fetch the dog, we are done with it."

Gugu's face was featured on TAC's first T-shirts declaring "HIV Positive," words that were to become a hallmark of their campaigning. Another TAC cofounder Mark Heywood told Ben:

> People now think of TAC as a big, powerful organisation. But it started with just a handful of people, in a community that was heavily traumatised, fearful, shamed, and ignorant of its rights. Civil society was not in a good place, either, at the time—struggling to reorientate from resisting apartheid, with many of its ablest leaders moving into roles in the new government.[3]

One catalyst to escalate pressure was the painful death of TAC volunteer Christopher Moraka from a thrush infection in July 2000, his immune system ravaged by AIDS. Fluconazole could have eased his pain and prolonged his life. But it was under the patent of US company Pfizer, which had a monopoly on its price. Just one 200 mg tablet cost US$13 over the counter at a private pharmacy in South Africa at the time. The cost to the public health system was US$4.10—but in practice, this was prohibitively expensive for general use. However, a high-quality generic version could be imported for thirty cents per pill from Thailand. In the same way, GlaxoSmithKline's AZT, a key antiretroviral drug, cost US$20 in South Africa at the time; its Thai equivalent just thirty cents.[4]

To highlight the drug-pricing scandal following Christopher's death, Zackie Achmat, openly HIV positive at a time when this was rare, flew to Thailand to buy five thousand capsules of the generic version of Fluconazole and imported them to South Africa "illegally" in the full glare of publicity—turning up the pressure on the companies. It was one of TAC's first acts of civil disobedience; it was not to be its last. TAC provocatively called it a defiance campaign, deliberately echoing the iconic 1950s civil disobedience Defiance Campaign, where non-white South Africans burned the hated government pass books that set down their racial category under the apartheid system. The battle to take on "big pharma" had shifted up a gear.

As well as pushing the issue up the media agenda, TAC had been building a grassroots movement that would grow to fifty thousand people in six hundred branches across South Africa. Mark Heywood explains:

> TAC was a social movement of poor people, many of them HIV positive or directly affected by the disease. It wasn't enough just to press the case at national level. We invested in building the skills and knowledge of local working-class leaders, who led grassroots work combining campaigning, human rights education, and literacy in HIV treatment. Our experience in the

> anti-apartheid struggle taught us that you need to build the power of those directly affected by the issue. That's missing from a lot of civil society initiatives for change today. But mass participation was undoubtedly a key element of our success.[5]

Mark acknowledges that this was a big investment. "It was the early days of digital campaigning—and we used things like email really well. But we never stopped organising face-to-face. There's no substitute for it." He continues:

> You need to treat people with respect. You shouldn't assume that because they are affected by the issue, somehow they should just have arguments handed down from the center on trust. In the branches, in rural areas and small towns across South Africa, members wanted to discuss questions like: "Why has human rights got anything to do with us getting treatment? Doesn't research justify the high cost companies want to charge? If we criticize the ANC government for inaction, isn't that betraying our long struggle for liberation?" They wanted to know the answers, because even people in their community affected by a lack of treatment still needed to be won over to the campaign. We need that in civil society movements today. We're too often speaking to echo chambers of the like-minded.

While building this grassroots movement, and the moral platform for action via media work, TAC opened a legal front. In January 2001, Mark got a call from Zackie saying they should meet with respected Johannesburg human rights lawyer Gilbert Marcus. Mark recalls:

> We met Marcus at his home and decided to seek the court's leave for TAC to intervene as an amicus curiae [friend of the court]. We intended to provide evidence as to how the amended law would improve the affordability of medicines for HIV and argue that the Government was acting on a constitutional duty to fulfil the right access to healthcare services mandated in section 27 of the Constitution. TAC framed the legal dispute as essentially a moral one between rich, hugely profitable pharmaceutical companies and poor people in life-or-death need of essential medicines; between rich companies wielding great economic and legal power (as well as their influence over the United States government and the WTO) and a newly democratic state seeking to keep a constitutional promise to protect the health of its people in the midst of the AIDS epidemic.[6]

They decided to make a bid to join the case, with a court date set for a couple of months' time later. Meanwhile, the international campaign had been growing. It was driven by solidarity with TAC's campaign and what was at stake in South Africa. But it was also part of a battle for more equal access to essential medicines affecting people worldwide. And this itself was one front in the wider struggle over how we manage the international economy and what we put at the heart of this: maximising profit, or people's right to equal life chances. This struggle against inequality can seem too big, too abstract to take on, and civil society ends up in generalised railing against globalisation and inequality, which changes little. Here was a campaign that was urgent, tangible, and vital to win in its own right and that could help advance the wider struggle.

## UNFAIR TREATMENT

Back in London, this meant Ben getting his head around the details of the gripping-sounding Trade-Related Aspects of Intellectual Property Rights (TRIPs) of the World Trade Organization (WTO) agreement. Like Harriet, Ben had spent many years working on the intricacies of trade policy for developing countries. But TRIPs was a new one on him. Looking into it further, he discovered how big pharma had lobbied rich country governments to insist that regulations on intellectual property be made part of the major WTO deal ten years earlier. If poorer countries wanted to be able to trade more of their goods with rich countries, they had to sign up to phasing in the TRIPs provisions, with the risk that this would also price them out of affordable drugs. And now the drug companies were determined to use the deal to squeeze anything that challenged their power to maximise their profits by enforcing patents.

With a deadline looming to submit written evidence for a House of Commons Select Committee inquiry, sparked by the profile of the South African court case, Ben worked late in the ACTSA offices in North London's fast-gentrifying Islington. The building had previously been the home of Nelson Mandela's African National Congress (ANC), where it had based its fight in exile against apartheid. A former Victorian shop, it had been bombed in 1982 by a group of apartheid regime spies, taking the whole back off the building and injuring caretaker Vernet Mbatha inside.[7] Whenever former activists from South Africa visited, they wanted the full tour of the small and cramped building where the forces of apartheid had blasted into a quiet London street.

Ben tried his best to marshal the case for why MPs should stand up to the British government. He knew it was not going to be easy. The minister for trade, Richard Caborn, had already replied to his call for Britain to support the South African government's right to use alternatives to the expensive big-brand drugs, saying these were "not the answer here" and their use "would undermine the willingness of the pharmaceutical industry to play a constructive role."[8] It was a bitter blow, coming from a Labour government big on its rhetoric of support for post-apartheid South Africa, and from a minister who had himself been on the national committee of the Anti-Apartheid Movement for years. But it showed the lobbying muscle of big pharma.

Even many in the NGO community were saying that providing these kinds of "first-world medicines" on a big scale was not realistic or appropriate in Africa and diverted focus from pushing education and prevention as the only viable solution.

In the US too, the industry persuaded the Clinton administration to place South Africa on an official trade "watch list," withhold the lower import taxes it was due, and even block aid—measures only overturned in the face of mounting protests from AIDS activists in a US election year. The EU followed suit with its trade commissioner Leon Brittan telling the South Africans to change course, arguing that the law would "negatively affect the interests of the European pharmaceutical industry."[9] He remained silent on the interests of the millions of South Africans sick and dying from HIV/AIDS.

Bent over his laptop, with only the spirits of past ANC officials for company in the office, Ben tried to switch from ranting protester mode to the sweet reason of his inside-influencer persona. He garnered all the pragmatic arguments to persuade the MPs on the committee: the huge extra costs of treating secondary diseases like resurgent TB, which AIDS was bringing in its wake; the evidence from countries like Brazil where generic drugs were saving thousands of lives of people with HIV; and chinks in the TRIPs agreement (in article 31 to be precise) permitting governments to override patents on grounds such as public interest and national emergency. But in the end, he had to bring it all back to fairness and equality:

> ACTSA recognises the need to provide for patent protection to stimulate and reward research and development of new medicines, but it also argues that a balance must be struck with protecting the rights of poor people to gain access to life-saving treatment. In an economically divided world, blanket application of such patents effectively means HIV/AIDS drugs will be largely unavailable in poor countries.[10]

It was clear that just presenting a rational policy case would never be enough: the noise had to crank up. In response to TAC's call for a day of action, with court proceedings due to begin on 5 March 2001, ACTSA worked with them and others worldwide to make sure the drug companies had nowhere to hide. As well as the APBI demonstration, they helped organise picketing outside the headquarters of British drug company GSK in West London—and ensured that the media were there to cover it. Staff peeped out from office windows as Ben and his fellow campaigners unfurled banners or chatted to tentative staff on their way into work. Many were unaware of the court case and were shocked by what their company was doing.

TAC and ACTSA appealed together for support in a joint letter of protest from international organisations.[11] In the United States, ACT UP, Africa Action, and other groups held noisy protests outside drug companies' New

York offices, as did activists in Canada, Brazil, Australia, the Philippines, and countries across Africa and Europe. This brought together groups active in the AIDS crisis—and which, like ACT UP, had campaigned for medical research on HIV/AIDS in the United States, when its stigma as a "gay" disease had blocked it—as well as those fighting global poverty or with an anti-apartheid heritage. Bridging coalitions like this deepened the well of support.

## BIG PHARMA LOSES BIG

Back in South Africa, TAC organised a five thousand–strong protest through Pretoria to the US Embassy. They had persuaded the leader of South Africa's powerful trade union movement COSATU, general secretary Zwelinzima Vavi, to head up the march, with many trade union members swelling its ranks.[12] What is more, COSATU agreed to join TAC's court bid to be heard as an "amicus curiae." The unions had played a central role in the struggle against apartheid, as one pillar of the so-called Tripartite Alliance along with the ANC and South African Communist Party, as well as backing civil society anti-apartheid coalitions such as the United Democratic Front. Securing their support was no mean feat, given their close links with the ruling ANC. While TAC was also aligned with the government on the court case, on other issues they were highly critical of the government, so some unions were wary of getting too close to TAC. Mark recalls:

> Zackie and I spent hours in meetings with the unions to persuade them to support us. Slowly we showed them that the issue of access to treatment was a vital, and winnable, fight for their members. They understood that our criticism of government—though sometimes fierce—was constructive and strategic, not gratuitous. It was a long, hard process. But all that work paid off when the trial was a key point cementing a relationship that brought the long-term organising muscle and mass membership of the trade union movement behind the campaign.[13]

The momentum of legal and media pressure, grassroots mobilisation, and alliance building in South Africa, together with coordinated international pressure, became unstoppable. In the March hearing, Judge Bernard Ngoepe agreed to TAC's amicus request, saying, "I am aware that the entire nation is interested and people beyond our boundaries."[14] When the court reconvened on 18 April, the drug companies' lawyers announced a stunning volte-face. They were unconditionally withdrawing their legal action and would pay all costs. After deciding to make South Africa a key battleground in their global strategy, it was a humiliating retreat and put them and the governments that had backed them into reverse. This was a turning point. The prices for antiretroviral drugs soon started falling. The idea that drug treatment was not realistic for African countries was overturned. Big pharma's confidence that it could work the corridors of power to fashion global trade rules for maximum profit without scrutiny took a hammering.

Companies had tried to persuade the public that this was a matter of national economic interest for the rich countries where the companies were based—against developing countries cheating them of earnings and jobs. Instead, civil society groups were showing that there was a greater common interest between citizens across borders, that our access to health should not just be based on ability to pay, and that the companies needed reining in. It was not that we wanted fewer global rules, just different ones. They sang from a TRIPs corporate-rights hymn sheet, and we from international declarations for human rights and equal access to health.

The issue has surfaced again in more recent battles about trade, including a possible UK-US trade deal following Britain's exit from the EU. Leaked documents showed that, between 2017 and 2019, drug pricing, extending patents, and weakening the ability of the UK's National Health Service to drive good deals had been a key part of discussions on a possible US-UK agreement—not only between the two governments but directly between British officials and US pharmaceutical interests.[15] The *British Medical Journal* reported that if the UK loses its ability to negotiate drug prices or to import generic drugs under a trade agreement with the US after Brexit, the NHS's drug bill could soar from £18 billion (US$23.2 billion) to £45 billion a year.[16]

The wider struggle between international collaboration, national self-interest, and private profit in tackling global health threats was thrown into relief again by the race to find treatments and a vaccine for Covid-19. Some rich nations used their power and deep pockets to push to the front of the queue at the expense of the common global interest to find a collective solution. President Trump offered "large sums of money" to try to grab exclusive rights to a vaccine being developed by German company CureVac, and announced his intention to withdraw the United States from the World Health Organization at the height of the crisis, claiming it was biased toward China.[17] President Biden committed to the United States rejoining the WHO as soon as he took office. The US government also bought up months' worth of the global supply of the drug remdesivir as soon as signs emerged that it might help treat Covid-19 patients. Its manufacturer, US pharmaceutical giant Gilead, charged prices estimated at over five hundred times the production cost, despite having had US$70.5 million from the public purse to develop the drug.[18] Other countries used their wealth to buy up in advance millions of vaccine doses still under development. Oxfam advocates Anna Marriott and Nabil Ahmed, writing in the *British Medical Journal*, reflected how this was "a stark reminder that the current system leaves all the power in the hands of pharmaceutical companies to decide who gets the medicines they need and who does not"—just as the battle over access to AIDS drugs had shown.[19]

Civil society groups pressed for a "people's vaccine," demanding that all vaccines, treatments, and tests be patent free, mass produced, distributed fairly, and made available to all people, in all countries, free of charge.[20] In a joint letter catalysed by NGOs, over 140 current and past world leaders and experts backed this call at the World Health Assembly in May 2020, making a direct connection with the previous struggle for access to HIV treatment: "We must learn the painful lessons from a history of unequal access in dealing with disease such as HIV and Ebola. But we must also remember the ground-breaking victories of health movements, including AIDS activists and advocates who fought for access to affordable medicines for all."[21]

In September 2020, the Covax initiative, co-led by the World Health Organization, announced that 156 countries covering two-thirds of the world's people, had signed up to the deal to underpin the fast and equal distribution of any new coronavirus vaccines across the world, at least to frontline health and care workers.[22] Despite flirting with vaccine nationalism earlier in the pandemic, Britain committed £500 million in aid to help 92 of the world's poorest countries access doses.[23] President Trump refused to allow the United States to back the initiative,[24] while Oxfam's Marriott and Ahmed argued that the scheme's "laudable aim is to improve vaccine access in poor countries, but crucially it does not challenge the model of pharmaceutical monopoly responsible for inequality of access in the first place."[25]

## THE TIDE TURNED

After the 2001 court case, TAC went on to fight many more battles to realise its goals. In particular, this included a dark period when President Thabo Mbeki questioned the science on the link between HIV and AIDS, plunging the government stance into what TAC dubbed "AIDS denialism"—and causing a new blockage to treatment with ARVs in the public health system. It was a bitter blow, but TAC stepped up its campaigning. Says Mark, "Our response was to consolidate people's power to make the social and economic rights given to them in the new constitution into a reality."

A series of hard-fought, but dramatic victories followed: winning a Constitutional Court challenge forcing the government to roll out ARV treatment to prevent mother-to-child transmission of HIV in 2002; pushing the government to grant access to its plan for the rollout of ARVs in 2004; securing prisoners the right to ARV treatment in 2006; and securing TAC's ultimate goal of a comprehensive, ambitious national strategy to treat and prevent HIV, adopted by the South African Parliament in 2007. Internationally, in the campaign's wake, the Doha Declaration on the TRIPs Agreement and Public Health was adopted by the WTO ministers in 2001, backing the right of "member states in circumventing patent rights for better access to essential medicines . . . [and] WTO members' right to protect public health and, in particular, to promote access to medicines for all."[26] It was an important principle to win, even if the struggle for developing countries to make it stick in the face of the power of the big drug companies remains a tough one in practice.

The results have been extraordinary. Today, South Africa has the world's largest public-provided ARV treatment program, mostly funded from domestic resources. The price of drugs for the public health system has plummeted, with a standard ARV treatment now 1 percent of what it cost in 2001. Mother-to-child HIV transmission has been slashed, with 53,000 babies a year being protected from contracting the virus.[27] Overall, South African deaths from AIDS have plunged by 50 percent in the last ten years alone.[28]

In part inspired by South Africa, there has been an international transformation in the strategy to tackle the disease. Back in 2001, even though we knew there were treatments that worked against the virus, most people would have thought such a goal was pie in the sky. Reaching millions of marginalised people with treatment seemed quite simply impossible.

Of course, HIV/AIDS remains a major challenge in South Africa, as it is around the world. Of course, progress would not have been possible without scientific advance. It needed the muscle of governments and UN bodies to put what civil society pressure had demanded into practice. But it was citizen action that, first, through the campaigns of activists such as ACT UP in the United States, pushed for the research needed when the disease was downgraded as a "gay plague", and, second, catalysed the opportunity held out by the new drugs into global change, by securing the decisive shift that ensured people with the disease won equal access to treatment, based on their need, not their ability to pay; a change that campaigners were told was totally unrealistic and that was fought tooth and nail by powerful interests. Today, over 23 million people are receiving life-saving antiretroviral therapy worldwide (up from just 685,000 in 2000), and global AIDS deaths have fallen 60 percent from their peak of 1.7 million a year in 2004.[29]

## LESSONS FOR CITIZEN ACTION

Mark Heywood reflected with Ben on some of the ingredients of success in TAC's campaign:

> Look, when we started out, we were swimming against the tide and fumbling our way to an approach. Of course, we made wrong turns and mistakes. We weren't experts in the disease. We were pissed off and angry at people dying

round us. But we did take political strategy seriously—grounding the campaign carefully in an analysis of our allies and enemies, and of what we needed to move to achieve specific campaign goals. . . . You have to have a clear political vision. Perhaps it was our early schooling as Marxist militants in the anti-apartheid struggle that helped there! We were also very inspired by the in-your-face campaigning of some of the international campaign groups like ACT-UP in the US that had put the issue on the public agenda. And just as they had organized those affected by the disease in the US—especially gay men—we did the same, but following the demographics of the disease in South Africa as it took hold across communities of poor, working class men and women.

As well as the movement's consciousness inherited from the anti-apartheid struggle, a clear focus on an urgent, tangible goal of access to treatment was crucial. Says Mark, "I always say, if you set out just to build a movement, you're likely to fail. But if you set out to build a campaign, then you can build a movement around it."

People at the grassroots were also directly empowered through what TAC calls "treatment literacy": learning about how they, their families, and communities could manage their own treatment, rebutting the patronising, racist arguments of the sceptics that poor African patients would find managing the regime too complex. This recipe of combining practical local action with policy-change campaigning stands in contrast to the way in which NGOs often separate the two—seeing each side as a possible distraction from the other. The opposite seems to be true, with hands-on action and campaigning each reinforcing local communities' resolve to do the other. Though outspoken, TAC was open-minded about building a range of alliances—with trade unions, churches, health professionals, academics, or lawyers—to buttress further the grassroots engagement.

TAC built democratic structures where all these interests could have their say in shaping strategy, but it also had a strong core leadership empowered to respond to obstacles and grab opportunities quickly. The campaign also deployed a rich range of tactics, switching between them at different stages: eye-catching media work, "lawfare" legal work, public protest, civil disobedience, marshalling evidence, gaining command of technical issues, and negotiation with policy makers when openings appeared. And persistence—lots of it.

One of the most remarkable features of the strategy, though, was how it combined this grassroots organising with national pressure and international campaigning. Strength and coordination at all levels like this is all too rare. International campaigns often find it tough enough to coordinate across national networks, but these alliances usually lack the depth into grassroots movements, too. So, while they may do useful work lobbying at a high level with policy makers, they struggle to mobilise the sustained political muscle needed to create political will. As one academic study of the campaign observes, "TAC relies both on transnational advocacy networks and grassroots mobilisation in ways that are similar to modes of activism that are increasingly described as 'globalisation from below' or 'grassroots globalisation.'"[30] Mark comments:

> The international dimension was crucial to our success in South Africa. To have pressure on the pharma companies back in their bases in Europe and the US was vital—as was the connection and encouragement of the wider AIDS movement from the US to China and in other African countries. Some of the big NGOs were able to provide evidence and policy insights on the international dimensions, like TRIPs, and breaking some of the myths on how medicine R&D actually works—and they really put this at the service of our movement at key points such as our legal challenges.

The campaign's impact spread wider, helping move the needle on corporate accountability and new international aid funding for HIV/AIDS, and breaking stigmas around groups of people such as sex workers. Victories on specific issues accumulated to reshape the whole approach to the problem. Often, civil society groups try to do the reverse by attempting to change ways of thinking on broad agendas—"overturn global inequality" or "equal rights for disabled people"—as the route then to achieve specific changes. Here was an example of success the other way around.

Of course, there were plenty of problems, major ups and downs. One issue was the impact of success itself. After such a string of so many successes, the organisation lost its way. Mark says:

> We weren't ready for when the adrenaline of constant wins stopped—and especially when we secured our big goal of a proper national treatment strategy. TAC was adrift for half a decade really after that. We also fell out over tactics sometimes—when to go in hard, when to be more conciliatory. . . . After our success, lots of money came at us from aid donors. It allowed us to do new things, but it nudged us more into service delivery, and away from campaigning and mobilisation. It tied us more and more into the cycle of applying and reporting on projects to aid donors. It drew our eye away from our grassroots. It made us less risk-taking. Then when the money dried up, as donors moved on, it was hard to adjust. But TAC has come through that and found its feet again.

## THE SALVE OF SOLIDARITY

The coronavirus pandemic and its global economic effects are visceral reminders that we are all part of each other, that we depend on one another to survive and thrive in our shared global home just as much as in our local neighbourhood. All the building of walls, populist macho pseudo-science, and othering of migrants and foreigners to deflect attention have not cut it in the face of the coronavirus. Human solidarity and sound science, across borders and communities, have. Harnessing these same engines through creative, tenacious civil society organising was key to turning the HIV/AIDS tide when it had seemed unstoppable and threatened to overwhelm entire societies, especially across Africa, with its devastating health and economic toll. Now, while HIV/AIDS remains a major challenge, the UN says the world has not just contained the disease, it could end HIV/AIDS altogether by 2030. The Covid-19 pandemic and its aftermath seemed just as overwhelming and intractable. Which is why civil society must again shape new kinds of global collaboration and local solidarity toward a world beyond Covid-19, nurturing hope again in the darkest of times.

*Chapter Eight*

# The Past as Prologue to Our Future

*Lessons from past struggles that made the "impossible" possible.*

Crises precipitate transformations, becoming markers of transition. A crisis forces a society to do things it barely dreamed of. It also exposes underlying fault lines and hastens change already underway, prompting deeper reflection that citizens can help shape. The movement of women into male roles as factory workers, bus conductors, and workers behind the battle lines in World War I, for example, does not explain on its own why women in Britain finally won the right to vote in 1918. The shakeup of the war was profound. But women's enfranchisement would not have happened without the highly organised, disruptive campaign mounted by the suffragettes in the decade before the war—and the threat that they would resume after it. As radical suffragette Evelyn Sharp reflected later,

> I cannot help regretting that any justification was given for the popular error which still sometimes ascribes the victory of the suffrage cause, in 1918, to women's war service. This assumption is true only in so far as gratitude to women offered an excuse to the anti-suffragists in the Cabinet and elsewhere to climb down with some dignity from a position that had become untenable before the war.[1]

By contrast, many progressives assumed that the 2008 financial crisis, having revealed the patent flaws of the global capitalist financial system, was bound to usher in radical change. In fact, the system survived largely intact—and the crisis paved the way for the rise of populist nationalism. Today, swathes of humanity are wrestling with the global fires of climate emergency, conflict, forced displacement, and inequality, doused with fuel from the coronavirus pandemic and its fallout. What changes will come out of this vast crisis—and what part can citizens realistically play in shaping that change?

We are at a junction. Down one path, fear and insecurity could lead to more demonising of the "other," increased isolation behind ever-higher national walls, and grabs for state surveillance and control in the name of safety. It could unleash an insistence that jobs and incomes can be restored only by a ruthless focus on the bottom line, with action on climate change or a fairer sharing of wealth dismissed as luxuries that can be ill afforded. Or, down a different route, the crisis could prompt a deeper reflection on the global threats we face—and how we can now work together to tackle them to rebuild a fairer, more sustainable global society.

Crucial insights can be gained from civil society's engagement with previous points of shift in history. Change makers have wrestled with recurring dilemmas about when to adopt which strategies in response: ferment noisy grassroots pressure from below or engage directly with policy makers as quiet insiders; shape soaring narratives that reimagine the world or advocate for change within a familiar story; focus on local action within communities' reach or on big-scale change that matches the challenges we face. For each generation, the tools, assumptions, and organisations we apply to these dilemmas are fashioned by what has gone before. But how—and why? This chapter is a whistle-stop tour, exploring some of the key trends and drivers in Western civil society from 1945 until now. Strong movements rediscover and redeploy strategies that worked in the past, even as they take advantage of emerging opportunities, and we believe that citizens will succeed in securing change by building on their current successes, flexing existing, underused muscles as well as developing new ones.

## UNITED WE STAND

The profound trauma of World War II, and the preceding global economic depression, which led to international governance changes, also saw civil society remake itself to restore a shattered globe. The town-twinning movement flourished across Europe and North America, for example, to build local-to-local peaceful links between citizens across nations, whether they had fought side by side or against each other, and NGOs sprang up to channel aid from ordinary people moved by the crises in Europe. Some, such as CARE and Oxfam, are leading organisations today, still working with refugees and people in humanitarian crises as well as transforming their remit into tackling the long-term causes of poverty.

Other groups focused on organising working-class people to win them a fairer deal—an approach that remained at the forefront of advancing social change in developed countries for some twenty-five years after World War

II, especially through developing new and existing trade unions and community-based networks. The hallmarks of this era were long-term local grassroots organising, door knocking, recruitment drives, and campaigns. Building and deploying an active membership—through strikes, direct action, and negotiating from strength—was central to the strategy for change, as well as being the main source of funding through many members each paying a small, regular amount.

Founded by the legendary Saul Alinksy in 1940, the Chicago-based Industrial Areas Foundation was based on his pre-war experiments in Chicago's "back of the yards" meatpacking neighbourhood, whose squalor, poverty, and pollution were made famous in Upton Sinclair's novel *The Jungle*. Alinsky's model focused on growing the power of communities at a local level. A cornerstone of the model was alliance building across religious, ethnic, and trade union groups to fight on common issues and build up local leaders. Organisation, not issue, was key—the community identifying its key concerns, distilled into disciplined campaigns focusing on "immediate, specific, and winnable issues." But it didn't stop there. As Mike Miller, a community organising veteran, now head of the ORGANIZE! Training Center in San Francisco reflects, "These are tools to build power that can subsequently address more deeply embedded problems. Success can be used to convince the sceptics on the sidelines to participate. When more people participate, more people power is built, and more recalcitrant issues can be addressed."[2]

The movement chalked up a host of victories: from defeating slum landlords to winning jobs and better wages for minorities, from securing better public services to stopping banks redlining poor or racially diverse districts as off-limits for loans. Once the campaign strategy was honed, community organisations used confrontational but nonviolent tactics to pile pressure on clearly identified targets, whether in city halls or board rooms—from sit-ins and boycotts to media stunts to embarrass opponents. Tried and tested over decades, the model still holds good. Having grown across the United States and beyond to Canada, Australia, the UK, and Germany, community organising continues to be used widely with thousands of religious congregations, NGOs, and unions for tangible, locally based wins, such as those of Citizens UK on living wages and sanctuary for refugees.

The trade unions played a leading role in reshaping the social and economic order in the post-war era, with citizens determined there would be no return to the poverty and industrial confrontation of the Depression. In continental Europe, in particular, this included models that embedded collaboration among unions, business, and government. Some economists refer to these decades as the "Golden Age of Capitalism"—the "great" era, perhaps, that Donald Trump or Brexiteers conjured up, which resonated so much in the once-booming industrial heartlands. And yet this was a period of strong international economic governance, and of peak trade-union membership. In

Britain, the unions boasted ten million members by the mid-1960s—44 percent of the workforce, nearly twice today's proportion.[3] The 1950s and 1960s saw workers winning better wages, workplace rights, and welfare protections, as well as suffering lower unemployment than in times before or after, when unionisation rates were lower.[4] Workers in North America and much of Europe were winning in the same ways, all the more remarkable given the continent's recent devastation. In many European countries, trade unions became part of a post-war social model, with a voice in how companies are run and in government policy making.

This period also saw the start of the great movements to throw off the chains of European imperial domination still holding across swathes of the developing world, starting with the winning of Indian independence following the civil disobedience campaigns led by Mahatma Gandhi after two hundred years of British rule. The growing momentum for change built by liberation movements from other colonies in Africa, Asia, and the Caribbean gathered pace during the 1950s, spawning support within coloniser nations through groups such as the Movement for Colonial Freedom. In the United States, the growing civil rights movement against the legalised segregation and discrimination faced by African Americans included campaigns to strike down the segregationist Jim Crow laws, which secured landmark Supreme Court rulings such as *Brown v. Board of Education* in 1954. While it would take the civil disobedience campaigns of the next decade to get many of these properly implemented in the South, the movement was gathering strength.

## THE RISE OF THE NEW SOCIAL MOVEMENTS

In the 1960s and 1970s, a panoply of new movements was noisily breaking through: civil rights, feminism, environmentalism, opposition to nuclear weapons, gay rights, international human rights, global economic justice, and solidarity with struggles against colonialism and white minority rule. These new social movements placed more emphasis on identity, solidarity with struggles across borders, and individual expression than the class-based movements that preceded them. This coincided with new strands of thinking on the left and the emergence of alternative lifestyles and the counterculture.

Feminism's challenge that the "personal is political" resonated widely, as movements including environmentalism took up the challenge that changing how we live might be just as important as changing policies. The 1960s witnessed an escalation of street protest and nonviolent direct action, from the American civil rights movement to the anti–Vietnam War protests and the first wave of the anti–nuclear weapons movement in Europe. In some cases, these escalated into full-on revolutionary movements. African American citizens secured federal protections on voting rights and against segregation and all forms of discrimination. In 1968, civil unrest brought France to the brink of government overthrow while the movement for "socialism with a human face" in Czechoslovakia was brutally crushed by Soviet troops following the Prague Spring uprising.

The 1960s and 1970s also saw the birth in the UK and United States of an extraordinary clutch of new campaign groups, many reflecting a more global outlook, that would go on to transform civic action: Greenpeace, Friends of the Earth, the Anti-Apartheid Movement, Stonewall, the Campaign for Nuclear Disarmament, and Amnesty International. The World Development Movement, where we both later worked, was founded in 1970. A host of smaller groups sprang up to rally action on specific issues: for example, solidarity campaigns for movements fighting Western-backed dictatorships in Latin America or to support leftist governments in Mozambique and Angola, which faced the merciless onslaught of the forces of apartheid South Africa and US-sponsored rebels.

These organisations often combined a mass membership with local groups—though sometimes "membership" was less formal than the trade union model of regular dues that gave people formal voting rights. They also developed larger professional headquarters staff to carry out research, high-level lobbying, and media promotion. Campaigns were largely devised at the centre, with materials produced and sent to individual members and local groups via national mass-mailing lists. They were able to coordinate national hits on decision makers through vehicles such as letter-writing campaigns, as well as elicit individual donations to finance their work. However, the organised pressure groups still maintained a close affinity with the wider social movements and political ideologies from which they had sprung—a connection that was eroded dangerously in later decades.

More sophisticated communication strategies developed in response to the television age and the media's role in shaping political agendas and "public opinion." Groups started packaging their campaigns to make a good media story, thus reaching more people more quickly—far beyond their existing support base. Creating news and good pictures was key. When Friends of the Earth (FoE) set up in Britain in 1971, two years after it did in the United States, one of their first campaigns was against companies introducing disposable plastic bottles instead of returnable glass ones. Media photographs of FoE activists dumping 1,500 disposable tonic bottles on the doorstep of Schweppes London headquarters brought the issue alive—and helped the group take off. As consumers look to ditch plastics, Schweppes must now wish it had paid more attention.

## NO SUCH THING AS SOCIETY

During the 1980s and 1990s, civil society had to respond to the lurch toward radical free-market economics ushered in by the Reagan-Thatcher era. Wider changes ate away at a model of mass-membership, locally-based organising: the rise of the individualistic consumer economy; falling numbers taking part in organised religion; and a reduction in trade union membership and power as a result of anti-union laws in the United States and UK (though less so in Continental Europe, where their role remains enshrined in the social contract, for example through their powerful role in the works councils as in Germany). In his seminal book *Bowling Alone*, Robert Putnam documents how, from parent-teacher associations to the Jewish service organisation B'nai B'rith, the proportion of Americans involved in voluntary associations with active local chapters grew steadily for much of the twentieth century and soared after World War II, peaking in the 1960s; then numbers declined, falling rapidly from the 1980s onward. In the 1990s, Putnam notes, "More Americans are bowling than ever before, but *league* bowling has plummeted"; now they bowled alone rather than in organised clubs.[5]

As is true today, however, plenty of people resisted the radical right's agenda. When in 1979 NATO announced plans to deploy over five hundred intermediate-range "tactical" nuclear missiles, mass opposition mushroomed across Europe. Central to his political awakening, as a schoolboy in Northamptonshire, Ben helped set up his first campaign group against the imminent arrival of Cruise missiles at the nearby Molesworth air base. The group's name Oundle Under Threat (OUT) reflected the sense of how close the danger of nuclear war felt. Their rudimentary efforts, with photocopied leaflets and publicity in the local paper, showed Ben how, even in a small conservative market town in the English Midlands, it was possible to win over people if you bothered to talk to them. It had other benefits, too: he met his first girlfriend.

This early experience also taught Ben the cost of taking a stand. He was proud of being admonished by a teacher for wearing a badge with the iconic Campaign for Nuclear Disarmament (CND) symbol; until, that is, he felt the fear—but also exhilaration—of seeing line after line of committed people lie down in front of the diggers trying to enter the base to build the silos, only to be dragged off to waiting police vans. Braver university friends gave up their studies to join groups that were cutting wire to enter nuclear weapons facilities and "disarm" them, ending up in jail. Permanent peace camps kept vigil at bases, led by the women at the Greenham Common air base, who brought feminism and antimilitarism together—and inspired Harriet, who joined in cutting the wire and dancing into the base, appropriately clad in a beret sporting the trademark CND symbol and a lumpy hand-knit stripy sweater from Peru. Huge marches were organised by a resurgent CND, the demonstrators decried as traitors by the tabloid press. Ben remembers "telephone trees" where one activist would ring another to mobilise direct, quick-fire action to disrupt—non-violently—military training exercises; something that could now be done with a one-thumb instant message to a WhatsApp group. To everyone's surprise, a few years later, disarmament talks got underway, culminating in a summit between President Reagan and Soviet leader Mikhail Gorbachev in Iceland in 1986 and, a year after that, the signing of a treaty to withdraw the new missiles on both sides. Campaigners celebrated.

Other titanic resistance campaigns failed to stop the onslaught as civil society battled the headwinds. The Reagan administration continued to reverse previous advances in environmental protection. In Britain, the 1984 miners' strike and the massive movement of solidarity failed to stop the pit closures, which decimated whole communities, including civic organisations such as the miners' clubs. The closures were a seismic defeat for the trade union movement, just as the Thatcher government had intended. Decades later, many such devastated communities would be among those abandoning their traditional support for Labour to back Boris Johnson's pro-Brexit Conservatives and their promise of "taking back control," thus winning him the 2019 general election.

More widely, civil society was fighting back—but it often felt on the back foot, trying to defend what it had won rather than advancing new fronts. Harriet and Ben worked together at WDM during this period, organising yearly letter-writing campaigns against another round of cuts in the international aid budget; each year it was cut again. At the same time, though, NGOs were developing a new tactic: to channel the rise of celebrity culture and a globalising media into international campaigning.

## MEDIA, CELEBRITY, AND THE ADVENT OF MASS CAMPAIGNING

In October 1984, BBC news reporter Michael Buerk broke a story from the plain outside Korem in Ethiopia about a "biblical famine, now, in the twentieth century." His report continued, "This place, say workers here, is the closest thing to hell on earth. Thousands of wasted people are coming here for help. Many find only death."[6]

TV images of forty thousand huddled, starving people shot around a shocked world; and viewers demanded action. In time, the response of global citizens to Ethiopia's famine shifted the focus onto the underlying issues of deepening poverty, international debt and unfair trade in Africa—and helped propel these up the political agenda through a series of campaigns by the major NGOs, often in effective coalitions. While Ben spent a student summer researching how Ethiopian and Eritrean refugees living in Sudan's cities were organising themselves into self-help organisations, back in London's Wembley Stadium and the John F. Kennedy Stadium in Philadelphia, Live Aid concerts were being broadcast to 1.9 billion people around the world to raise money for famine relief. Live Aid represented a breakthrough moment—creating awareness of global poverty among a wider audience—although critics attacked the portrayal of white saviours rescuing helpless Africans, which perpetuated damaging stereotypes.

In the chill of the Reagan-Thatcher era, Live Aid's stance for global solidarity generated a powerful shot of energy. The prime mover behind the concert, former Boomtown Rats frontman Bob Geldof, later reflected, "We took an issue that was nowhere on the political agenda and, through the *lingua franca* of the planet—which is not English but rock'n'roll—we were able to address the intellectual absurdity and the moral repulsion of people dying of want in a world of surplus."[7] From fundraising for famine relief, Geldof, Bono, and other stars swung behind campaigns to tackle international causes of poverty, at just the time that many large aid charities had moved into campaigning, arguing that their relief and development programs were not delivering enough change.

Three years later, 600 million people in 67 countries rocked to another global concert, celebrating Nelson Mandela's seventieth birthday and calling on the apartheid South African government to release him from nearly three decades of political imprisonment. But, as Ben heard from former leaders of the Anti-Apartheid Movement when he later took up the reins of its successor organisation Action for Southern Africa, it had taken a lot of behind-the-scenes persuasion by music promoter Tony Hollingsworth and Jerry Dammers of ska band the Specials before they backed the plan. They feared a concert could dilute the campaign objectives activists had fought hard for years to advance; objectives such as the release of all political prisoners—not just Mandela—and sanctions against the apartheid regime, which would have been too political for the broadcasters to air.

Ultimately, however, in consultation with the still-banned ANC in South Africa, the Anti-Apartheid Movement recognised the value of building support from so many new people beyond the activist core and backed the concert, thus ramping up the pressure on their governments to press harder for an end to apartheid. For the concert's finale, performers from the all-star line-up came together to sing what became a generation's defiant anthem for a different future, not just for South Africa, but for the world. Even as the regime showed little sign of releasing him from his bleak Robin Island cell, millions of us sang along to Dammers's words: "Free, free Nelson Mandela!" Led by the relentless pressure of the movements in South Africa, but supported by an upsurge of international solidarity, two years later Nelson Mandela walked free. Four years after that the new, non-racial, democratic South Africa was born.

While earlier campaigns gained power from large memberships, including in affiliated organisations such as trade unions or faith groups, the millions watching Mandela's birthday concert provided a new support base. It was a breath-taking scale of engagement. The brilliance of the Anti-Apartheid Movement was to bring these two bases together. But did going wide add to or erode going deep? That was the question plaguing campaigners who became hooked on harnessing the power of massive-scale support through campaign coalitions and international alliances to push harder on issues like aid, trade, international debt, and arms sales. At the same time, traditional charities transitioning into this new model of campaigning met the alarm of establishment bodies. An inquiry by the regulator, the Charity Commission, in 1990 found that Oxfam had overstepped the line "between stating a possible solution to a problem in reasoned fashion and campaigning to have that solution adopted." In a decision that had obvious ramifications for other organisations with charity status, Oxfam was ordered to cease its "unacceptable political activities."[8] But the global campaign genie was out of the bottle and ever smarter approaches brought global problems into sharp public focus, with rules on charities' campaigning widened in time also.

Never was the challenge of wrestling a complex subject into a bite-sized campaign starker than with the foreign debts crippling many developing countries and the brutal cuts in health and education forced on them by the International Monetary Fund (IMF) to keep debt repayments flowing from poor to rich nations. The public, campaign experts worried, would never get their heads around complex global financial flows or acronyms that made your head spin. At WDM, we prided ourselves on having already pushed the boat out with a booklet catchily titled *Piggy Banks*—but with a target audience limited to geekier WDM members, journalists, and lobbyists. It was a longstanding and important area of work for us, but not one we had managed to scale up. "That's page 12 of the *Financial Times* stuff—you can't make a mass campaign out of it," one colleague argued before we sat down with other NGOs to form a grand coalition. Little did we know.

The truth we learned is that every issue, no matter how complex, can be made accessible. That was the genius of the Jubilee 2000 campaign dreamed up by eccentric former diplomat Bill Peters and retired politics lecturer Martin Dent, who called for the coming millennium to mark an end to developing countries' crippling debts. NGOs, churches, and trade unions united in a coalition that spread to over forty debtor and creditor countries. People formed human chains from Birmingham to Cologne, with a simple demand to governments: "Cancel the debt." Straight to the point. Simple. And it worked, over time helping to secure packages of relief and write-offs of up to US$100 billion of debt. Former Jubilee 2000 director Ann Pettifor makes the parallels with another complex issue distilled into a clear focused campaign people can unite behind: "What we did achieve happened because we had a real movement behind it," she says. "And it's the same, what's happening now with the climate."[9]

If people will take to the streets to demand changes to complex financial dealings that hurt developing countries, any issue can be made accessible. Gritty rights-based campaigns began to take centre-stage, no longer the oddball little sister to charities' "good works." Slowly, government and corporate leaders began to realise that, far from hiding around the nearest corner, they wanted to be associated with these campaigners and their sound bite demands for a better world. Body Shop founder Anita Roddick stood out with her mixture of activism and cruelty-free products and her shops promoting campaigns on everything from saving the rainforests to freeing long-incarcerated Black Panther members in the United States.

Decades of grassroots efforts on the horrifying problem of landmines left behind after the guns fall silent finally found success with another breakthrough of clarity into a world of entrenched and complex arguments. Today, no one justifies the use of landmines, which indiscriminately maim or kill civilians decades later. But at the end of the twentieth century, fierce debates raged as militaries argued that they needed landmines in their arsenal. All that changed when Princess Diana visited Angola courtesy of the Halo Trust, in January 1997, stepping out onto an active minefield.[10] This simple, extraordinary gesture elevated the profile of the coalition campaign by the International Campaign to Ban Landmines (ICBL) and contributed to the ultimate passing of the Ottawa Mine Treaty banning the use, production and transfer of antipersonnel mines. It was signed by 122 states—not including the United States—on 3 December 1997, just three months after the princess was killed in a car crash.

An iconic example of celebrity endorsement, it enabled a cultural shift, like being against apartheid and stopping smoking in public places, that now seem so obvious and yet were so hotly contested for so long. Harnessing celebrity, music and popular culture became powerful routes to reach out and win wider audiences—and thus secure gains. While campaigners worry about dumbing down campaigns or diverting energy from building grassroots support, the impulse to reach out to wider audiences beyond the committed activist base remains as important as ever.

## PHILANTHROCAPITALISM AND GOVERNMENTS JOIN FORCES

After the Berlin Wall came down, international civil society was pushed to the front as a vehicle to usher post-Communist nations onto the path of liberal capitalist democracies. During the 1990s, funds poured in from Western governments and the foundations set up by new philanthropists such as Microsoft founder Bill Gates, Hungarian-born investor George Soros, and eBay founder Pierre Omidyar, who had made their money through global financial investment and tech booms. With an instinctive global outlook, these new "venture philanthropists" wanted to go beyond traditional good works and invest in models promising a big reach on human rights, international development, and government accountability—as well as in building the strength of civil society itself, especially in developing and post-Communist countries. They were prepared to pour funds into existing organisations, but also into new networks springing up to enable civil society to collaborate better across borders.

Government funding to international NGOs multiplied. Such funding had a longer pedigree in the Nordic nations, in tune with their traditional state-civic partnership models, but it now widened as NGOs' public profiles and international presence grew, and because governments were interested in funding areas such as "democratisation" where they believed NGOs could deliver most effectively.

Some of the 1960s generation of causes that had morphed into major NGOs were now putting their shoulders behind expanding beyond their traditional base in Western countries, often becoming international federations so they could better influence governments, global companies, and international organisations such as the UN or World Bank. Many such international NGO families, from Fairtrade International to Amnesty International or Human Rights Watch, have enjoyed enormous success. At the same time, they often struggled to balance the passions of members in different nations, as well as the power imbalances between national member organisations with funds and those without—all while seeking the breakthrough of a global movement. Harriet carries the scars of trying to balance the needs of Fairtrade in consumer markets with the needs for Fairtrade among the farmers and workers of Africa or Latin America. It does not make for an easy life, but it is deeply democratic and, at its best, empowering, with each party learning from others' perspectives. Finding effective ways for groups to collaborate across borders on common global challenges—from climate change and tax avoidance to health—keeps activists awake at night.

The rise of the global NGO networks and high-profile coalition campaigns represented a major kickback from civil society to the free market revolution. In a hostile environment, their strategy was to harness features of the era such as globalisation, mass consumption, and celebrity culture into tools for change. Critics on the left were quick to dismiss this as capitulation to these powerful forces for small, incremental gains, but they offered routes for civil society to fight for and win important tangible gains, such as more and better aid, debt write-offs for developing countries, a big new international fund to tackle AIDS across the world, and a set of new international goals helping drive big cuts in global poverty.

## Chapter 8

## TOO CLOSE FOR COMFORT

Despite signs of progress, cracks were emerging. We were eating away at problems, but they were growing bigger, from soaring inequality to the escalating scale of the climate crisis. Many organisations, especially in the environmental and global-justice movements, had long been calling for system change, not just reforms. But the 2008 financial crash both proved them right and took attention away from the necessary transformations. Tensions mounted between those arguing for limited but "achievable" change and those advocating taking on some of the bigger but harder to shift issues. Realisation was also dawning about the cost, as well as benefits, of getting closer to power.

In 2005, Harriet travelled with Tanzanian coffee farmer and cooperative leader Raymond Kimaro, one of Fairtrade's founding fathers, to join the Make Poverty History demonstration for international aid and trade justice outside the G8 Leaders' Summit in Gleneagles, Scotland. Some 500 UK member organisations and faith groups joined forces while 225,000 people processioned, danced, and sang through Edinburgh's streets with colourful banners rippling in the wind. A string of Live 8 concerts rocked around the world as celebrities and pop stars roused the public, thousands sported white wristbands, and lobbyists ran up and down the G8 power corridors.

Here was civil society creating the public endorsement that governments—some at least—needed and wanted. As Harriet remembers, advisers to then–Prime Minister Tony Blair and Chancellor Gordon Brown had called in Fairtrade and many other NGOs in the run-up to the summit, encouraging the action that would give them the mandate they needed to win international agreements. NGO lobbyists argued that this insider work was a savvy strategy if our aim was maximising policy change. Radical critics were furious, believing the cosy relationship was undermining civil society's critical edge. Fierce behind-the-scenes rows erupted over whether to welcome or condemn the final result, which chalked up tangible wins but was, of course, never enough.

The next time the summit came to Britain, in 2013, it was after the global crash, and NGOs came together once again to push for commitments on global poverty. Heading up Bond, the membership network of British international NGOs, Ben was in the thick of the debate. One group was against the whole idea and lobbied him in no uncertain terms. They said the proposed coalition was dominated by the big, established organisations, failed to involve the trade unions, and was not radical enough. Ben felt that the dark economic picture underscored the importance of mounting a stand together. He tried—but failed—to persuade them to stay and shape the more radical stance.

Among those who stayed in the coalition, in the months before the summit, Ben chaired heated coalition board meetings, with some NGO chiefs insisting the focus needed to be on limited but winnable goals, such as backing child nutrition programs: "We can bring major businesses and foundations in behind it—and use this to swing the governments into support," they argued. Others insisted the focus should be on structural causes of poverty, such as transnational companies avoiding taxes. The debates went on as the clock ticked away toward the summit. Finally, an approach was hammered out that straddled both. But the experience of the coalition had distilled out wider questions on future strategy for internationalist civil society.

## COUNTER-EVENTS ON THE WORLD STAGE

In parallel, another branch of civil society was growing, demanding sweeping global system change. Labelled the "anti-globalisation movement," many of its protagonists preferred the term "counter-globalisation," as they advocated global connections while rejecting the dominant neoliberal free-market model. They criticised the relentless pressure for global trade rules and privatisation stacked in favour of multinational companies. The movement was a coalescing of more radical strands from the movements for global justice, liberation solidarity campaigns, feminism, and green politics.

Tracing back a few decades, this movement and the mainstream NGOs—while separate strands—were interwoven in a closer ecosystem for global change. But the strands slipped apart over time, weakening their collective strength. This branch of the movement not only advocated more radical change but also sought to challenge the fundamental values underpinning mainstream thinking. This was at the heart of the gatherings to shadow the big global set-pieces of the powerful, such as the G7, through events such as The Other Economic Summit (TOES), later to develop into leading green think tank the New Economics Foundation. TOES was launched in 1984 to "build an international citizen coalition for a new economics grounded in social and spiritual values to address concerns the G7 consistently neglects," remembers one of its organisers, green economics thinker James Robertson.[11]

The way these two strands could create greater impact by weaving together made an early impression on Ben during his first trip to the annual meeting of the World Bank and IMF in Berlin, in September 1988, the year before the Berlin Wall came down. The Western nations hoped that meeting in free West Berlin would be a defiant declaration of Western democracy as the cracks in the Eastern bloc opened. They had not counted on West Berlin as a haven of anti-establishment leftism—partly because people living there were not subject to the military draft. Bedding down in a rough-and-ready hotel in the bohemian quarter, Ben was blown away by the scale and creativity of the opposition he encountered and inspired by activists' energetic gatherings. It brought together his direct-action baptism in the British peace movement and his role at the time as a rookie campaigns officer for a respectable NGO that was also organising pressure in Berlin.

Another young activist Ben met in Berlin, Jan, had gotten out of Poland after being involved in the Solidarity opposition to the Communist regime and was now active in the global-justice movement. Encountering someone from the other side of the Iron Curtain was unusual enough back then, but Ben was equally unprepared to see Jan's pass for the official conference venue and asked how he had gotten it. "I'm not an activist, I'm a journalist," Jan laughed, whipping out the crumpled copy of his organisation's newsletter—which looked even more basic than WDM's—and promptly clinched another reporter's pass at the accreditation desk for Ben. Once inside, they chatted to officials and the gaggle of other NGO types before duly heading to the media area to type up copy for their campaign newsletters, alongside reporters from Reuters and the *New York Times*—trying not to attract attention, although overindulging in the free drinks was a bit of a giveaway.

Outside, Ben and Jan joined the twenty thousand protesters—from black-clad anarchists to parents with children—in a march organised by seasoned Berlin militants to protest against hard-line IMF austerity and privatisation programs being imposed across the developing world. Suddenly, they came to a mass of cars with their drivers standing by, blocking a key interchange. As police sirens wailed, an almighty traffic jam stretched back, pinning in the official cars of ministers trying to get to the conference. "Who is causing the jam?" Ben asked a Berliner on the march. "The taxi drivers, of course!" she laughed. Before the police could arrest them, having successfully delayed the meeting and made their point, they hopped back into their cabs and melted away. Whenever NGO strategists talk earnestly of an insider-outsider strategy, Ben remembers those formative Berlin days when he ricocheted from one to the other. Jan ended up as a senior official at the European Commission.

Ben did not know it at the time, but the Berlin protests were a key moment in a growing movement of demonstrations and international civil society counter-events at the World Bank, IMF, and WTO meetings. The gap between the militant anti-globalisation movement outside and the suited-up NGOs inside widened over time. This came to a head a decade later at the 1999 WTO meeting in Seattle, which descended into running battles between protesters and the police, as the front windows of symbols of corporate globalisation such as McDonalds and Starbucks were smashed in. For companies, this was the wakeup call to the growing public disquiet with their global domination and behaviour. For the big NGOs, it was too hot to handle, and they pulled back. Following Seattle, the first World Social Forum (WSF) gathered in 2001 to explore what the counter-globalisation movement was for, not just what it was against, under its banner "Another World Is Possible." Rooted in Latin American civil society, forged in the heat of the struggles against military dictatorship, it was linked to a resurgent left winning elections in the "pink tide" sweeping the continent, with Brazilian civil society hosting the first gathering in Porto Alegre.

A deliberate counterpoint to the growing profile of the World Economic Forum in Davos, the talking shop of the international capitalist system, the WSF was held in Tunis in 2015, four years after citizens had overthrown the country's dictator as part of the Arab Spring. Hosting the WSF was an expression both of Tunisian civil society's pride in its achievements and its desire for solidarity with the fragile citizen revolution. Ben attended, participating in the plethora of events, stalls, and debates of movements seeking liberation and radical reshaping of the global order. But there was also animated discussion about future strategy. Some argued that, while the movement's commitment to deep participatory methods, and shunning anything that smacked of hierarchical organisation was laudable, it was a block on planning and prioritising action to advance a program of change. Others countered that down that path lay the trap big NGOs had fallen into of chasing incremental reform when radical change was needed—of becoming part of the very system they said they wanted to change. Ben was welcomed into a large tent by a man with a gracious smile and desert headdress from the Polisaro Front, who had led the forty-year campaign for independence from former Spanish Western Sahara, now occupied by Morocco. Having long supported the solidarity campaign backing their brave struggle, Ben was inspired again by their defiant speeches and liberation songs, even though the end of their long, courageous battle for their homeland seemed as far away as ever.

## DAWN OF THE CYBER-CAMPAIGNERS

Counter-globalisation activists were quick to grasp the potential of digital technology to serve their movement—especially driven by the practical imperative of working across distances. The Seattle protests were a turning point. Organising under the banner "Mobilization against Corporate Globalization," rudimentary by today's standards, the campaign website was one of the earliest examples of online campaign organising, bringing a disparate movement together.[12] As the new digital activists bent over their computers in Seattle, they had little idea of just how profoundly the digital revolution was to reshape the world as well as activist strategies. Soon, digital technology was transforming protest movements and wider politics, especially as the technology moved from weighty mainframes to laptops to the palm of the hand.

While existing campaign organisations struggled to keep up by retrofitting a digital approach onto an existing way of working, they were overtaken by a new generation of digital-first campaigns bursting onto the scene. Early out of the gates was MoveOn in the United States, calling on decision makers to "move on" from impeaching President Clinton to more pressing issues. Others based in North America included Avaaz, with an international focus, and Change.org, both set up in 2007; SumOfUs, on international corporate accountability; and Leadnow.ca in Canada. The movement spread internationally with GetUp in Australia, UpLift in Ireland, and Campact in Germany. Rather than define themselves by a single issue, these groups used the new technology to build vast lists of supporters cheaply and quickly, based on broad shared values, and mobilised them with quick-fire action emails and to sign petitions on a host of issues.

Avaaz claim over 55 million supporters worldwide. Their cofounder, and executive director Ricken Patel says, "Our mission is to close the gap between the world we have and the world most people everywhere want. Idealists of the world unite!"[13] A British-Canadian dual national, he grew up in rural Canada after his family had to flee Uganda in the 1970s when Idi Amin expelled the Asian community. The nearest school was a First Nations school on a reservation where the painful consequences of the long destruction of the Cree nation were all around. "It was a deep annihilation of a people's culture and it was conscious," he recalls.[14] He developed a strong desire from an early age to make the world a better place, combined with an entrepreneurial streak drilled into him by his father. After working for NGOs in conflict zones, he came across MoveOn and, with others, saw how tech could be harnessed to tackle global problems and engage a new generation of younger digital-savvy citizens worldwide. He dismisses the critics who say that their approach is "clicktivism," low-commitment activism for the lazy who only spend a second signing an online petition to salve their conscience: "To reduce our actions down to clicking is silly. It's what happens after the clicks—how we use that support—that's what brings about incredible change."[15] They have helped win campaigns on everything from defending a more plural media to blocking Rupert Murdoch's takeover of broadcasting giant BSkyB and collaborating with others to build pressure for international action on climate change at the Paris conference in 2015.

One obvious strength of digital campaigners is agility, responding to the headlines within minutes. The digital-first groups can add surge pressure at key moments, maximising response rates through sophisticated use of data. For example, before sending out an email action to a wide group of supporters, they will do rapid real-time testing of how to frame it and see what gets the most bites. Some organisations, such as Change.org, enable people to use their platform to start their own petitions, thus democratising action. Fully funded by small donations from their members, they are independent from big donors. Inevitably, the digital-first organisations need to tack back and forth across their diverse supporters' pet issues to keep them engaged and to keep funds flowing, which means they are responsive to their members but perhaps not quite as free as it might seem to set new agendas for maximum impact.

While this new wave has broadened its range of techniques, the online petition still remains central, albeit its effectiveness has declined since the early days. "If you want your local fire chief to do something more on an issue and they haven't ever had a petition, then it'll still work. But many decision makers have become inured to them," Michael Silberman, global director of MobLab and a veteran digital campaigner, told us.[16] MobLab was started as an internal cell in Greenpeace set up by former CEO Kumi Naidoo to bring the dynamism of the digital campaigning world inside a 1960s-born pressure group after the crushing disappointment of the UN Climate Change Conference in Copenhagen in 2009. Michael believes digital techniques are "brilliant tools, but they're still tools. They have to be part of a coherent strategy for social change, and part of a mix of tactics to achieve change." Much effective civil society change requires persistent long-term pressure and building; otherwise, headline-grabbing "concessions" by policy makers quickly evaporate once the heat is off.

In response, digital-first groups have increasingly recognised the need to combine online action with offline activism and are engaging in deep reflection and reviewing their strategies. These groups depend less on direct engagement with decision makers or on negotiating only when they have generated enough pressure. The digital campaign groups' international network, OPEN, says it pursues an "outside power theory of change, which primarily relies on the collective force of large-scale citizen participation to move public and private sector decision-makers towards just outcomes."[17] Indeed, practically speaking, it would be impossible to support the full spectrum of pressure across media, lobbying, and protest across the range of issues they target.

At the critical moment we face now as global citizens to shift our current path, civil society will draw on its rich heritage of vision, learning, and struggle, reinterpreted for our new times. This will be crucial to the new strategies for winning citizen-powered change at the global scale and pace that is demanded by the raging global fires.

*Chapter Nine*

# The Three Wheels of Change

*How movements are charting new ways forward that everyone can join.*

A new era of citizen-powered change is taking shape, gaining traction even amid the extreme and escalating challenges facing our world. It is a movement fuelled by hope. As Rebecca Solnit argues, in her brilliant case for "hope in the dark," we never know how our positive action might eventually contribute to change:

> Sometimes one person inspires a movement, or her words do decades later; sometimes a few passionate people change the world; sometimes those millions are stirred by the same outrage or the same ideal, and change comes upon us like a change of weather. All that these transformations have in common is that they begin in the imagination, in hope. To hope is to gamble. It's a bet on the future.... Hope just means another world might be possible, not promised, not guaranteed. Hope calls for action; action is impossible without hope. [1]

But we also know that action by citizens flourishes where they see how it fits into a coherent strategy—how their efforts contribute to a stream of change and how they can join others to create rivers of transformation. People want to be part of something bigger than themselves. Often, other than in large visible events such as demonstrations, the collective scale of dispersed, diverse movements is hard for people to see, yet they work away, providing the underpinnings of change. Solnit notes:

> After a rain mushrooms appear on the surface of the earth as if from nowhere. Many do so from a sometimes-vast underground fungus that remains invisible and largely unknown. What we call mushrooms, mycologists call the fruiting body of the larger, less visible fungus. Uprisings and revolutions are often

> considered to be spontaneous, but less visible long-term organizing and groundwork—or underground work—often laid the foundation.[2]

A people-powered movement is developing across the world from the last decade of protest into what we believe will become a crucial decade of progress on the global challenges. Its urgency will be catalysed by the terrible direct and indirect cost of the Covid-19 pandemic, driven by people's determination that the world must now choose a new path of global cooperation and human solidarity.

As we mentioned at the start of this book, the change we see coming can be imagined as a three-wheeled cycle ridden by us citizens, its wheels representing our three instincts to believe, battle, and build. The front wheel gives us our beliefs, the values of the good society to inspire, motivate, and guide us; the two back wheels are, on one side, our campaign battles to wrest changes from the powerful and, on the other, our building, through our actions and choices, of the living alternatives that prefigure a better future. Each wheel of change reinforces, and relies upon, the other—and the biggest breakthroughs will happen where they work in synergy, gaining momentum together as when you power your cycle down a long, gentle slope.

## BATTLE: CAMPAIGNING FOR CHANGE

The campaigns for change will be tough and hard fought to overcome the powerful forces they face, even if they will be emphatically nonviolent. They will deploy a savvy strategy of approaches that win specific gains for social justice and sustainability, while also advancing the bigger struggle for system change. And they will use some of the tactics that follow to win.

### Pick the Right Dominos

In the current hostile climate, there is a temptation to retreat into defending what is under threat or trying to squeeze under the radar whatever limited gains we can. But, as veteran campaigner George Lakey argues, we should learn lessons from the last global lurch to the right of the 1980s, when many movements went on the defensive. He says this was a big mistake. And the exceptions, notably the campaign for LGBTQ rights, prove the rule:

> If the LGBTQ movement had chosen early in the decade to join the others, it would have focused on defending protections against discrimination previously won in some cities and towns. Instead, even while some homophobes talked about sending gay men to camps to isolate "the gay disease" of AIDS, the movement stepped up to confront Reagan and the medical-industrial complex. After winning, LGBTQ people stayed on the offensive demanding equal marriage, then equality in the military. . . . As a gay man I marvel at the degree of

acceptance of sexual and gender minorities that I would not have believed possible in my lifetime.[3]

In the same way today, bold, front-foot campaigns will be the mostly likely to win through. These combine big, concrete, overarching goals with cleverly finding the specific dominos that campaigners can knock down to set off a chain reaction of victories toward much bigger change. The climate movement takes an uncompromising position on the need for a huge and rapid scale of transition from the carbon economy, while breaking it down into specific battles toward that goal—for example, pressing a university to divest from fossil fuels or a government to enable all schools to reach zero carbon. That is exactly the kind of strategic mix that, we believe, will win.

## Structure and the Street—Bridge the Gap

One important trend is the coming together of spontaneous street mobilisations and bottom-up, digital-fuelled hashtag movements with the sustained strategic pressure that organisations deliver. Both approaches increasingly realise they need each other. By combining street and structure, they can win big campaign breakthroughs they could not achieve on their own. This requires some tough rethinking and realignment on both sides. Michael Silberman of MobLab told us:

> With the professionalization of organizations in the past few decades, there has been a huge decline in the exercising of our real "citizen muscle." Digital has hurt us in that way. We felt like we could build big lists, raise money rapidly and so keep building momentum and mobilize people. It made us think that we didn't need deeper grassroots power and membership building. . . . But in terms of confronting the larger systemic challenges we have underinvested in organizing and local leadership development for decades, and it left us weakened. But we're really seeing that start to shift.

Insider-track influencing will be another key ingredient to add to the mix. But in the populist age, this approach will need to be part of something bigger to once again win a place at the negotiating table that some NGOs had taken for granted. These organisations need to pivot their strategy to this new reality, or risk losing traction. At the same time, many protest movements recognise that broad-brush opposition is not enough, even when this can put large numbers on the streets.

Central to bridging the gap will be a renewal in grassroots organising. Partly, this will be powered by the groundswell of ordinary people propelled into action by the climate crisis, by rising conflict and inequalities, or by populist shockwaves—people who are now moving from single protests to sustained activism. Dana Fisher from the University of Maryland tracked people who joined the

2017 Women's March in the United States, many of whom did not see themselves as activists. "All of their levels of civic engagement went up," she said. "The same people who marched in the streets at the seven biggest protests that have taken place since Trump's inauguration went back to their communities and attended town hall meetings, lobbied elected officials, registered voters, wrote postcards and knocked on doors." [4] As Michael Silberman also put it, "We should never organize a demonstration without knowing what we're going to ask people to do the morning afterwards."

Slowly, established organisations are rediscovering this strength and aligning it with the power of digital into what Canadian campaigner Matt Price calls "the old art and new science of winning campaigns"[5] —an approach sometimes defined in the jargon as "engagement organising" or "directed-network campaigning." Campaigning advice group NetChange found this approach has been behind many of the North American campaigns in the last ten years that delivered major policy change from government or corporates—such as the Fight for $15 campaign (see chapter 6). According to their study, the approach also scored well on "force amplification"—the ability to start with modest resources but go on to build strong movements. Organisations using these combined strategies have outperformed "institutional heavyweight" organisations running traditional, highly resourced, professional pressure campaigns from the centre.

But they have also done better than "grassroots upstarts" such as the Occupy Wall Street network, which were largely driven by self-starting supporters coordinating action through an open and horizontal decision-making structure. They grew rapidly and created a lot of noise on the issues, shifting many people's perceptions for good—but were less skilled at converting this into tangible concessions from the targets.

The directed-network campaigns are usually led by a central body that frames the issues and coordinates efforts to key goals, but then leaves plenty of freedom and agency to grassroots supporters and allies on tactics and approach at the local level.[6] Jason Mogus and Tom Liacas of NetChange conclude:

> Directed-network campaigns succeed because they are aligned with new sources of self-organized people power but maintain enough centralized structure to focus it on clear political and cultural targets. In other words, they successfully marry new power with old power. By opening to new models of organizing in a network society, directed-network campaigns generate greater public engagement and achieve rapid scale with relatively few resources at the outset. With an executive structure that establishes strategic direction and carefully manages resources, these campaigns have what it takes to survive in an advocacy landscape now saturated with information and calls to action that compete for our attention.[7]

## Embrace Full-Stack Campaigns

In the tech world, the "full-stack" trend is toward developers who understand both the front-end, customer-facing part of computer systems and the back-end, hidden elements, such as databases. It comes from a realisation that system designers produce their best work when they can see the whole picture. The same principle applies to successful campaigns, which need integrated, full-stack thinking to win.

So, while we are currently in a "movement moment" with a welcome renaissance of grassroots organising, this will not be a silver bullet. The shift back to building in-person grassroots power and nurturing local leaders must be part of better deploying the full armoury of campaign techniques. Critical here is to harness—but not fetishise—digital power and to ensure that it supports the other arms of the campaign, rather than being removed into a world of its own. Breakthrough campaigns will succeed by better allowing tactics to flow freely from campaign objectives, deploying a creative range in different phases, until the goal is secured. Outrage, ridicule, evidence, humour, persistence, force of numbers, sweet reason, and inspiration: all will be needed in the campaign battle ahead. One-trick-pony campaigning—whether the online petition or policy briefing, the big demonstration or lobbying meeting—are not going to cut it. Exactly this full stack of tactics and approaches was critical, for example, to the success of the Treatment Action Campaign in securing access to AIDS drug treatments (see chapter 7).

## COME TOGETHER

Successful groups will often embrace campaigning together through alliances, coalitions, and joining hands across issues. As peacebuilders support campaigns for government action to tackle poverty or climate change, for example, the connections forged strengthen civil society's pitch for big, bold changes that will address the interrelated root causes. As well as better general working between social movements and civil society organisations, the breakthrough campaigns will build wider, creative coalitions across, say, NGOs, faith groups, organisations of indigenous peoples or women, and trade unions; and they will be focused not on symptoms but causes.

In one sense, the case for civil society coming together for one big push seems a no-brainer. But there are reasons it does not happen more often. Some are understandable but ultimately less important—such as organisational brand competition for funding or profile, or concern about working with people who do not share one's entire worldview. But there are other, more knotty reasons. For example, small groups may feel they have less influence than the larger ones. Or, in the bid to bring in a range of groups, coalitions may lose focus and end up with a vague, lowest-common-denominator position that does nothing to worry power holders. Or the coalition takes a Christmas-tree approach to policy demands, each organisation adding its own pet cause—with no one ready to say no or suggest an order of priority—until none can benefit. What is more, the time and effort spent managing a coalition and its structures absorb resources and can sap commitment.

But bringing together diverse support bases, resources, and skill sets from different organisations and constituencies—not to mention the authority and credibility of diverse voices speaking as one—can also bring an unparalleled power to a campaign. It will often be the only route to achieve cut-through in a crowded and divided political landscape, as shown by the environmental movement's coordinated global approach in the run-up to the Paris UN climate conference in 2015, which secured important new international commitments. And the strength of opponents, from fossil fuel companies to populists, is focusing people's minds on joining forces. Thankfully, civil society has been developing better practical strategies we can use to avoid or manage the pitfalls of coalition working, to help support more effective working together.

Crisis Action is one organisation that emerged to address this challenge. Guy Hughes set it up out of his frustration at the failure of the 2003 protests against the Iraq War, where millions around the world crowded into the streets to try to stop the US-led military intervention. He believed that, while bigger coalitions were the key to change, they were often not effective and agile. Crisis Action was designed to fill this gap by focusing specifically on supporting coalitions of organisations across different mandates—whether human rights, humanitarian, or peacebuilding—to create smarter, more effective ways to protect civilians in conflict. Guy's initiative continues to secure significant successes in the face of some of the toughest challenges: an amazing legacy for a young man whose life was cut short by a tragic mountaineering accident.

When Ben was at Crisis Action working on contentious issues such as the impact on civilians of the Israeli government's blockade of Gaza, he was amazed by the power that could be achieved by two particular principles of the model: having an organisation like Crisis Action that was not competing for the public limelight itself as an honest broker between groups, and the opt-in coalition in which (while every participating organisation was part of the alliance and its guiding strategy) not everyone had to opt in to every activity. This allowed the coalition to remain coherent without having to run every action at the pace of the slowest, meaning more gets done more quickly. On the Gaza siege, Crisis Action pulled together a diverse coalition across the European Union—working in collaboration with both Israeli and Palestinian human rights groups—securing media coverage for a forgotten issue and lobbying EU governments and the European Commission, which resulted in the lifting of some restrictions on goods needed by civilians in Gaza.[8]

Another approach to successful coalitions is "white-label" campaigning where groups create a single campaign identity—a name or hashtag slogan for example—for the issue at stake, as Fight for $15 did on the campaign for a better minimum wage. This identity fronts the campaign, engaging the public, media, and decision-makers while the institutions behind it remain in the engine room, actively involved but in the background. The white-label approach enables the campaign to be used and interpreted by a whole range of activists and local groups, giving them much greater agency over tactics toward the agreed-upon overall aim. It also means that the campaign takes flight more organically online. Done right, this approach can transform the member management and coordination drag often experienced by more rigid coalitions into a brilliantly diverse patchwork of action that still adds up to a lot more than the sum of its parts. A framework is created in which each group can contribute to the whole using their specific heritage and supporter base, instead of loads of different organisations all doing little bits of the same tactic. Also known as the "flotilla approach" to coalitions, it involves agreeing to an overall direction to reach a specific destination, but everyone does not have to be on the same ship to get there.

## BUILD: CONSTRUCTING THE ALTERNATIVE FUTURE

A Chinese proverb says, "I hear and I forget; I see and I remember; I do and I understand." Nothing beats creating the living alternative for engaging people in understanding the problems and the solutions. So it is encouraging to see that, alongside winning bigger, bolder battles, citizens are increasingly taking the future into their own hands. They will scale up these already myriad efforts to imagine and fashion real "prefigurative" change between the cracks of the current system.

If campaigning is vertical, where we target those in power to wrest changes from the existing system, then building the alternative is horizontal, where we collaborate with other citizens, developing the power to transform the system from the grassroots. Citizens are doing this in so many ways: cooperatives (selling products or providing housing) that operate within the wider capitalist economy while rejecting its fundamental principles of profit and competition; Fairtrade ensuring farmers get a fair price for their crops, irrespective of the global market price; citizen peacebuilders reaching across battle lines to forge lasting peace beyond diplomats and the warring parties; refugee groups in camps generating renewable electricity.

American radical social thinker Erik Olin Wright set out to show how a strategy of nurturing change between the gaps of the current world could forge a transformation to a post-capitalist world without violent revolution. He argued, "We can get on with the business of building a new world, not from the ashes of the old, but within the interstices of the old."[9] He saw a path to genuine transformation through "eroding" instead of "smashing" capitalism. This path would not settle for "taming" capitalism; neither could it be mistaken for simply "escaping" capitalism through a hippy counterculture-style "turn on, tune in, drop out" to exit the rat race. Rather, he advocated building "real utopias" to erode the current system from within. These, he said, would transform "the nowhere of utopia into the now-here of creating emancipatory alternatives of the world as it could be in the world as it is." Wright used an analogy to picture how this strategy could transform the current system over time:

> Think of a lake. . . . In such an ecosystem, it is possible to introduce an alien species of fish not "naturally" found in the lake. Some alien species will instantly get gobbled up. Others may survive in some small niche in the lake, but not change much about daily life in the ecosystem. But occasionally an alien species may thrive and eventually displace the dominant species. The strategic vision of eroding capitalism imagines introducing the most vigorous varieties of emancipatory species of non-capitalist economic activity into the ecosystem of capitalism, nurturing their development by protecting their niches, and figuring out ways of expanding their habitats. The ultimate hope is that eventually these alien species can spill out of their narrow niches and transform the character of the ecosystem as a whole.[10]

Sometimes this approach is dismissed by those who say it is naive to erect tiny models of an alternative—no matter how well crafted—when the juggernaut of the existing system thunders on, either crushing them in its path or rushing past unhindered. Better to focus on changing the path of that system truck. Worse still, the energy people spend on such initiatives is diverted from campaigning to change the system. Or, they say, people can become so compromised by functioning within the existing system, they end up being little more than an ethical "wash" for the governments or corporations they have to work with.

It is true that these are dangers that need to be guarded against, but they are not inevitable. The horizontal movement for more sustainable, equal, and inclusive ways of living, working, and resolving human challenges is blooming. It uses a host of innovative models, delivers across an ever-wider range of needs—from providing social care to banking to transport—and at a scale not seen, at least in the West, for years. As Neal Lawson of Compass says, "There is a cacophony of trial, experimentation and innovation going on. . . . People are sharing, caring, communing, creating, building, producing, inventing and supporting—as never before."[11]

In this, they are empowering communities, creating the more decentralised, democratised economy every day while proving the case that alternative models do work, that people do care about the ethics of the products they buy, or do want more safe cycle routes to get to work and school, and so create the mandate and the conditions for wider change by companies and governments. The living alternatives are at their best when they work alongside campaigning for changes in wider policies—campaigns that are also enriched by what they can show about viable new ways of doing things, the two back wheels powering the tricycle forward and guided by the beliefs of the front wheel. Living alternatives give people the opening to live by their values today, putting them into practice immediately. And the process itself of working together to create those models becomes part of the wider societal shift. The ever-growing living alternatives movement will be a defining part of the wider citizen-led push for change in the next decade, firing people's imaginations and investing the wider movement with a sense of positive, living human vision. The strongest alternative approaches will be set apart by a number of features.

## Challenge Systems, Not Symptoms

As the renaissance of living alternatives has gathered pace, it has begun pushing for wider culture and system changes, thus becoming much more than a radical outsider counterpoint. For example, civil society shifted the debate around business and sustainable development away from add-on "corporate social responsibility" to focus on the impact of the core business model on environmental sustainability or exploitation in the supply chain. While, of course, yawning gaps remain between this discourse and realities on the ground, civil society bringing alternative models together with campaigning pressure is now moving the focus onto ownership and who calls the shots: citizens and communities, or private owners and companies dominated by short-term goals of returning maximum quarterly profits to shareholders?

With much wider questioning of our current global models of capitalism, military-based security, and domineering relationship with nature than has been the case for decades, civil society models that offer real alternatives to the current failing system will gain traction. "We're in a time when people are much more open to radical economic ideas," says Michael Jacobs, an academic and former adviser to Prime Minister Gordon Brown.[12] In a barren landscape of thin, old-style answers to the big problems society faces, far-reaching, innovative civil society alternatives will stand out and gain momentum, whether cities aiming for carbon-free economic prosperity or communities welcoming refugees. The citizen alternatives increasingly challenge the grip of the powerful ideology promoted by vested interests that say that there is no viable alternative, despite the faults of the current system. They show every day that the alternatives are alive, kicking, and ready to go. And many of these campaigns and alternatives that were on the fringes yesterday are in the political mainstream today, from the Green New Deal to community ownership models of key utilities such as water or rail.

Movements will break through by providing a beacon or living prototype that is viable and inspiring beyond the remorseless logic of profit, competition, or centralised, state-imposed solutions to local challenges. And they will demonstrate the ability to scale up, growing beyond the cracks in the system to start colonising and blooming more widely across whole sectors. This will demand active strategies, especially via the growth in networks and alliances at local, national, and international level, becoming more than the sum of their parts. But there will also be a key role for carefully constructed strategic alliances between citizen groups and other sectors, particularly municipalities and provincial-level governments as interest rises in local solutions.

## Develop a Movement

In the period ahead, the living alternatives movement is set to extend its base and reach. In part, this will be through a burgeoning new network of thinkers and innovators powering new models of change, particularly around new democratic economic alternatives. Groups like Democracy Collaborative in the United States—famous for their pioneering of new solutions such as community wealth building to address the industrial decline of Cleveland—or Common Wealth in Britain are finding a huge thirst among the rising generations.[13] As the old paradigm of neoliberal economics seems increasingly in crisis and bereft of ideas, intellectual energy has moved to these ideas. As Common Wealth put it, "After a long winter in which ideas about economic alternatives were largely banished from public consideration, the seeds of a new economic consensus might be beginning to sprout."[14]

These trends tap into the wider affinity of the millennial generations with business models that go beyond the traditional bottom line and the potential of technology to power them. The interest is not just in intellectual concepts but career paths away from the big corporations struggling to persuade young talent that they can offer the sense of purpose this new cohort craves. Increasingly, too, links are being made across environmental and social-justice drivers with initiatives to develop alternatives that combine the two. The Green New Deal is one manifestation of this as a policy platform for national governments that is also central to the new wave of the living alternative movement. It is breaking from the stereotype that such alternative models are the preserve of more privileged, fashionable ecowarriors or artisan-fruit-gin-sipping hipsters. Instead, it plumbs the deep vein of community and economic alternatives organised by working-class communities—for example, today's credit union movement or the pioneering ME Solshare in Bangladesh, which enables people with solar panels to trade energy with their neighbours, creating a community grid or network.

Another part of building the impact of the alternatives is finding better ways to connect a multitude of positive, but disconnected initiatives into more coherent local ecosystems and national and international networks. Positive action builds positive action. Community energy groups, for example, see part of their role as demonstrating to their neighbours that solar is successful and can provide economic benefits to communities facing fuel poverty as well as contributing to tackling climate change.

**Tech to Transform**

Our age of distributed networks and online connectivity has immense potential to link more people into common voices and collaboration for alternatives. Civil society has made great strides in harnessing this collaborative power; the potential is clear through examples from Wikipedia to Freecycle, the Library of Things, Borroclub, and local networks setting off a full-scale counterrevolution enabling people to recycle, share, and donate through crowdfunding. Of course, big tech has been a powerful counterforce, centralising power, data, wealth, and control, and extracts a price from the human sharing via networks, as with Uber, Airbnb, and Facebook, denting hopes that the digital revolution would lead to more common human endeavour outside the market. Nevertheless, a new wave of alternative initiatives winning people over to tech models that serve a social purpose will be a critical terrain in the phase ahead, for example in setting up cooperatively run digital platforms. There has been an explosion of work and thinking about how tech can nurture collaborative, citizen-based alternatives. While ever more numerous bright ideas will bubble up through decentralised initiatives, the focus in the next phase may be on scaling up those with the most potential for expansion, while ensuring that the systems are in place to prevent them being hijacked by those seeking to monetise and make profit from them.

## BELIEVE: TOWARD THE GOOD SOCIETY

If our campaigning and living alternatives wheels provide the practical power to drive us forward, our front wheel of beliefs will steer us to our destination. Our beliefs reflect the better world we are aiming for, as well as who we are and how we go about achieving that new world. Both of us believe that these principles of practice—of how we do things—are an essential part of change-making: the end does not justify the means. A campaign that succeeds in achieving a change in policy but does so in a way that fails to empower the very people with whom it is supposed to be in solidarity cannot be called a real success. Our mantra must be, as the Gandhian saying has it: "Be the change you want to be in the world."

For many years, mainstream politics proceeded on the basis of consensus over broad, liberal, democratic values; the discussion was more about specific aims and how to achieve these. Mainstream civil society often went along with this and was so absorbed in technical delivery of programs and campaigns for specific changes that it lost sight of its role in influencing broader values. But renewing a big, common vision of the good society is now a pressing priority as deep-seated divisions, fragmentation, and despair have strengthened their grip in so many communities, and the Covid-19 pandemic has stripped our society and each of us back to reflecting on the fundamentals of what really matters.

Civil society can and must rise to the urgent task of renewing and restoring our shared values, locally, nationally, and globally. Without strengthening this shared moral underpinning, our change wheels of campaigning and building living alternatives will founder against the values of the old order. If we get things right, "a strong civil society [can] make society civil and strong," in the words of thinker Michael Edwards.[15] As citizens, it is up to us to develop a new culture based on what we value and prioritise as communities and as a society. *New York Times* columnist David Brooks makes the following argument:

> I think the people in the social sector are finding, willy-nilly, new ways to live. Moreover, the values emerging there are the values America needs most right now. They are the values of community building, relationship, healing and transcending difference. If the early 2000s were defined by the Silicon Valley hackers, and the 1980s were defined by the Yuppies, and the 1960s were defined by the hippies, I believe the coming years will be defined by some of the people in this sector, who are living most urgently to build a new social fabric, who are working most urgently to build a new power dynamic, and who are thus addressing the central problem of our time.[16]

Of course, many principles underpin what drives civil society action for change, but what follow are three particular ones we see as central for our times.

## Empowerment

Much recent divisive politics has been driven by people's sense that they have lost control and agency over their lives, both individually and as communities. Populists have exploited this to offer empty answers through blaming "the other" for taking this away, while we have become self-absorbed consumers and individuals venting at the world in what one former Twitter enthusiast, White House correspondent Maggie Haberman, called the "anger video game" of social media.[17]

By contrast, we need to renew that metaphorical public square where citizens come together equally across their differences to identify problems, find ways to solve them, and work out a better future together. Long part of civil society thinking on the importance of defending the realm of a common "public sphere," it would also help renew our fractured democracy. Activists can contribute to this vision by breaking out of our tendency to address only other activists, becoming more willing to engage with others who do not seem to share our complete worldview. This will be critical in the interests of fairer, more genuine societal engagement as well as of building broader, stronger coalitions of support.

Rising to this vision also means championing the values of civility in public discourse: renewed respect for our fellow citizens whoever they are, and belief in the potential of all people for responsible self-governance and agency. A belief in empowering people and enabling all to participate is underpinned by a commitment to inclusive approaches and to equality, where everyone can expect fair outcomes and influence in shaping their own and their community's life. As the rallying cry of the disabled people's rights movement goes, "Nothing about us, without us."

## Collaboration

Collaboration is a central value to guide a civil society strategy for change, and one that has enabled so many inspiring initiatives to overcome hurdle after hurdle. Belief in the value of cooperation runs counter to the ideology of individualism and competitiveness constantly beamed at us; but it actually goes with the grain of our nature as human beings. While competitiveness is part of who we are—and can be one spur to human progress and satisfaction—all the evidence shows that we are just as hard-wired to be collaborative, cooperative, compassionate. These characteristics are core to our flourishing and very survival.

Research by the Common Cause Foundation on common values shows that three out of four people place more emphasis on compassionate values than selfish values, irrespective of their background or beliefs.[18] And yet, at the same time, three out of four people also believe their fellow citizens hold selfish values to be more important than compassionate ones. "They can't both be right," as co-ops champion Ed Mayo observed to Ben. He says this mismatch matters because by believing, wrongly, that everyone else is mainly selfish, citizens are much less likely to feel responsible for their community, get involved, or work with others: "It is the powerbrokers in society who constantly promote the myth of competition as the main path to improvement and fulfilment—from the classroom onward. It is only by changing our values frames that we recognise that our place is in a moral community."

The drive for cooperation is, in part, born out of collective self-interest: mutual aid in the face of adversity. But cooperation extends from this into a value much in need of revival and cherishing in civil society: solidarity—that sense of shared equal interest and common struggle that motivates action across geographies, languages, and issues, powered by the human spirit.

## Hope

Vivien Leigh said, "Life is not about waiting for the storm clouds to pass. It is about learning to dance in the rain." Right now, it is pouring out there, yet citizens are in the midst of the deluge doing their thing, finding hope and optimism for the future. As Rebecca Solnit reminded us, hope is the wellspring of action because you need to believe that better is possible in order to act.

When the two of us reflect on the many extraordinary individuals we have met driving initiatives for change, it is striking that they have always been powered by hope. Yes, their actions have been born out of anger over injustice, compassion over suffering, dread at the future of a planet whose balance has been disturbed. But it is always hope that turns this into a project for change and, crucially, for sustaining the mission through thick and thin. We have always known that these hopes are fragile—indeed, been brutally reminded on the many, many occasions that cherished plans and projects have been thwarted, slowed, dashed by external adversaries, internal disagreements, flakiness, and, well, just getting things plain wrong. But this is all part and parcel of creating change. We both believe that the biggest danger for citizen action is not in having hopes that are too high but in setting our sights too low. Time and again, citizens acting together with high ambitions have fashioned change everyone said was impossible.

Hope also sustains the vital role of civil society as an incubating space for ideas, pioneering practice, and action-orientated analysis; these are all needed to power new initiatives, movements, and people prepared to fund and support crazy ideas, some of which may fail but so many of which will flourish. In the commercial world, about 80 percent of new products fail, but companies are ready to take that risk to find the 20 percent that will succeed. So too must civil society be ready to take risks and fail in order to unleash the major leaps forward. And for this, it also needs bold, creative leadership.

Every one of us has the capacity to hope and to see the pathways ahead. Citizen action is about harnessing that hope behind collective efforts to bring about change. The global fires are burning high. But from a million examples of citizen action across the world, we know that a bunch of hopeful, determined people with a fine plan can unleash the power of the human spirit to confront these fires and build a more sustainable, peaceful world. And along the way, they will encounter the sheer thrill, the irrepressible joy, the fun and laughter of cooperating with others for that better future.

On our own, too often, we can all feel overwhelmed and powerless. But like the individual starlings that flock together to create awe-inspiring, collective, fast-moving patterns in the sky, we can see off the dangers that threaten our world while also building something better and so much more beautiful.

# Notes

## PROLOGUE

1. Frank Edwards, Hedwig Lee, and -Michael Esposito, "Risk of being killed by police use of force in the United States by age, race-ethnicity, and sex," *Proceedings of the National Academy of Sciences* (Washington, DC, August 2019), 116 (34).
2. Ibram X. Kendi, "Is this the beginning of the end of American racism?," *Atlantic*, September 2020.
3. *Guardian*, 7 June 2020.
4. Arundhati Roy, "The pandemic is a portal," *Financial Times*, 3 April 2020.

## 1. THE JOURNEY TO CHANGE

1. World Development Movement changed its name to Global Justice Now in 2015.
2. Tim Lankester, *The Politics and Economics of Britain's Foreign Aid: The Pergau Dam Affair* (Abingdon: Routledge, 2013), 112.
3. Lankester, 112.
4. Lankester, 140.
5. Sir Tim Lankester, speaking at the Politics and Economics of Britain's Foreign Aid: The Pergau Dam Affair event organized by the Institute of Government, 25 October 2012. https://www.instituteforgovernment.org.uk/events/politics-and-economics-britains-foreign-aid-pergau-dam-affair.
6. House of Commons International Development Committee, *Definition and Administration of ODA* (HC547, 2017–19, June 2018).
7. *Financial Times*, 16 June 2020.
8. Speaking on BBC Radio, *Today*, 2 September 2020.
9. Bob Seely and James Rogers, *Global Britain: A Twenty-First Century Vision* (London: Henry Jackson Society, 2019).
10. Arundhati Roy, *War Talk* (Boston: South End Press, 2003).

## 2. CITIZENQUAKE

1. Robin Wright, "The story of 2019: Protests in every corner of the globe," *New Yorker*, 30 December 2019.
2. Erica Chenoweth and Maria J. Stephan, "How the world is proving Martin Luther King right about nonviolence," *Washington Post*, 18 January 2016. Working with Maria Stephan, Chenoweth performed an extensive review of the literature on civil resistance and social movements from 1900 to 2006—a data set then corroborated other experts in the field. While they focused specifically on nonviolent attempts to bring about regime change, other evidence indicates a similar upsurge in wider civil society action to press for system change short of actual regime change. A movement was considered a success if it fully achieved its goals both within a year of its peak engagement and as a direct result of its activities. See also: Erica Chenoweth, "The Rise of Nonviolent Resistance," *PRIO Policy Brief 19*, (Oslo: Peace Research Institute Oslo, 2016).
3. Wright, "The story of 2019."
4. The original email is reproduced on the website of the then Adbusters editor, Micah White, which he co-wrote with Kalle Lasn. See: https://www.micahmwhite.com/occupywallstreet.
5. Joseph Stiglitz, "Of the 1%, by the 1%, for the 1%," *Vanity Fair*, 31 March 2011.
6. CBC News, "Wall Street naked performance art ends in arrests," CBC Radio Canada, 2 August 2011.
7. Jana Kasperkevic, "Occupy Wall Street: Four years later," *Guardian*, 16 September 2015.
8. *Guardian*, 19 May 2014.
9. *Guardian*, 4 May 2010.
10. *Guardian*, 7 November 2019.
11. Naomi Larsson, "The sounds of banging pots are leading a protest movement in Chile," *Latino USA*, 24 October 2019.
12. Amanda Taub, "'Chile Woke Up': Dictatorship's legacy of inequality triggers mass protests," *New York Times*, 3 November 2019.
13. Cas Mudde and Roger Eatwell, *Western Democracies and the New Extreme Right Challenge* (London and New York: Routledge, 2004).
14. For more on populism, see also: Roger Eatwell and Matthew Goodwin, *National Populism: The Revolt against Liberal Democracy* (London: Pelican, 2018) and Jan-Werner Müller, *What Is Populism?* (London: Penguin, 2017).
15. *Guardian*, 19 December 2017.
16. Declan Walsh and Max Fisher, "From Chile to Lebanon, protests flare over wallet issues," *New York Times*, 23 October 2019.
17. Hardy Merriman, "Lessons of uprisings around the world: The present moment, and possible future," *International Center on Nonviolent Conflict Blog* (Washington, DC: ICNC, 21 November 2019). https://www.nonviolent-conflict.org/blog_post/lessons-of-uprisings-around-the-world/.
18. Paul Mason, *Why Its Kicking Off Everywhere: The New Global Revolutions* (London and New York: Verso, 2012), 69.
19. *Financial Times*, 17 July 2019. Also, OECD, *OECD Employment Outlook 2020: Worker Security and the COVID-19 Crisis* (Paris: OECD), July 2020.
20. Henry Timms and Jeremy Heimans, *New Power: Why Outsiders Are Winning, Institutions Are Failing, and How the Rest of Us Can Keep Up in the Age of Mass Participation* (London: Picador, 2019), 8.
21. *Daily Telegraph*, 3 September 2014.
22. Michael Edwards, *Thick Problems and Thin Solutions: How NGOs Can Bridge the Gap* (The Hague: HIVOS, 2011).
23. Sheila McKechnie Foundation, *Social Power: How Civil Society Can 'Play Big' and Truly Create Change* (London: SMK, 2018), 6. This was the report of SMK's Social Change

Project to which Ben contributed in its early stages. The full report can be found at: https://smk.org.uk/social-change-project/social-power-report/.

24. Sheila McKechnie Foundation, *Social Power*, 44.
25. Interview with the authors, January 2020.
26. Interview with the authors, January 2020.
27. Sarah Repucci, *Freedom in the World 2020: A Leaderless Struggle for Democracy* (Washington, DC: Freedom House, n.d.). For an overview see: https://freedomhouse.org/report/freedom-world/2020/leaderless-struggle-democracy.
28. Maria Stephan, "What we get wrong about protest movements," United States Institute for Peace Podcast, 19 December 2019.
29. David Kode and Mathew Jacob, *India: Democracy Threatened by Growing Attacks on Civil Society* (Johannesburg: CIVICUS, November 2017), 1.
30. *Financial Times*, 27 December 2019.
31. CIVICUS, *The State of Civil Society Report 2019* (Johannesburg: CIVICUS), 2019, 6.
32. César Muñoz Acebes and Daniel Wilkinson, *Rainforest Mafias: How Violence and Impunity Fuel Deforestation in Brazil's Amazon* (New York: Human Rights Watch, 2019).
33. Richard Kerbaj, "Charities chief goes to war on Islamists," *Times*, 20 April 2014.
34. Tania Mason, "Commission unfairly targets Muslim charities, says think tank," *Civil Society News*, 17 November 2014,.
35. For figures on estimated numbers of Muslim-based registered UK charities see: https://www.themuslim500.com/guest-contributions-2019/the-two-most-important-institutions-for-british-muslims/; and for total numbers of charities see: https://www.gov.uk/government/publications/charity-register-statistics/recent-charity-register-statistics-charity-commission. Creation of new category quoted by Tania Mason, "Commission unfairly targets."
36. Randeep Ramesh, "Charities can fund Cage campaign group, commission agrees," *Guardian*, 21 October 2015.
37. We are thinking here particularly of media analysis—but it has also been true of academic research historically. However, since the 1970s, theoretical and empirical work has grown into an established field of social movement studies—though this still tends to be based more in social science than in political studies.
38. Mark Engler and Paul Engler, *This Is an Uprising: How Nonviolent Revolt Is Shaping the Twenty-First Century* (New York: Nation Books, 2016), xx.
39. As Grainne Healy, co-director of the YES campaign for same-sex marriage in Ireland put it: "Our communications started with values. Our research told us that the electorate believed in love, equality, fairness, generosity, and being inclusive. These were what it meant to be Irish." For more background on the campaign see: Gráinne Healy, Brian Sheehan, and Noel Whelan, *Ireland Says Yes: The Inside Story of How the Vote for Marriage Equality Was Won* (Sallins: Merrion Press, 2016).
40. Hilary Wainwright, "A new politics from the left?," *Open Democracy*, 20 May 2016. These concepts of power also draw on the ideas of American pioneer of organisational theory Mary Parker Follett. As Wainwright goes on to say, this concept also has profound implications for how we think about human creativity: "Power as transformative capacity arises from both our individual creative capacity and our character as social beings. It rests on the importance of collaborative human creativity." See also: Hilary Wainwright, *New Politics from the Left* (Cambridge: Polity Press, 2018).
41. Neal Lawson, *45° Change: Transforming Society from Below and Above* (London: Compass, 2019), 43.
42. Some accounts attribute this story to President Lyndon B. Johnson with Martin Luther King Jr. However, the FDR and Randolph version seems to be the origin. See: https://changewire.org/how-does-great-change-happen/.

## 3. THE TIMED TEST WE CANNOT FAIL

1. World Meteorological Organisation, "2019 concludes a decade of exceptional global heat and high-impact weather," WMO Press Release—03122019, 3 December 2019.
2. CIVICUS, "An open letter to our fellow activists across the globe: Building from below and beyond borders" (Johannesburg: CIVICUS, 18 July 2014).
3. Greta Thunberg, "Greta Thunberg to world leaders: 'How dare you—you have stolen my dreams and my childhood,'" Greta Thunberg, at the United Nations Climate Action Summit, video source from UNTV Reuters, 23 September 2019.
4. Damian Carrington, "School climate strikes: 1.4 million people took part, say campaigners," *Guardian*, 19 March 2019.
5. Chika Unigwe, "It's not just Greta Thunberg: Why are we ignoring the developing world's inspiring activists?," *Guardian*, 5 October 2019.
6. Sonya Elks, "Schools challenged to teach climate change as students join Greta strikes," Thomson Reuters Foundation, 27 February 2020.
7. Interview with the authors, April 2020.
8. Sandra Laville, "UK citizens' climate assembly to meet for first time," *Guardian*, 22 January 2020.
9. Martin Luther King Jr., The Quest for Peace and Justice, Martin Luther King's Nobel Lecture, Auditorium of the University of Oslo, 11 December 1964.
10. Gail Bradbrook, "Fir Farm 2019," YouTube, uploaded 20 July 2019. https://www.youtube.com/watch?v=ubFN73mZT4Q.
11. Andrew Napier, "Hampshire farmers join Extinction Rebellion protests in London with pink tractor," *Hampshire Chronicle*, 13 October 2019.
12. *Daily Mail*, 7 October 2019.
13. At a public meeting in Cambridge, February 2019, attended by the author.
14. Phoebe Weston, "'Untold human suffering': 11,000 scientists from across world unite to declare global climate emergency," *Independent*, 5 November 2019.
15. *Metro*, 10 October 2019.
16. UK Department for Business, Energy & Industrial Strategy, "UK becomes first major economy to pass net zero emissions law," press release, 27 June 2019.
17. Jessica Long, Lizzie Gordon, and Ruth Townend, *Now What, Climate Change and Coronavirus* (London: IPSOS Mori, June 2020).
18. Long, Gordon, and Townend.
19. Caroline Lucas, "Theresa May's net-zero emissions target is a lot less impressive than it looks," *Guardian*, 12 June 2019.
20. Paula A. Davies and Michael D. Green, "European Commission formally announces green deal," *Environment, Land & Resources* (Latham & Watkins, 16 December 2019).
21. David Robson, "The '3.5% rule': How a small minority can change the world," *BBC Future*, 14 May 2019.
22. Erica Chenoweth, "It may only take 3.5% of the population to topple a dictator—with civil resistance," *Guardian*, 1 February 2019.
23. Umair Irfan, "Fossil fuels are underpriced by a whopping $5.2 trillion," Vox, 17 May 2019.
24. Damian Carrington, "Fossil fuels subsidised by $10m a minute, says IMF," *Guardian*, 18 May 2015.
25. David Coady, Ian Parry, Nghia-Piotr Le, and Baoping Shang, "Global fossil fuel subsidies remain large: An update based on country-level estimates," IMF Working Paper 19/89, (Washington, DC: IMF, May 2019), 5.
26. Carrington, "Fossil fuels subsidised."
27. Grant Wilson, Iain Staffell, and Noah Godfrey, "Britain's electricity since 2010: Wind surges to second place, coal collapses and fossil fuel use nearly halves," *The Conversation*, 6 January 2020.
28. Jennifer Deol, "Five people-powered movements that took on Big Oil, and won," 350 Canada, 17 February 2020.

29. Influence Map, *Big Oil's Real Agenda on Climate Change: How the Oil Majors Have Spent $1 Billion since Paris on Narrative Capture and Lobbying on Climate* (London: Influence Map, March 2019).
30. Sandra Laville, "Top oil firms spending millions lobbying to block climate change policies, says report," *Guardian*, 22 March 2019.
31. Catherine Howarth, quoted in Influence Map, *Big Oil's Real Agenda*.
32. Laville, "Top oil firms spending millions."
33. Sandra Laville and David Pegg, "Fossil fuel firms' social media fightback against climate action," *Guardian*, 10 October 2019.
34. Laville and Pegg.
35. Neela Banerjee, Lisa Song, and David Hasemyer, "Exxon's own research confirmed fossil fuel's role in global warming decades ago," *Inside Climate News*, 16 September 2015.
36. Banerjee, Song, and Hasemyer.
37. Ben Chapman, "Gas companies spend €104m lobbying to ensure Europe remains 'locked in' to fossil fuels for decades, report finds," *Independent*, 31 October 2017.
38. Belén Balanyá and Pascoe Sabido, *The Great Gas Lock-In: Industry Lobbying behind the EU Push for New Gas Infrastructure* (Brussels: Corporate Europe Observatory, October 2017), 4.
39. Chapman, "Gas companies spend €104m lobbying."
40. Corporate Europe Observatory, "Cut gas, oil and coal out of our politics," 24 October 2019.
41. Jackie Wills, "Carbon Tracker has changed the financial language of climate change," *Guardian*, 15 May 2014.
42. Edward Helmore, "Activists cheer BlackRock's landmark climate move but call for vigilance," *The Guardian*, 15 January 2020.
43. Benjamin Hulac, "This group coined 'carbon bubble.' Its influence is growing," *E&E News, Climate Wire*, 11 December 2018.
44. Pilita Clark, "Mark Carney warns investors face 'huge' climate change losses," *Financial Times*, 29 September 2015. See also: Jessica Shankleman, "Mark Carney: Most fossil fuel reserves can't be burned," *Guardian*, 13 October 2014.
45. Hulac, "This group coined 'carbon bubble.'"
46. Jamie Henn, "Our collective story is inspiration to go big in 2010," 350.org, 13 January 2010. For more see: https://350.org/go-big/.
47. Desmund Tutu, "We need an apartheid-style boycott to save the planet," *Guardian*, 10 April 2014.
48. Go Fossil Free, "1000+ Divestment Commitments," Go Fossil Free, data accessed April 2020. https://gofossilfree.org/divestment/commitments/.
49. Bill McKibben, "Money is the oxygen on which the fire of global warming burns," *New Yorker*, 17 September 2019.
50. Carey L. Biron, "Al Gore backs growing fossil fuel divestment campaign," Guardian, 11 February 2013.
51. Joe Romm, "Bill McKibben reviews 'Straight Up,' challenges me to offer 350.org advice. I accept!," Think Progress, 12 July 2010.
52. Mike Dougherty and Elizabeth Gribkoff, "Climate change: Why Bill McKibben keeps fighting after 30 years," The Deeper Dig podcast, VTDigger, 18 September 2019.
53. Ella Nilsen, "The new face of climate activism is young, angry—and effective," Vox, 17 September 2019.
54. Ryan Grim and Briahna Gray, "Alexandra Ocasio-Cortez joins environmental activists in protest at Democratic Leader Nancy Pelosi's Office," The Intercept, 13 November 2018.
55. Danielle Kurtzleben, "Rep. Alexandria Ocasio-Cortez Releases Green New Deal Outline," NPR, 7 February 2019.
56. Richard Orange, "'Inspirational': Alexandria Ocasio-Cortez applauds mayors' Global Green New Deal," *Guardian*, 9 October 2019.
57. Ruarí Arrieta-Kenna, "The Sunrise Movement actually changed the democratic conversation. So what do you do for a sequel?," *Politico*, 16 June 2019.
58. Arrieta-Kenna.

59. Global Witness, *Enemies of The State?* (London: Global Witness, 2019).
60. At a conference in London attended by the author.
61. For more detail see: Adam Corner, Christina Demski, Katherine Steentjes, and Nick Pidgeon, *Engaging the Public on Climate Risks and Adaptation: A Briefing for UK Communicators* (Oxford: Climate Outreach, 2020). This report builds on the findings of the *RESiL RISK survey: British Public Perceptions of Climate Risk, Adaptation Options and Resilience* (RESiL RISK, March 2020).
62. European Commission Directorate-General for Communication, *Special Eurobarometer 490, Climate Change* (Brussels: European Union, 2019), 4. See also: "Eurobarometer survey confirms public support for energy policy objectives," European Commission, 11 September 2019.
63. Carol Davenport, "California sues the Trump administration in its escalating war over auto emissions," *New York Times*, 20 September 2019.
64. Community Energy Scotland, "The Future of Community Energy," 13 February 2020.
65. In discussions with the author, April 2020.
66. Brian Kohler, "Just Transition—A labour view of Sustainable Development," CEP vol. 6, no. 2, Summer 1998.
67. Sandeep Pai and Savannah Carr-Wilson, "Renewable energy: Planning a just transition," *Ecologist*, 28 November 2018. See also the book by the same authors: *Total Transition: The Human Side of the Renewable Energy Revolution* (Calgary: Rocky Mountain Books, 2018).
68. Orange, "'Inspirational.'"
69. Richard Orange, "Ocasio-Cortez tells world's mayors drastic action needed on climate crisis," *Guardian*, 11 October 2019.
70. In a letter on 31 March 2020, the Environmental Protection Agency told all government and private sector players that the agency did not expect power plants, factories, or other companies to meet environmental standards and reporting of pollution during the crisis time, adding that it would not pursue penalties if companies broke the rules. See Sophie Lewis, "'An open license to pollute': Trump administration indefinitely suspends some environmental protection laws during coronavirus pandemic," CBS News, 31 March 2020.
71. Press Association, 21 September 2020.
72. In discussions with the author, April 2020.

# 4. THE DOVES TAKE ON THE DRONES

1. Interview with the author, February 2019.
2. A global symbol of peaceful protest, he has been erased in China, including on the largest public social media platform Weibo—although on the anniversary in 2013, one Weibo user managed to slip past the censors by replacing the tanks in the photo with giant yellow rubber ducks. Consequently, "big yellow duck" was added to the government blacklist.
3. World Bank, *Pathways for Peace: Inclusive Approaches to Preventing Violent Conflict* (Washington, DC: World Bank, 2018), 12.
4. Institute for Economics and Peace, Global *Terrorism Index 2017* (Sydney: IIEP, 2017), 35.
5. Organisation for Economic Co-operation and Development, *States of Fragility 2016: Understanding Violence* (Paris: OECD Publishing, 2016), 16.
6. OECD, 57.
7. Action on Armed Violence, "Explosive violence in 2019," AOAV, 7 January 2020.
8. Philippe Bolopion, "Atrocities as the new normal," Human Rights Watch, 10 December 2018.
9. International Network on Explosive Weapons, "INEW call commentary," accessed January 2020. http://www.inew.org/about-inew/inew-call-commentary/.
10. 5.6 million internally and 6.6 externally displaced, according to Human Rights Watch quoting Syrian Observatory for Human Rights (SOHR), see: "Syria: Events of 2018," Human Rights Watch, accessed December 2019. https://www.hrw.org/world-report/2019/country-

chapters/syria. The Syrian Observatory for Human Rights (SOHR) estimated the death toll since the start of the war to be as high as 511,000 as of March 2018.

11. From March 2011 to March 2020, at the hands of the main perpetrator parties in Syria of which 956 were killed by ISIS, only slightly more than 924 by US-led coalition forces. See: Syrian Network for Human Rights, "Child Death Toll," 24 September 2018. http://sn4hr.org/blog/2018/09/24/child-death-toll/.

12. According to SNHR. See note 11.

13. Afaq Hussain and Riya Sinha, *Trading Confidence: A Compelling Case for Cross Line of Control Trade* (London and New Delhi: BRIEF and Conciliation Resources, 2016).

14. Council on Foreign Relations, "Women's Participation in Peace Processes," CFR, 30 January 2019. https://www.cfr.org/interactive/womens-participation-in-peace-processes.

15. Zoë Gorman and Grégory Chauzal, "Establishing a regional security architecture in the Sahel," *SIPRI Backgrounders*, Stockholm International Peace Research Institute, 25 June 2018. https://www.sipri.org/commentary/topical-backgrounder/2018/establishing-regional-security-architecture-sahel. See also: Kevin Sieff, "The world's most dangerous U.N. mission," *Washington Post*, 17 February 2017.

16. International Alert, *If Victims Become Perpetrators: Factors Contributing to Vulnerability and Resilience to Violent Extremism in the Central Sahel* (London: International Alert, June 2018).

17. Bate Felix and Aaron Ross, "U.N. says Malian forces executed 12 civilians at a market," *Reuters*, 26 June 2018.

18. Story told at the RISING 19 Global Peace Forum, Coventry, 14–16 November 2019, attended by the author.

19. Keir Mudie, "Sadiq Khan will use Glasgow method to beat knife crime and clean up London's violent streets," *Mirror*, 22 September 2018.

20. Michelle Cottle, "How Parkland students changed the gun debate," *Atlantic*, 18 February 2018.

21. Emily Witt, "How the survivors of Parkland began the Never Again movement," *New Yorker*, 19 February 2018.

22. Michael Silberman, "Can NGOs and social movements be authentic allies?," openDemocracy, 28 January 2020.

23. Nicole Gaudiano and Fredreka Schouten, "Gun-control groups team with students to turn Parkland shooting anguish into activism," *USA Today*, 15 December 2019.

24. Ruth Igielnik and Anna Brown, "Key takeaways on Americans' views of guns and gun ownership," Pew Research Center, 22 June 2017.

25. Total gun violence deaths: 15,348 plus 24,090 suicides in 2019; see: "Gun Violence, Past Tolls," Gun Violence Archive, data sources verified, 7 April 2020.

26. John Foley, "Exclusive—FedEx drops NRA deal by snail-mail," *Reuters*, 30 October 2018.

27. BBC News, "President Obama tears up during gun control speech," YouTube, posted 5 January 2016. https://www.youtube.com/watch?reload=9&v=ZJCiDrqjjz8.

28. Darran Simon, "Trayvon Martin's death sparked a movement that lives on five years later," CNN, 27 February 2017.

29. Black Lives Matter, "Her Story," accessed January 2020. https://blacklivesmatter.com/herstory/.

30. Based on numbers participating in protests across the US, according to a range of polling data sources, as synthesised here: Larry Buchanan, Quoctrung Bui, and Jugal K. Patel, "Black Lives Matter may be the largest movement in U.S. History," *New York Times*, 3 July 2020.

31. Patrisse Khan-Cullors, "Q&A: Patrisse Khan-Cullors: 'My favourite word? Freedom,'" interview by Rosanna Greenstreet, *Guardian*, 24 March 2018.

32. Frank Leon Roberts, "How Black Lives Matter changed the way Americans fight for freedom," ACLU, 13 July 2018.

33. Data released according to a 2016 study for the National Bureau of Economic Research states that roughly 6,000 Tunisians have left home to join ISIS ranks; see: Ian Bremmer, "The top 5 countries where ISIS gets its foreign recruits," *Time*, 14 April 2017.

34. According to the Global Peace Index the total global cost of conflict was US$14.3 trillion in 2016. That is eleven times the size of total foreign direct investment. See: Institute for Economics & Peace, *Global Peace Index 2017: Measuring Peace in a Complex World* (Sydney: IEP, June 2017), 5.

35. World spending on the military is now 76 percent higher than the post–Cold War low in 1998. The US remained by far the largest spender and spent almost as much on its military in 2018 as the next eight largest-spending countries combined. "The increase in US spending was driven by the implementation from 2017 of new arms procurement programmes under the Trump administration," says Dr Aude Fleurant, director of the SIPRI AMEX program. China, the second-largest spender in the world, increased its military expenditure by 5.0 percent to $250 billion in 2018, the twenty-fourth consecutive year of increase. See: SIPRI, "World military expenditure grows to $1.8 trillion in 2018," SIPRI for the media, 29 April 2019.

36. Institute for Economics and Peace, Global *Terrorism Index 2017*, 73.

37. Lindsey Doyle, "The Global Fragility Act of 2019 (GFA)," InterAction, 28 May 2019.

38. Included in the 2018 *Merriam-Webster's Dictionary*.

39. Pieter D. Wezeman, Aude Fleurant, Alexandra Kuimova, Nan Tian, and Siemon T.Wezeman, "Trends in international arms transfers, 2018," *SIPRI Factsheets* (Stockholm: SIPRI, March 2019), 1.

40. SIPRI, "Global arms trade: USA increases dominance; arms flows to the Middle East surge, says SIPRI," SIPRI, 11 March 2019.

41. Saferworld, "Landmark decision from the UK Court of Appeal: Secretary of State acted irrationally and unlawfully with respect to arms exports to Saudi Arabia," *Saferworld*, 20 June 2019.

42. World Bank, *Pathways for Peace* , 154.

43. United Nations Environment Programme, *From Conflict to Peacebuilding: The Role of Natural Resources and the Environment* (Nairobi: UNEP, February 2009), 8.

44. Izzeldin Abuelaish, *I Shall Not Hate: A Gaza Doctor's Journey on the Road to Peace and Human Dignity* (New York: Bloomsbury, 2012).

45. Izzeldin Abuelaish, "Bringing a heavy dose of hope," accessed February 2020. https://izzeldin-abuelaish.com/cmap-dr-izzeldin-abuelaish-bringing-a-heavy-dose-of-hope/.

# 5. SEEDS OF HOPE AMONG DISPLACED LIVES

1. She was at the North East Refugee Service supporting refugees in the North East of England.

2. Alf Dubs, "We simply can't turn our backs on vulnerable refugee children," *Guardian*, 10 January 2020.

3. Dubs.

4. Interview with author, Cambridge, UK, March 2019. For more, see Louisa Waugh's blog, 31 December 2019 at https://www.the-waugh-zone.org/.

5. UNHCR, *Global Trends: Forced Displacement in 2019* (Copenhagen: UNHCR, 2020), 2.

6. UNHCR, "Worldwide displacement tops 70 million, UN refugee chief urges greater solidarity in response," UNHCR press release, 19 June 2019.

7. In 2018, the US received the highest number of new individual applications for asylum (254,300), followed by Peru (192,500), Germany (161,900), France (114,500), and Turkey (83,800). See: UNHCR, *Global Trends*.

8. Andrew Jack, "Refugee Forum highlights slow progress on forced migration," *Financial Times*, 29 December 2019.

9. Jack.

10. Amnesty International, "Canada's win-win solution for welcoming refugees," accessed January 2020. https://www.amnesty.org/en/i-welcome-community-2/stories-of-welcome/community-sponsorship-in-canada/.

11. From 175 countries, settling in 160 cities. See: Government of Canada, "Refugees and asylum: Thank you Canada: Privately-sponsored refugees from coast to coast," 9 April 2019. https://www.canada.ca/en/immigration-refugees-citizenship/services/refugees/40-years-psr.html.
12. Amnesty International, "Canada's win-win solution."
13. Tom Rowley, "A Welsh town shows Britain a new way to welcome refugees," *Economist*, 5 July 2018.
14. Her full name is withheld to protect her identity and privacy. To read more, see: Lin Taylor, "Virtuous circle: Rescued refugee seeks to save others," Thomson Reuters Foundation, 1 August 2019.
15. Andy May, "Neil Jameson CBE, Citizens UK founder and executive director, to step down in August 2018," Citizens UK website, 14 December 2017.
16. See Paolo Freire, *Pedagogy of the Oppressed* (London: Penguin, 1996—first published in Portuguese in 1968) and Augusto Boal's Theatre of the Oppressed series of theatre analyses and critiques first developed in the 1950s.
17. Interview with the authors, March 2020.
18. Didier Caluwaerts and Kris Deschouwer, "Building bridges across political divides: Experiments on deliberative democracy in deeply divided Belgium," *European Political Science Review* vol. 6, no. 3, August 2014.
19. Carolyne Abdullah, Christopher F. Karpowitz, and Chad Raphael, "Equity and Inclusion in Online Community Forums: An Interview with Steven Clift," Journal of Public Deliberation vol. 12, no. 2, 13 October 2016, 5.
20. Michele Gelfand, "Authoritarians thrive on fear. We need to help people feel safe," *Guardian*, 2 January 2020. Figures from Pew Research Center findings: Jynnah Radford, "Key findings about US immigrants," Pew Research Center, 17 June 2019.
21. In November 2019.
22. Aljazeera, "European Commission takes Hungary to court over migrant law," Aljazeera.com News, 16 July 2019.
23. Amnesty International, "France: Man who gave tea to migrants acquitted of baseless charges," Amnesty International, 21 November 2019.
24. In July, Amnesty International issued a report documenting the Trump administration's use of the criminal justice system to threaten, intimidate, and punish activists, lawyers, journalists, and humanitarian volunteers from challenging—or simply documenting—the systematic human rights violations that US authorities have committed against migrants and asylum seekers. Erika Guevara-Rosas, Americas director at Amnesty International, said: "The Trump administration is wrong to try to prosecute people who are only trying to save lives. By threatening Dr Warren with a decade in prison, the US government sought to criminalise compassion and weaponize the deadly desert against people who make the perilous journey to the United States in search of safety." See: Amnesty International, *USA: 'Saving Lives Is Not a Crime': Politically Motivated Legal Harassment against Migrant Human Rights Defenders by the USA* (Amnesty International: July 2019).
25. UNHCR, *Desperate Journeys: Refugees and Migrants Arriving in Europe and at Europe's borders* (Geneva, January 2019).
26. Peter Martin, "What working on a Mediterranean rescue boat taught me about the politics of asylum," *New Statesman*, 31 March 2019.
27. Doctors Without Borders, "Mediterranean: MSF rescue ship Aquarius forced to terminate operations," 6 December 2018. https://www.doctorswithoutborders.org/what-we-do/news-stories/news/mediterranean-msf-rescue-ship-aquarius-forced-terminate-operations.
28. Peter Martin, "In the new climate of fear, our rescue boat turned away from people drowning," *New Statesman*, 27 June 2018.
29. Jo Cox MP, maiden speech to the House of Commons, Hansard vol.596, col.675, 17 June 2016.
30. Interview with the authors, 2020.
31. More in Common, *Attitudes Towards National Identity, Immigration and Refugees in Germany* (London and Berlin: Purpose Europe/More in Common, July 2017), 5.

32. Charlotte Edmond, "84 percent of refugees live in developing countries," World Economic Forum website, 20 June 2017.
33. Thanassis Cambanis, "Syria's Humanitarians Are Going Broke," Foreignpolicy.com, 29 June 2015.
34. G. Hassan, L. J. Kirmayer, A. MekkiBerrada, C. Quosh, R. el Chammay, J. B. Deville-Stoetzel, A. Youssef, H. Jefee-Bahloul, A. Barkeel-Oteo, A. Coutts, S. Song, and P. Ventevogel, *Culture, Context and the Mental Health and Psychosocial Wellbeing of Syrians: A Review for Mental Health and Psychosocial Support Staff Working with Syrians Affected by Armed Conflict*, (Geneva: UNHCR, 2015), 39.
35. Data reported to UN Office for the Coordination of Humanitarian Affairs (OCHA) Financial Tracking Service in: Development Initiatives, *Global Humanitarian Assistance Report 2017* (Bristol: Development Initiatives, 2017), 73.
36. Danny Sriskandarajah, "Five things international NGOs are blamed for," CIVICUS, 13 June 2016. https://www.civicus.org/index.php/media-resources/op-eds/858-five-things-international-ngos-are-blamed-for.
37. Cambanis, "Syria's Humanitarians Are Going Broke."
38. Cindy Chungong, "Beyond the media frenzy, Boko Haram survivors need real support," International Alert, 14 April 2018. https://www.international-alert.org/blogs/beyond-media-frenzy-boko-haram-survivors-need-real-support. The author visited the displaced people's camps in Maiduguri in June 2018, with Cindy Chungong, then head of International Alert Nigeria.
39. Not his real name.
40. Karen McVeigh, "UN states agree historic global deal to manage migration crisis," *Guardian*, 10 December 2018.
41. The US described the pact as "an effort by the United Nations to advance global governance at the expense of the sovereign right of states." McVeigh "UN states agree historic global deal."
42. UNHCR, "UN Human Rights Committee decision on climate change is a wake-up call according to UNHCR," UNHCR press release, 24 January 2020.
43. Kanta Kumari Rigaud et al., Groundswell: Preparing for Internal Climate Migration, (Washington, DC: World Bank, 2018), xvii.

# 6. THE 99 PERCENT FIGHTS BACK

1. After a long period of being pushed off the international agenda, there has been some renewed progress on an international framework for accountability on transnational companies. One important step was the UN adopting the "protect, respect, remedy" framework in 2008, and then the Guiding Principles for Business and Human Rights in 2011—the first official UN human rights corporate responsibility initiative. At the core of the approach is: the duty of government to protect human rights; the corporate responsibility to respect human rights; and the people's ability to seek remedy from corporate-linked human rights abuse. And crucially, this includes the notion of extraterritorial obligations including for transnational companies and their corporate supply chains. So while the approach has no legislative power and has been criticised as lacking bite and power, it does represent a significant step that UN member states (as well as civil society and forward-thinking businesses) have started to recognise the need to go further to assert responsibility in global supply chains. For more on this see: Office of the United Nations High Commissioner for Human Rights, *Guiding Principles on Business and Human Rights: Implementing the United Nations "Protect, Respect and Remedy" Framework* (Geneva: United Nations, 2011). NGOs and trade unions have also been involved in work in this area by the OECD and EU.
2. To explore this in greater detail and for more on the wider story of Fairtrade see: Harriet Lamb, *Fighting the Banana Wars and Other Fairtrade Battles* (London: Random House, 2008).

3. Fairtrade International, "Fairtrade Global Sales Overview," https://www.fairtrade.net/impact/global-sales-overview.
4. Fairtrade International, "Fairtrade Impact." https://www.fairtrade.net/impact.
5. Fairtrade International, "New guidance from Fairtrade boosts action to protect farmers and workers during Covid-19 pandemic," 1 April 2020.
6. SOMO research article, April 1990, quoting *Manager Magazine* no. 4, 1990.
7. Fairtrade Foundation, "New EU Procurement Directives and Fairtrade," Fairtrade Foundation, 2014.
8. Malcolm Gladwell, *The Tipping Point: How Little Things Can Make a Big Difference* (New York: Little, Brown and Company, 2000).
9. Peter Chapman, "Review of 'Cocoa,' by Kristy Leissle," *Financial Times*, 12 February 2018.
10. Barry Callebaut Group, "Full-Year Results Fiscal Year 2018/19 of the Barry Callebaut Group: Press release," 6 November 2019.
11. Make Chocolate Fair, "Cocoa prices and income of farmers," European Make Chocolate Fair Campaign, accessed December 2019. https://makechocolatefair.org/issues/cocoa-prices-and-income-farmers-0.
12. School of Public Health and Tropical Medicine, Tulane University, *Survey Research on Child Labor in West African Cocoa Growing Areas* (New Orleans: Tulane University, 2015).
13. STOP THE TRAFFIK, *Dark Chocolate: Understanding Human Trafficking in the Chocolate Supply Chain* (London: STOP THE TRAFFIK, 2018).
14. True Price, *Cocoa Farmer Income: The Household Income of Cocoa Farmers in Côte d'Ivoire and Strategies for Improvement* (Amsterdam/Bonn: True Price/Fairtrade International, April 2018).
15. Brennan Weiss, "Ghana is safe and stable, but its young people are still risking their lives to cross to Europe," *Quartz Africa*, 13 June 2017.
16. E. Higonnet, M. Bellantonio, and G. Hurowitz, *Chocolate's Dark Secret* (Washington, DC: Mighty Earth, 2017).
17. International Cocoa Organization, *Declaration of the Fourth World Cocoa Conference, Berlin* (Abidjan: ICCO, May 2018).
18. For more on the work of the Global Living Wage Coalition and their methodology see: https://www.globallivingwage.org/.
19. A. Rusman et al., *Cocoa Farmer Income. The Household Income of Cocoa Farmers in Côte d'Ivoire and Strategies for Improvement* (Bonn/Amsterdam: True Price/Fairtrade International).
20. The principles for how this could work in practice have been pioneered by campaigners on other products. For example, civil society has been in the vanguard of securing arrangements that manage the EU's trade to ensure that only timber from sustainable sources is imported from developing countries, and timber illegally logged in rainforests is kept out through the innovative Forest Law Enforcement, Governance and Trade (FLEGT) scheme. Overseen by a collaboration between governments, business, and civil society in both importing and exporting countries, it illustrates how social and environmental aims can be reconciled with economic ones, without this turning into a punitive block on developing countries' exports.
21. World Bank, *Global Economic Prospects: June 2020* (Washington, DC: World Bank, 2020).
22. For more on this idea see: Christophe Guilluy, *Twilight of the Elites: Prosperity, Periphery and the Future of France* (New Haven: Yale University Press, 2019).
23. Joseph Stiglitz, "Conquering the great divide," *Finance & Development* (Washington: IMF, September 2020).
24. UN Department of Economic and Social Affairs, *World Social Report 2020: Inequality in a Rapidly Changing World* (New York: UN DESA, 2020), 1.
25. UN DESA, 2020, see note 24. It is important to note this increase in inequality has not been the case everywhere; there is no law dictating it has to be so. For example, most countries in Latin America and the Caribbean have become more equal since 1990—admittedly often from very unequal starting points, as have a number of countries across Africa and Asia. It is

possible this may not last in Latin America as governments that implemented redistributive policies in countries like Brazil and Bolivia have given way to governments that reject these policies.

26. Facundo Alvaredo, Lucas Chancel, Thomas Piketty, Emmanuel Saez, and Gabriel Zucman, *World Inequality Report 2018* (Paris: World Inequality Lab, 2017).

27. Alvaredo et al.

28. Oxfam International, "World's billionaires have more wealth than 4.6 billion people," Oxfam International Press Release, Nairobi, 20 January 2020.

29. Ortenca Aliaj, "Ray Dalio: Tackle inequality or face a violent revolution," *Financial Times*, 5 November 2019.

30. Although it was worth noting that the rate of increase in inequality slowed after the 2008 crash as overall economic growth slowed. It is unclear what the long-term economic impact of the Covid-19-linked recession will be, but many projections estimate that is likely to exacerbate inequality without major change in policy frameworks.

31. World Bank, "The World Bank in Republic of Korea: Overview," World Bank, April 2018. Already a poor country, its economy was left shattered further after the Korean War. Real GDP grew by 10 percent a year on average between 1962 and 1994. https://www.worldbank.org/en/country/korea/overview.

32. Richard Baldwin, *The Great Convergence: Information Technology and the New Globalization* (Cambridge, MA: Harvard University Press, 2016).

33. UNDP, *Human Development Report 2019—Beyond Income, Beyond Averages, Beyond Today: Inequalities in Human Development in the 21st Century* (New York: UNDP, 2019).

34. UN Inter-agency Group for Child Mortality Estimation, *Levels and Trends in Child Mortality: Report 2018—Estimates Developed by the UN Inter-Agency Group for Child Mortality Estimation*, (New York: UN-IGME, 2018).

35. UN DESA, *World Social Report 2020*.

36. UNDP, *Human Development Report 2019*.

37. Thomas Piketty, *Capital and Ideology* (Cambridge, MA: Harvard University Press, 2020).

38. Kevin Rawlinson, "UK Uncut protesters blockade Vodafone stores across country," *Guardian*, 14 June 2014.

39. Tax Justice Network, "Transfer Pricing," TJN, accessed January 2020. https://www.taxjustice.net/topics/corporate-tax/transfer-pricing/.

40. Nicholas Shaxson, "How to make multinationals pay their share, and cut tax havens out of the picture," *Guardian*, 27 January 2020.

41. Patricia Cohen, "Wealth inequality rising fast, Oxfam says, faulting tax havens," *Boston Globe*, 18 January 2016.

42. Bibi van der Zee, "Holy cow, taxman! Featherweight activist battles the dodgers," *Guardian*, 7 July 2011.

43. OECD/G20 Base Erosion and Profit Shifting Project, *Addressing the Tax Challenges of the Digitalisation of the Economy: Policy Note* (Paris: OECD, 2019).

44. The European Court of Human Rights, *In the Case of Steel and Morris v. the United Kingdom* (Final Judgment, Strasbourg, 15 February 2005, Para. 89).

45. Sarah O'Connor, "One in 10 UK workers in insecure employment, says TUC," *Financial Times*, 16 December 2016.

46. TUC, *Living on the Edge* (London: TUC, 2016).

47. TUC, *Organising Precarious Workers: Trade Union and Co-operative Strategies: A report for the TUC from Co-operatives UK and the Co-operative College* (London: TUC, 2017).

48. Yvonne Roberts, "The tiny union beating the gig economy giants," *Guardian*, 1 July 2018.

49. Roberts.

50. Living Wage Foundation, "What Is the Real Living Wage?," Living Wage Foundation, accessed November 2019. https://www.livingwage.org.uk/what-real-living-wage.

51. Living Wage Foundation, "Women continue to be hit hardest by low wages in the UK," LWF Press release, 10 November 2017.

52. Ben Jackson and Steve Percy, "A Living income for cocoa farmers: How we can secure change in the global chocolate business," unpublished report prepared for Fairtrade Foundation, 2019.
53. Tom Liacas, "Fight for $15: Directed-network campaigning in action," MobLab website, 8 September 2016.
54. Liacas.
55. For a great, pithy history of the cooperative movement, see: Ed Mayo, *A Short History of Co-operation and Mutuality*, (Manchester: Co-operatives UK, 2017).
56. Robin Murray, "Global civil society and the rise of the civil economy," in Sabine Selchow, Mary Kaldor, and Henrietta Moore, *Global Civil Society 2012: Ten Years of Critical Reflection* (London: Palgrave Macmillan, 2012), 147.
57. United Nation Department of Economic and Social Affairs, Division for Social Policy and Development, *Measuring the Size and Scope of the Cooperative Economy: Results of the 2014 Global Census on Co-operatives* (New York: UN, 2014).
58. Peter Utting, Nadine van Dijk, and Marie-Adélaïde Matheï, *Social and Solidarity Economy: Is There a New Economy in the Making?* (Geneva: United Nations Research Institute for Social Development, 2014).
59. Utting, van Dijk, and Matheï.
60. Social Platform, "Maximising the potential of social economy and social enterprises: Contribution to the plenary session on the importance of social economy, of the EU Employment, Social Policy, Health and Consumer Affairs Council meeting," Milan, July 2014.
61. Utting, van Dijk, and Matheï, *Social and Solidarity Economy*.
62. Interview with the author, February 2020.
63. Utting, van Dijk, and Matheï, *Social and Solidarity Economy*, 27.
64. Robin Murray, *Danger and Opportunity: Crisis and the New Economy* (London: Nesta/Young Foundation, 2009).
65. Brian Groom, "A third of start-ups aim for social good," *Financial Times*, 15 June 2018.
66. Simon Borkin, *Platform co-operatives—solving the capital conundrum* (London: Nesta and Co-operatives UK, 2019).
67. Co-operatives UK, "New pilot 'accelerator' launched for UK Platform Co-operatives," Co-operatives UK press release, 20 March 2018.
68. Michelle Stearn, "Green Taxi Cooperative: Building an alternative to the corporate 'Sharing Economy,'" The Democracy Collaborative Blogspot, 19 May 2016.
69. David Barnett, "Can we trust Wikipedia? 1.4 billion people can't be wrong," *Independent*, 18 February 2018.
70. Robin Murray, "Global Civil Society and the rise of the civil economy," OpenDemocracy, 3 May 2012.
71. For John's seminal analysis stemming from his time at the Highlander Center, see: John Gaventa, *Power and Powerlessness: Quiescence and Rebellion in an Appalachian Valley* (Urbana: University of Illinois Press, 1980). For his more recent reflection on the post-Trump context see: John Gaventa, "Power and powerlessness in an Appalachian valley," *The Journal of Peasant Studies* vol. 46, no. 3, 2019. And for more global work: John Gaventa and Rajesh Tandon, *Globalising Citizens: New Dynamics of Inclusion and Exclusion* (London and New York: Zed Books, 2010). See also: Jodie Thorpe and John Gaventa, "Democratising Economic Power: The Potential for Meaningful Participation in Economic Governance and Decision-Making," IDS Working Paper 535 (Brighton: Institute of Development Studies, 2020).
72. John Duda, "The Italian region where co-ops produce a third of its GDP," *YES!*, 5 July 2016.
73. Shannon Rieger, "Reducing Economic Inequality through Democratic Worker-Ownership" (New York: The Century Foundation, August 2016).
74. James Sullivan, "Dairy co-op raises €6m through Parmesan wheels," *Co-op News*, 17 February 2016.
75. International Labour Organization, "The COVID-19 outbreak update from Legacoop, Italy," ILO, 27 March 2020. https://www.ilo.org/global/topics/cooperatives/news/WCMS_739990/lang--en/index.htm.

# 7. A TALE OF TWO PANDEMICS

1. Steven Robins, "'Long live Zackie, long live': AIDS activism, science and citizenship after apartheid," *Journal of Southern African Studies* vol. 30, no. 3, 2004.
2. Mark Heywood, *Get Up! Stand Up! Personal Journeys towards Social Justice* (Cape Town: Tafelberg, 2017), 109. Mark's gripping memoir of his lifelong involvement in citizen struggles against apartheid and for social justice in South Africa since shine an insightful light on what helps and hinders movements' success. He currently edits the online news site on activism and citizen struggles, Maverick Citizen.
3. Interview with the author, January 2020.
4. Action for Southern Africa, "Memorandum submitted by Action for Southern Africa (ACTSA)," *House of Commons Select Committee on International Development Report—HIV/AIDS: The Impact on Social and Economic Development, Appendices to the Minutes of Evidence* (HC 2000-01 (354-II) (London: The Stationery Office, March 2001).
5. Interview with the author, January 2020.
6. Heywood, *Get Up! Stand Up!*, 116.
7. In 1999 General Johann Coetzee, former head of the South African security police, and eight other officers confessed to organizing the bombing on government orders, in return for amnesty from the country's Truth and Reconciliation Commission. There have been persistent allegations that Prime Minister Margaret Thatcher's government had been informed who was responsible for the bombing by British intelligence but decided to allow them to escape back to South Africa to avoid a confrontation with the apartheid regime.
8. Samanta Sen, "British NGOs support Pretoria against pharmaceutical firms," *Inter Press Service*, 16 April 2001.
9. ACTSA, "Memorandum submitted by Action for Southern Africa."
10. ACTSA.
11. Joint open letter from Mark Heywood (TAC) and Aditi Sharma (ACTSA), February 2001—published with a call to action by the Africa Policy Information Center, Washington, DC. http://www.africafocus.org/docs01/tac0102.php.
12. Heywood, *Get Up! Stand Up!*, 116.
13. Interview with the author.
14. Heywood, *Get Up! Stand Up!*, 117.
15. Anthony Barnett, "My investigation into a US trade deal shows it really could cost the NHS millions," *Guardian*, 27 November 2019.
16. Elisabeth Mahase, "NHS and drug prices could be included in US-UK trade deal, leaked documents suggest," *British Medical Journal*, 27 November 2019.
17. Aitor Hernández-Marales, "Germany confirms that Trump tried to buy firm working on coronavirus vaccine," *Politico*, 15 March 2020.
18. Nabil Ahmed and Anna Marriott, "A call for a people's vaccine," *BMJ Opinion*, 16 July 2020.
19. Ahmed and Marriott.
20. Oxfam International, "World leaders unite in call for a people's vaccine against COVID-19," Press Release, *Medium*, 4 May 2020.
21. Oxfam International, "World leaders unite."
22. Peter Beaumont, "'Landmark moment': 156 countries agree to Covid vaccine allocation deal," *Guardian*, 21 September 2020.
23. Anna Gross and Jim Pickard, "Johnson to boost WHO backing with £571m vaccine pledge," *Financial Times*, 25 September 2020.
24. Emily Rauhala and Yasmeen Abutaleb, "U.S. says it won't join WHO-linked effort to develop, distribute coronavirus vaccine," *Washington Post*, 1 September 2020.
25. Ahmed and Marriott, "A call for a people's vaccine."
26. World Trade Organization, *Doha, WTO Ministerial: Declaration on the TRIPS agreement and public health*, 14 November 2001.
27. UNAIDS, *Communities at the Centre: Global AIDS Update 2019* (Geneva: UNAIDS, 2019).

28. UNAIDS, "Country Profile: South Africa," UNAIDS, accessed December 2019. https://www.unaids.org/en/regionscountries/countries/southafrica.
29. UNAIDS.
30. Steven Robins, and Bettina von Lieres, "AIDS activism and globalisation from below: Occupying new spaces of citizenship in post-apartheid South Africa," *IDS Bulletin: New Democratic Spaces* vol. 35, no. 2, 2004. They draw on: Arjun Appadurai, "Grassroots globalization and the research imagination," in Joan Vincent (ed.), *The Anthropology of Politics: A Reader in Ethnography, Theory and Critique* (Malden MA: Blackwell Publishers, 2002).

# 8. THE PAST AS PROLOGUE TO OUR FUTURE

1. Evelyn Sharp, *Unfinished Adventure: Selected Reminiscences from an Englishwoman's Life* (London: Faber and Faber, 2009; first published 1933).
2. Mike Miller, "Alinsky for the Left: The Politics of Community Organizing," *Dissent*, Winter 2010.
3. For 1960s figures, see: Roger Undy, "Trade Union Organisation: 1945 to 1995," *Britain at Work: Voices from the Workplace 1945–1995* (London: London Metropolitan University 2012). http://www.unionhistory.info/britainatwork/narrativedisplay.php?type=tradeunionorganisation. For contemporary numbers see: Carl Roper, "Trade union membership is growing, but there's still work to do," TUC, 2018. https://www.tuc.org.uk/blogs/trade-union-membership-growing-there percentE2 percent80 percent99s-still-work-do.
4. Timothy J. Hatton and George R. Boyer, "Unemployment and the UK labour market before, during and after the Golden Age," *European Review of Economic History* vol. 9, no. 1, 2005, 35–60. It was also a period of increasing economic productivity—an issue all sides agree is a chronic problem facing Britain today (as well as, to some extent, the United States). Of course, this is not to say trade unions were the only factor at work in this period of sustained economic growth. However, it is important to rebalance the airbrushing out of the role of the trade unions in securing significant advances for workers and the economy during this period from the highly selective nostalgic populist narratives of today.
5. Robert D. Putnam, *Bowling Alone: Collapse and Revival of American Community* (New York: Simon & Schuster, 2000), 112.
6. BBC News, 24 October 1984. Clip available at: https://www.youtube.com/watch?v=XYOj_6OYuJc.
7. Simon Garfield, "For Bob Geldof, Live Aid changed everything," *Observer*, 17 October 2004.
8. Maggie Black, *A Cause for Our Times: Oxfam—The First Fifty Years* (Oxford: Oxford University Press, 1992), 283.
9. Dave Morris, "Ann Pettifor makes the case for the Green New Deal," *Financial News*, 14 October 2019.
10. Caroline Hallemann, "Why Diana's fight against landmines was so remarkable," *Town and Country*, 18 August 2017.
11. Quoted in Rajni Bakshi, *An Economics for Well-Being* (Mumbai and Bangalore: Centre for Education and Documentation, 2007).
12. An archive copy of the website can be found here: https://web.archive.org/web/19991127195837/http://www.seattle99.org:80/.
13. Ed Pilkington, "Avaaz—the online activist network that is targeting Rupert Murdoch's bid," *Guardian*, 24 April 2011.
14. Robert Butler, "The man behind Avaaz," *1843 Magazine*, May/June 2013.
15. Andrew Anthony, "Ricken Patel: The global leader of online protest," *Observer*, 17 March 2013.
16. Interview with the authors, January 2020.
17. From the OPEN website—an international network bringing such digital-first campaign groups together. See: https://the-open.net/network#dna.

## 9. THE THREE WHEELS OF CHANGE

1. Rebecca Solnit, *Hope in the Dark: Untold Histories, Wild Possibilities* (Edinburgh: Canongate, 2016), 3–4.
2. Solnit, *Hope in the Dark*, xii.
3. George Lakey, *How We Win: A Guide to Nonviolent Direct-Action Campaigning* (Brooklyn: Melville House, 2018), 23.
4. Michelle Goldberg, "1, 2, 3, 4, Trump Can't Rule Us Anymore," *New York Times*, 21 October 2019.
5. Matt Price, *Engagement Organizing: The Old Art and New Science of Winning Campaigns* (Vancouver: UBC Press, 2017).
6. Jason Mogus and Tom Liacas, *Networked Change: How Progressive Campaigns Are Won in the 21st Century* (Vancouver: NetChange, 2016).
7. Mogus and Liacas.
8. For an excellent overview of Crisis Action learnings on coalition working, see: Nick Martlew, *Creative Coalitions: A Handbook for Change* (London: Crisis Actions/Matters of the Earth, 2017). Interactive online version here: https://crisisaction.org/wp-content/pdf/creative-coalitions-a-handbook-for-change.pdf.
9. Erik Olin Wright, "How to be an anticapitalist today," *Jacobin Magazine*, February 2015. For Wright's brilliant analysis and case in full see: Erik Olin Wright, *Envisioning Real Utopias* (London and New York: Verso, 2010).
10. Wright.
11. Neal Lawson, *45° Change: Transforming Society from Below and Above* (London: Compass, 2019).
12. Michael Jacobs, "Capitalism is in crisis. And we cannot get out of it by carrying on as before," *Guardian*, 8 November 2019.
13. For more on Cleveland and wider application of this model see: Ted Howard and Marjorie Kelly, *The Making of a Democratic Economy: How to Build Prosperity for the Many, Not the Few* (San Francisco: Berrett-Koehler, 2019).
14. Thomas M. Hanna and Mathew Lawrence, *Ownership Futures: Towards Democratic Public Ownership in the 21st Century* (London: Common Wealth and Democracy Collaborative, 2020).
15. Michael Edwards, *Civil Society* (Cambridge: Polity, 2009), 84.
16. David Brooks, "Looking to civil society for the values that shape a culture," *Stanford Social Innovation Review*, 14 June 2018.
17. Max Greenwood, "Top New York Times reporter: Twitter 'no longer works' for me," *The Hill*, 22 July 2018.
18. Common Cause Foundation, *Perceptions Matter: The Common Cause UK Values Survey* (London: Common Cause Foundation, 2016). For more on the Common Cause Foundation's work see: https://valuesandframes.org/.

# Index

Abuelaish, Izzeldin, 86
Achmat, Zackie, 138, 139
ACLU (American Civil Liberties Union), 97
Action Aid, 124
Action for Southern Africa (ACTSA), 137–38, 141–43
ACT UP, 142–43, 146, 147
Adams, Richard, 113–14, 115–16
African National Congress (ANC), 141, 196n7
Ahmed, Nabil, 144–45
Algeria, 13, 17
Alinksy, Saul, 153
alliances. *See* collaboration
Alsuleman, Ayham, 95
alternative models, 175–79
Amazon rainforests, 55
American Civil Liberties Union (ACLU), 97
American Petroleum Institute, 45
Amnesty International, 27, 90, 99, 161, 191n24
ANC (African National Congress), 141, 196n7
Anderson, Eric Clinton, 14
anger, 93
Anti-Apartheid Movement, 158–59
anti-globalisation movement, 163–65
antiretroviral drugs (ARVs). *See* HIV/AIDS pandemic

APBI (Association of the British Pharmaceutical Industry), 137–38
Apple analogy, 41–42
Arab Spring, 11–13, 165
Arguedas, Carlos, 110
arms industry, 1–5, 83–85, 156–57. *See also* military expenditures; peace campaigns
ARVs (antiretroviral drugs). *See* HIV/AIDS pandemic
Ashden organization, 56, 63
Asociacíon Bananos Ecológicos de la Línea Noroeste (Banelino), 112–13, 115
al-Assad, Bashar, 67
Association of the British Pharmaceutical Industry (APBI), 137–38
astroturfing, 45
asylum seekers, 97–98. *See also* refugees
Attenborough, Sir David, 41
Australian movements, 166
Austrian movements, 66
authoritarian regimes, 25–26, 83–85
Avaaz, 106, 166

Badasu, Delali Margaret, 117
Bamba, Sindou, 117–18
banana workers, 109–13
Banelino (Asociacíon Bananos Ecológicos de la Línea Noroeste), 112–13, 115
Bangladeshi movements, 56, 178

Basmeh & Zeitooneh (Smiles and Olives), 102–3, 104–5
"battle" instinct, 170–75
Ben Ali, Zine al-Abidine, 12
Berlin protests, 163–64
Bhushan, Chandra, 61–62
Biden, Joe, 144
big pharma, 141–43, 144–45. *See also* HIV/AIDS pandemic
Bindmans (law firm), 2–3
Black Lives Matter (BLM) movement: about, 76–78; climate activists and, 38; protests, ix–x; social media and, 22; supporting Sunrise, 55
Blackrock, 48
Blair, Tony, 162
Blazevic, Sara, 53
BLM. *See* Black Lives Matter (BLM) movement
Body Shop, 160
Boko Haram, 22, 105–6
Bond network, 28, 162
*Bowling Alone* (Putnam), 156
BP (formerly British Petroleum Company), 45
Bradbrook, Gail, 39, 40
Brazilian Amazon killings, 27
Brexit, 19–20, 97
bridges, taking of, 40
#BringBackOurGirls, 22, 105
Bristol Harbor protests, ix–x
Bristow, Giles, 60, 63
British actions. *See* United Kingdom
Brooks, David, 180
Brown, Gordon, 106, 162
BSkyB, 166

C40 gathering, 62
CAAT (Campaign Against the Arms Trade), 84, 85
Caborn, Richard, 141
*cacerolazo* (Chilean protests), 17–19
Cage (organisation), 28
Cambanis, Thanassis, 104
Campact movement, 166
Campaign Against the Arms Trade (CAAT), 84, 85
Campaign for Nuclear Disarmament (CND), 156–57
Campanale, Mark, 47–50
Canada: Leadnow.ca, 166; refugees welcomed in, 89–90, 95–96
Canning Town Group, 41
capitalism: alternatives to, 129–31, 177–79; "Golden Age of," 153–54; Occupy movements, 14–15, 48, 55, 172. *See also* global inequalities
carbon bubble theory, 49
Carbon Tracker, 47–49, 51
CARE, 152
Carney, Mark, 49–50
Catholic Charities, 103
Cayman Islands, 125
celebrities and social movements, 118, 157–60, 162
challenge funds, 106
change: "battle" instinct, 32, 170–75; "belief" principles of practice, 32, 170, 179–82; "build" strategies, 32, 175–79; crises as markers of, 151–52; hope fueling, 32, 169–70, 182; social movements winning with 3.5%, 42–43; yearning for, 20–21. *See also* citizen movements; social movements
Change.org, 100, 166–67
Charity Commission, 28, 159
Charles, Prince of Wales, 62–63
Chenoweth, Erica, 13, 42–43
Chevron, 45
children and young people: abductions of Chibok schoolgirls, 22, 105–6; child labor, 116–18; ISIS attracting youth, 78–79; legislation drafted by students, 37–38; mobilising citizen movements, 21; peace campaigns through technology, 78–79; peace education classes, 102–3; school strikes, 22, 33, 36–38; Syrian conflict and, 67–68, 89–90
Chile's citizen protests, 17–19
chocolate trade, 117–19
Christensen, John, 123–24
Christian Aid, 124
citizen assemblies, 93–94
citizen movements: balancing with traditional NGOs, 25; ballot box compared to, 29–31; common characteristics, 20–22; hope and, 182;

# Index

new generation taking power in, 20–22;
new world order for, 22–25; power of,
7–9; right-wing and authoritarian
responses to, 25–28. *See also* change;
social movements; *specific protests and
movements*
Citizens UK, 90, 93, 95, 128, 153
CIVICUS, 26–27, 36, 103
civility, 181
civil rights movements, 31, 154–55
civil society: climate change and, 36;
commonalities across borders, 144;
defined, 5–6; focusing on global
inequalities, 122–23; pressing issues,
6–7, 31–32; refugees and, 107–8;
tipping point and, 116
Clift, Steven, 96
Climate Change Act (UK), 35
Climate Change Conference talks (COP),
35, 62
climate movement: 350.org, 36–37, 50–53,
55, 60; battle strategies, 171;
community energy groups, 179; conflict
and, 85–86; Extinction Rebellion,
38–42, 43; Global Green New Deal, 55,
62; green justice, 61–63; Green New
Deal, 54, 55, 178; political action,
52–56; public engagement, 56–57;
refugees displaced by, 107; school
strikes, 33, 36–38; urgency of, 33–35.
*See also* fossil fuel
Clinton, Hillary, 50
CND (Campaign for Nuclear
Disarmament), 156–57
Coalition of Ivorian Human Rights Actors
(RAIDH), 117–18
coalitions. *See* collaboration
cocoa farming, 117–19
coffee prices, 112
collaboration: across borders, 161;
approaches to, 173–75, 181; flotilla
approach, 175; power of creativity and,
185n40; technology for, 179
Colorado Rising grassroots group, 45
Colotl, Jessica, 97
Colson, Edward, 1
Columbia's peace process, 71
Common Cause Foundation, 181
commons, governance of, 59

Common Wealth, 178
community energy, 60
Compass think tank, 31
concerts as mass demonstrations, 158, 162
Conciliation Resources, 70–71
conflict diamonds, 85
conflicts: climate and, 85–86;
humanitarian aid and, 66; peace seeking
after (*see* peace campaigns); record
number of, 66; sources of, 66
contact democracy, 96
cooperation. *See* collaboration
cooperatives, 129–31, 132–35, 175
COP (Climate Change Conference talks),
35, 62
Corporate Europe Observatory, 46
COSATU (South African trade union), 143
Costa Rican banana workers, 109–11
Côte d'Ivoire's cocoa farmers, 117–18
counter-globalisation movement, 163–65
Covax initiative, 145
Covid-19 pandemic: Black Lives Matter
protests and, x–xi; climate change
threat rising with, 42; COP26 and,
62–63; economic impact of, 119–23;
environmental protection laws
suspended during, 188n70; globally
connected society and, 6–7, 147–48;
inequality and, 194n30; migrants' vital
role in, 98; national populism and, 80;
public fundraising and, 104; struggles
with vaccine nationalism, 144–45;
unemployment rates during, 21
Cox, Jo, 100
credit union movement, 131, 178
criminalisation of compassion, 98–100
Crisis Action, 174
Criticalmass.com, 51
Crowther, Bruce, 114
cyber-campaigns, 165–67
Czechoslovakian movements, 155

d'Aguila, Raul, 115
Dalio, Ray, 121
Dammers, Jerry, 158–59
Daqneesh, Omran, 67–68
Davos, World Economic Forum at, 23, 165
Defence Export Services Organisation
(DESO), 4

Democracy Collaborative, 178
Democratic Republic of the Congo, 85
Dent, Martin, 159
de Pena, Marike, 112–13, 115
DESO (Defence Export Services Organisation), 4
developing countries: blaming "the frontier" for inequalities, 122; foreign debts crippling, 159–60. *See also specific countries*
Diana, Princess, 160
digital technology. *See* technology
directed-network campaigns, 128–29, 172
disabled people's rights movement, 181
disposable plastic bottles, 155
District Mineral Foundation (DMF), 61–62
diversity of voices, 173–75
divisiveness in politics, 180–81
Dlamini, Gugu, 138–39
DMF (District Mineral Foundation), 61–62
Draghi, Mario, 16
Dreamers, 97
Drobac, Peter, 131
Dubs, Alf, 87
Durrell, Gerald, 34

ECGD (Export Credit Guarantee Department), 83
economic alternatives, 177–79
E-Democracy, 96
Edwards, Michael, 23, 180
EENews.net, 49
Egeland, Jan, 89
electoral politics, 29–31
empowerment, 180–81
*The End of Nature* (McKibben), 49
energy gardens, 60
engagement organising, 172
Engel, Eliot, 82
Engler, Mark, 29
Engler, Paul, 29
environmental issues. *See* climate movement
Ethiopian famine movement, 157–58
Ethiopian refugees, 101
Ettadhamen data collection, 78–79
euro crisis, 16
European Code of Conduct, 84
European Green Deal, 42

European Occupy movement, 14–17
European Union and Fairtrade, 116
#*EvasionMasiva,* 17–19
Everytown for Gun Safety, 75
"exhausted middle," 100
Export Credit Guarantee Department (ECGD), 83
#ExtendTheWelcome campaign, 95
Extinction Rebellion (XR), 38–42, 43
Exxon/ExxonMobil, 45, 46, 47

Fairbnb.coop, 132
Fairtrade global movement: banana workers and, 110–13; changing government and businesses, 115–16; development of, 24, 113–15; Fairtrade Towns, 114; highlighting inequalities, 116–19; single-mindedness of, 34; success of, 161, 175
faith communities, 93–94
fear and refugees, 96–98
feminism movement, 154, 156
Fernandez, Sabrina, 75
Fight for $15 campaign, 172, 175
Finance Uncovered, 124
financial cooperatives, 131
financial crisis of 2008, 14, 35, 151–52, 162. *See also* Occupy movements
financial investments in peace, 79–83
Finegan, Benjamin, 55
Finland's carbon neutral goal, 42
Fisher, Dana, 171–72
FLEGT (Forest Law Enforcement, Governance and Trade) scheme, 193n20
flotilla approach to coalitions, 175
Floyd, George, ix–x, 77
FoE (Friends of the Earth), 2, 34–35, 155
Follett, Mary Parker, 185n40
force amplification, 172
Forest Law Enforcement, Governance and Trade (FLEGT) scheme, 193n20
fossil fuel: coal mining communities, 61; divestment movement, 51–52; #FossilFreePolitics, 47; investors in, 47–50; lobbying power of, 44–47; need for non-proliferation treaty, 50; subsidies for, 43–44
Foster, Anne Lee, 45

Francis, Pope, 108
Freedom House, 25–26
*Freedom in the World 2020*, 25–26
French protests, 17, 155
#FridaysforFuture, 37
Friedman, Milton, 18
Friends of the Earth (FoE), 2, 34–35, 155
"the frontier," 122
full-stack campaigns, 173

G7 gatherings, 163
G8 Summit, 124, 162–63
Garza, Alicia, 76–77
gas companies, 46. *See also* fossil fuel
Gaventa, John, 133
Gaza blockade, 174
Geldof, Sir Bob, 118, 158
Germany: Campact movement, 166; civilian harm, 66; refugee crisis and, 101, 107; *Seefuchs* boat, 99–100
GetUp movement, 166
*gilets jaunes* protests, 17
Glasgow's violent crime, 74
Global Fragility Act, 82
Global Green New Deal, 55, 62
global inequalities: alternatives to market capitalism, 129–31; banana workers, 109–13; chocolate trade, 117–19; Covid-19 and, 119–23; financial crash of 2008 and, 121; Global Living Wage Campaign, 118; increases in, 194n30; peace investments, 79–83; precarious workers, 125–28; tax issues, 121, 123–25. *See also* Fairtrade global movement
global issues: "great convergence" trend, 121; interconnectedness, 34. *See also* climate movement; Covid-19 pandemic; HIV/AIDS pandemic; peace campaigns; refugees
Global Peace Index, 81
Global Witness, 55, 86
GlobeScan poll, 42
Go Fossil Free campaign, 51
Gonzalez, Emma, 75
Gordon, Fay, 58
Gore, Al, 33
government, 37–38, 106, 119. *See also* politics; *specific governments*

grassroots activists: international campaigning, 147–48; renewal of, 171, 173; transforming the possible, 35–36. *See also* citizen movements; climate movement
"great convergence," 121
Greek movements, 16, 87–88
Green New Deal, 54, 55, 178
Green Party, 42
Greenpeace, 25, 37, 53, 167
Green Taxi Cooperative, 132
Griffiths, Rachel, 91–92, 93–94
gun reform, 74–76
Gun Violence Archive, 75–76

Haberman, Maggie, 180
Hallisso, Fadi, 102, 104
Halo Trust, 160
hashtag movements, 171; #BringBackOurGirls, 22, 105; *#EvasionMasiva,* 17–19; #ExtendTheWelcome campaign, 95; #FossilFreePolitics, 47; #FridaysforFuture, 37; #MeToo movement, 22, 42; #NeverAgain, 74–76; #ShellKnew exposé, 46; #TeachtheFuture, 37–38; #TheWorld?Refugees, 106. *See also specific hashtag movements*
Heimans, Jeremy, 22
Henderson Global Investors, 48
Henn, Jamie, 50–51
Henry Jackson Society, 5
Herne Hill Welcomes Refugees, 90–91, 95
Heywood, Mark, 24, 139–40, 146–47
"hidden middle," 101
*Hidden Tribes* report (More in Common), 100
HIV/AIDS pandemic: ACTSA protesters, 137–38; arguments for fairness, 141–43; denialism of, 145; drug companies capitulation, 143–44; full-stack campaigning for drug treatments, 173; future eradication of disease, 149; lessons from citizen action, 146–48; mobilising for generic drug availability, 138–41; victories, 145–46
Hollingsworth, Tony, 158–59
Hong Kong, 17

hope for the future, 32, 169–70, 182
Howarth, Catherine, 45
Hughes, Guy, 174
Human Rights Watch, 27, 161
Hungarian criminalisation of compassion, 98
Hungarian NGOs, 26

Ibrahim, Abir Haj, 65, 67–68, 71
Ibrahim, Zamzam, 37–38
ICBL (International Campaign to Ban Landmines), 160
Iceland's citizen protests, 15
I-change (organisation), 79
IMF (International Monetary Fund), 44, 159–60, 163–64
immigration restrictions, 38. *See also* refugees
*An Inconvenient Truth*, 33
Independent Workers Union of Great Britain (IWGB), 127
India: Centre for Science and Environment, 61–62; CIVICUS report on, 26–27; trade and, 70–71
Indignados ("the outraged ones") movement, 16–17
Industrial Areas Foundation, 153
InfluenceMap think tank, 45
*Inside Climate News*, 46
insider-track influencing, 171
Intergovernmental Panel on Climate Chage (IPCC), 35
International Alert, 25, 68–69, 72, 102
International Campaign to Ban Landmines (ICBL), 160
International Criminal Court, 80
International Day of Climate Action, 51
International Monetary Fund (IMF), 44, 159–60, 163–64
international trade rules, 20
international vision. *See* collaboration; global inequalities
IPCC (Intergovernmental Panel on Climate Chage), 35
IPSOS Mori, 42
Iraqi protests, 13
Iraqi refugees, 92
Irish movements, 166
*I Shall Not Hate* (Abuelaish), 86

ISIS, attraction to, 78–79
Islamist extremists, 28
Italy: as anti-immigrant, 19–20, 99–100; cooperatives in, 130; Emilia Romagna's social economy, 134–35
IWGB (Independent Workers Union of Great Britain), 127

Jacobs, Michael, 177
Jameson, Neil, 93
Jeyarajah, Nick, 91–92
jihadists in Mali, 71–73
Johnson, Boris, 5, 97
Joint Chamber of Commerce and Industry (JCCI) for Jammu and Kashmir, 70–71
Jones, Dagan, 40
Jones, Paul Tudor, 121
Joseph Rowntree Charitable Trust (JRCT), 28
Jubilee 2000 campaign, 159–60
*The Jungle* (Sinclair), 153
"just transition," 61

Kagera Co-operative Union, 34
Kendi, Ibram X., x
Kenya's Ushahidi app, 79
Khadhraoui, Rym, 98–99
Khan-Cullors, Patrisse, 77
Kimaro, Raymond, 162
Kimberley Process, 85–86
Kindertransport rescue mission, 87
King, Martin Luther, Jr., 81
King, Sir David, 41
Kingston, Phil, 41
Klein, Naomi, 49
knife crime, 73–74
Kohler, Brian, 61
Kurdi, Alan, 89–92, 106

Lagarde, Christine, 125
lake analogy, 176
Lakey, George, 170
landmines ban, 160
Lankester, Sir Tim, 3–4
LaShelle, Emily, 54
Lawson, Neal, 31, 176
Leadnow.ca, 166
League Party in Italy, 19–20

Lebanon: protests in, 12–13, 17; refugees in, 101–3
legislation drafted by students, 37–38
Leigh, Vivien, 182
Leonard, Annie, 53
letter campaigns, 83–84
lexicographers, 82–83
LGBTQ movement, 170–71, 185n39. *See also* HIV/AIDS pandemic
Liacas, Tom, 129
libel claims, 125–26
lifestyle choices, 56–57
Line of Control, 70–71
Live 8 concerts, 162
Live Aid concerts, 158
living alternatives, 175–79
living wage campaigns, 125–29
localisation of humanitarian aid, 103
London City Airport shutdown, 41
London School of Economics (LSE), 44

Make Poverty History campaign, 162
Malaysian weapons deal, 1–2
Mali peace campaigns, 71–73
Mandela, Nelson, 158–59
March for our Lives movement, 75
Margolin, Jamie, 54
Marjory Stoneman Douglas High School, 74–76
Markey, Edward, 54
Marriott, Anna, 144–45
Martin, Trayvon, 76–77
Mason, Paul, 21
mass mobilisation through social media, 21–22, 78
matriarchy theory of organizing, 58–59
Maucher, Helmut, 116
Mayo, Ed, 130–31, 133–34, 181
Mbeki, Thabo, 145
McCaul, Michael, 82
McDonald's restaurants, 125–26
McKibben, Bill, 49, 50–53, 63
Medellin, Columbia, 56
media, 155
"mediated mobilisation," 78
Mehmet, Kamillo, 59
Merkel, Angela, 107
ME Solshare, 178
#MeToo movement, 22, 42

Mexican border wall, 89
Mexico and Fairtrade, 112–13
Middle East's "stability first," 26
military expenditures, 81, 190n35. *See also* arms industry
Miller, Mike, 153
miners' strike, 157
mining and conflict, 85
minority groups as activists, 38
MINUSMA, 72–73
Moberadoon network, 68, 70
"Mobilization against Corporate Globalization," 165–66
MobLab, 167, 171
Moraka, Christopher, 139
More in Common organisation, 100–101
Morris, David, 126
Morrison, Scott, 61
Mortensen, Gemma, 100–101
Mossack Fonseca (law firm), 125
Movement for Colonial Freedom, 154
MoveOn, 166
Moyer-Lee, Jason, 127
Mubarak, Hosni, 11
Mumber, Pierre, 98–99
Murdoch, Rupert, 166
Murphy, Paul, 84–85
Murray, Robin, 130, 131
mushroom analogy, 169–70
Muslim-based charities, 28, 103
Myanmar conflicts, 85

Nafziger, Gloria, 90
Naidoo, Kumi, 167
National Rifle Association (NRA), 75–76
natural disasters and humanitarian aid, 66
natural resources and conflict, 85–86
negative peace, 71
Nepal's community rebuilding, 71
NetChange, 129, 172
net zero goals, 35, 39, 40, 42
#NeverAgain, 74–76
New Economics Foundation, 163
Newsom, Gavin, 59
Ngoepe, Bernard, 143
NGOs. *See* nongovernmental organizations (NGOs)
Nicaraguan coffee farmers, 34
Nigerian abductions, 22, 105–6

Nkoli, Simon, 138
No More Deaths, No Mas Muertes, 99
nongovernmental organizations (NGOs): global influence of, 161; governments working with coalitions, 162–63; localisation of humanitarian aid and, 103; needing to campaign, 100–101; peacebuilding and, 81–82; public fundraising and, 104; traditional role of, 22–25; unprepared for refugee crisis, 89
nonviolent civil disobedience, 13, 40–43, 184n2
Northern Ireland's community rebuilding, 71
Norway's carbon neutral goals, 42
NRA (National Rifle Association), 75–76
nuclear missile disarmament, 156–57

Obama, Barack, 31, 50, 76
Ocasio-Cortez, Alexandria, 54, 62
Occupy movements, 14–15, 48, 55, 172
Offenheiser, Raymond C., 123
Ogoni people protests, 55–56
Omidyar, Pierre, 161
OPEN network, 167
OpenStreetMap, 78–79
Orbán, Viktor, 26
ORGANIZE! Training Center, 153
Ostrom, Elinor, 59
Otero, Agamemnon, 57–61
The Other Economic Summit (TOES), 48, 163
Oundle Under Threat (OUT), 156
"the outraged ones" (Indignados) movement, 16–17
Oxfam: collaborating with grassroots activism, 25; fundraising by, 103; ordered to cease political activities, 159; post-World War II, 152; on wealth inequalities, 120

Pakistan and trade, 70–71
Pakistani refugees, 101
Panama Papers, 125
Pancho Lara, Francisco, 69
pandemics. *See* Covid-19 pandemic; HIV/AIDS pandemic
Paris Agreement, 45, 59, 174
Parkland shootings, 74–76

Parmesan-making cooperative, 134–35
Patel, Ricken, 166
peace campaigns: arms sales and, 83–85; Black Lives Matter and, 76–78; Campaign for Nuclear Disarmament, 156–57; challenges of, 73; citizen voices in, 70–71, 175; investments and, 79–83; knife crime and, 73–74; in Mali, 71–73; #NeverAgain, 74–76; +Peace coalition, 81–83; in Syria, 65, 67–69; technology and, 78–79; in Tianemen Square, 65; tools for peace building, 80–83; women in, 71
Pelosi, Nancy, 53, 54
Pergau Dam project, 1–5
Peters, Bill, 159
Pettifor, Ann, 159–60
pharmaceutical industry, 141–43, 144–45. *See also* HIV/AIDS pandemic
Philippines peace campaigns, 69
Piketty, Thomas, 122
Pinochet era, 18
place-based activism, 59
platform cooperative, 132
Podemos political party, 16–17
Politico, 54–55
politics: ballot box compared to citizen movements, 29–31; Podemos party, 16–17; political elites, 119. *See also* government; populism; *specific countries*
populism: authoritarianism and xenophobia, 89; bleakness of, 6–7; Covid-19 pandemic and, 80; exploiting divisiveness, 180–81; as nationalist movement, 19–20; refugee crisis and, 97; rise of, 19–20, 151–52; trade wars and, 122
positive peace, 71
post-Communist nations, 160–61
poverty, 66, 122–23. *See also* global inequalities
power. *See* social power
Price, Matt, 172
printing press blockades, 41
progress. *See* change
Protect Colorado grassroots group, 45
protest movements. *See specific movements*

Putnam, Robert, 156

racism, 77. *See also* Black Lives Matter (BLM) movement
Radiohead, 34–35
RAIDH (Coalition of Ivorian Human Rights Actors), 117–18
Randolph, A. Philip, 31
Rashid, Afsheen, 57
Read, Rupert, 41
Reagan-Thatcher era, 156–58
"recovered factory" movement, 131
Rees, Marvin, x–xi
Refugee Convention, 107
refugees: Basmeh & Zeitooneh working with, 102–3, 104–5; citizens organising for, 93–94; communities welcoming, 89–92, 94–96; criminalisation of compassion, 98–100; Dreamers, 97; fear and, 96–98; generating renewable energy, 175; global commitment to help, 106–8; images of, 89; migrants rescued on *Seefuchs,* 99–100; Moberadoon network and, 67–69; numbers of, 101; World War II and, 87, 88; xenophobia and, 89
religious support for NGOs, 103
Repowering (energy group), 57–61
resistance. *See* nonviolent civil disobedience
right-wing populism, 19–20, 97. *See also* populism
Rix, Debbie, 89–90
Roberts, Frank Leon, 77–78
Robertson, James, 163
Robins, Mark, 49
Robins, Nick, 49
Roddick, Anita, 160
Roddick Foundation, 28
Romm, Joe, 52
Roosevelt, Franklin D., 31
Rose, Madeline, 81–83
Roy, Arundhati, xi, 8
Rwandan positive peace, 71

Sabido, Pascoe, 46
Sadri, James, 104
Salvini, Matteo, 19–20, 135
Samos Volunteers, 87–88

"Sardines" movement, 135
Saudi Arabia in Yemen, 84–85
Save the Children, 103
school strikes, 22, 33, 36–38
Seattle protests, 165–66
seed collectors, 55
*Seefuchs* boat, 99–100
SEIU (Service Employees International Union), 129
September 11 attack, 85–86
Service Employees International Union (SEIU), 129
Shanks, Will, 39
ShareAction, 45
Sharma, Y. V., 70–71
Sharp, Evelyn, 151
Shatila refugee camp, 101–2
Shawcross, William, 28
Shawky, Nirvana, 11–13
Sheila McKechnie Foundation, 24
Shell and Shell Canada, 44, 45, 55–56
#ShellKnew exposé, 46
Silberman, Michael, 75, 167, 171, 172
Silva, Dilma Ferreira, 27
Sinclair, Upton, 153
social economy, 132–35
social media, 21–22, 78
social movements: celebrities' involvement, 157–60; counter-globalisation movement, 163–65; crises as markers of change, 151–52; cyber-campaigns, 165–67; in 1960s and 1970s, 13, 154–55; in 1980s and 1990s, 13, 156–61; in post-Communist nations, 160–61; post-World War II, 152–54; suffragette movement and WWI, 151; winning with 3.5%, 42–43. *See also* change; citizen movements; nongovernmental organizations (NGOs); nonviolent civil disobedience; refugees; *specific protests and movements*
social power, 24, 30–31
social service cooperatives, 134
"Social Stock Exchange," 50
SOHR (Syrian Observatory for Human Rights), 188–89n10
Solnit, Rebecca, 169–70, 182
Soros, George, 26, 160–61

South African movements: Action for Southern Africa, 137–38, 141–43; Anti-Apartheid Movement, 158–59; civil society and positive peace, 71; COSATU, 143; Treatment Action Campaign, 24, 138–41, 143, 146–48, 173. *See also* HIV/AIDS pandemic
South Korea's economic development, 121
Spain's citizen protests, 16–17
The Specials, 73–74, 158–59
Sriskandarajah, Danny, 25, 103–4
Staple, Christine "Sugary," 74
Staple, Neville, 73–74
starlings analogy, 7–8
Steel, Helen, 126
Stephan, Maria, 26
Step It Up, 50
Stern, Nicholas, 44
Stiglitz, Joseph, 14, 120
"Stop Soros" laws, 26
Stop the City protest, 48–49
street mobilisation, 171–72
structural racism, 77
Sudan protests, 12–13
suffragette movement, 151
Sunak, Rushi, 5
Sunrise movement, 53–55
Swiss cooperatives, 130
Syrian Network for Human Rights, 67
Syrian Observatory for Human Rights (SOHR), 188–89n10
Syria's crises: challenge fund for, 106; civilian casualties, 66–69; organisations combining into one campaign, 104; peace campaigns, 65, 67–69, 70, 71. *See also* Ibrahim, Abir Haj; refugees

TAC (Treatment Action Campaign), 24, 138–41, 143, 146–48, 173
Tahltan First Nation, 44
Tahrir Square protests, 11–13
Take the Squares movement, 16–17
tax inequalities, 121, 123–25
Tax Justice Network, 123–24
#TeachtheFuture, 37–38
technology: for collaboration, 179; cooperative platforms, 132–34; for counter-globalisation, 165–67; established organisations and, 172; importance of harnessing, 31, 173; for peace campaigns, 78–79; social media, 21–22, 78
Temponi, Gilson, 27
Tennessee Highlander Center, 133
Teppermarlin, Alice, 116
terrorism: abuse claims, 28; Boko Haram abductions, 22, 105–6; ISIS attracting young people, 78–79
theatre for change, 93–94
350.org, 36–37, 50–53, 55, 60.. *See also* McKibben, Bill
Thunberg, Greta, x, 36–37
Tiananmen Square, 65
Tikka, Zuni, 14
timber imports, 193n20
Timms, Henry, 22
tobacco lobbyists, 35, 46
TOES (The Other Economic Summit), 48, 163
"tools of conviviality," 134
Total (oil company), 45
town-twinning movement, 152
track three diplomacy, 70
track two diplomacy, 70
Trade-Related Aspects of Intellectual Property Rights (TRIPs), 141
trade unions, 143, 153–54, 197n4
Treatment Action Campaign (TAC), 24, 138–41, 143, 146–48, 173
trends. *See* change
TRIPs (Trade-Related Aspects of Intellectual Property Rights), 141
Trump, Donald J.: Amnesty International and, 191n24; Covid-19 vaccine rights, 144–45; immigration policies, 97; Paris Agreement, 59. *See also* populism
Tunisia, 12–13, 78, 165
Turkey's refugees, 89, 101–3
Tutu, Desmond, 51
Twin Towers attack, 85–86

Uganda coffee cooperative, 34
Uganda refugee communities, 101
UK Uncut, 123–24
*Unburnable Carbon* (Robins and Robins), 49
Underground train stoppage, 41

# Index

UNHCR (United Nations High Commission for Refugees), 88, 103
unions, 127–28
United Kingdom: arms sales, 83–85; assemblies and commission on climate change, 39–40; asylum seekers, 97–98; Brexit, 19–20, 97; Cage (organisation), 28; climate change legislation, 35, 37–38; cooperatives, 130; Covid-19 vaccination assistance, 145; electricity supply, 44; Export Credit Guarantee Department, 83; Glasgow's violent crime, 74; homelessness, 122; international NGOs attacks, 27–28; Kindertransport rescue mission, 87; mergers in government, 4–5; Occupy movement in London, 14–15; precarious workers, 125–28; refugees sponsored in, 90–92; social movements of 1960s and 1970s, 155; trade deal with US, 144. *See also* Fairtrade global movement; *specific organizations and movements*
United Nations: Charter of 1945, 79; Climate Action Summit, 37; Climate Change Conference, 35, 167; Convention on Refugees, 88; Copenhagen Climate talks, 51; Environment Programme, 86; Global Compact on Migration, 107; High Commission for Refugees, 88, 103; Human Rights Committee, 107; Intergovernmental Panel on Climate Change, 35; military rules of engagement, 66; MINUSMA, 72–73; "protect, respect, remedy" framework, 192n1
United States: cost of fossil fuel subsidies, 43–44; history of resistance, 43; Mexican border wall, 89; minimum wage campaign, 128–29; social movements of 1960s and 1970s, 155; supporting oil/gas extraction, 44–45. *See also specific organizations and movements*
United Voices of the World, 127
United We Dream, 97
University of Maryland studies, 97
UpLift movement, 166

Ushahidi app, 79
US Institute of Peace, 26
utopias, 176

values, 179–82
venture philanthropists, 161
violent crime, 73–74
violent extremism. *See* terrorism
vocabulary for peace building, 82–83
von der Leyen, Ursula, 42

Wainwright, Hilary, 30
Wales community group, 95
Walker, David, 28
Warren, Scott, 99
water scarcity and conflict, 86
Waugh, Louisa, 87–88
WDM (World Development Movement), 1–5, 83, 109–11, 155, 157
wealth of top 1%, 120–21
Welton, Alli, 52
Whan, Eric, 42
white-label campaigning, 175
WHO (World Health Organization), 80, 144, 145
Wilde, Oscar, 111
Wiwa, Ken Saro, 55–56
women, 71. *See also* feminism movement
Woods, Darren, 47
World Bank, 107, 119, 163–64
World Development Movement (WDM), 1–5, 83, 109–11, 155, 157
World Economic Forum (Davos), 23, 165
World Health Organization (WHO), 80, 144, 145
World Humanitarian Summit, 103
World Refugee Forum, 89, 107
#TheWorld?Refugees, 106
World Social Forum (WSF), 164–65
World Trade Organization (WTO), 141
Wright, Erik Olin, 175
WSF (World Social Forum), 164–65
WTO (World Trade Organization), 141

xenophobia, 89, 100–101
Xingu Seed Network, 55
XR (Extinction Rebellion), 38–42, 43

Yemen and Saudi Arabia, 84–85

YES campaign, 185n39
young people. *See* children and young people

Zero Hour, 54
Zimmerman, George, 76–77

# About the Authors

**Ben Jackson** led the successor to the Anti-Apartheid Movement, launched Shelter's biggest campaign to end bad housing, and convened international NGO coalitions to protect civilians in conflict as UK director of Crisis Action. He has been a board member of Friends of the Earth, the CEO of Bond—the UK network for international development NGOs—and an adviser to the government and NGOs. He is now director of the Asylum Reform Initiative, a coalition campaign for deep change in Britain's asylum system. He studied at St. John's College Oxford and has been a visiting fellow at the Institute of Development Studies, University of Sussex. He is the author of *Poverty and the Planet* (1990).

**Harriet Lamb** spent fifteen years growing Fairtrade into a grassroots phenomenon in the UK and globally. She has headed the peacebuilding organisation International Alert and now leads Ashden, which backs innovative solutions to climate change. Her awards include a CBE, Cosmopolitan Eco-Queen, and Credit Suisse Businesswoman of the Year. She is an honorary fellow at Trinity Hall Cambridge, has honorary PhDs from Aston and Exeter universities, and was a 2019 visiting fellow at Clare College, Cambridge. She is the author of *Fighting Banana Wars and Other Fairtrade Battles* (2008), on which she and Ben also collaborated; that book has been translated into Swedish and Korean.

\* \* \*

Harriet and Ben each have thirty years of experience leading campaigns to secure change and driving civil society innovation. They campaigned together early in their careers, winning a pioneering court case forcing the British government to return to the aid budget the £234 million misused on the Pergau Dam project as a sweetener for an arms deal.